Conducting Research

Conducting Research

Patrick J. Schloss
BLOOMSBURG UNIVERSITY

Maureen A. Smith
BUFFALO STATE COLLEGE

Merrill,
an imprint of Prentice Hall
Upper Saddle River, New Jersey   Columbus, Ohio

Library of Congress Cataloging-in-Publication Data

Schloss, Patrick J.

    Conducting research / Patrick J. Schloss, Maureen A. Smith.

      p. cm.

    Includes index.

    ISBN 0-02-407370-9

    1. Research—Methodology.   I. Smith, Maureen A.

    II. Title.

    Q180.55. M4S35 1999

    001.4'2—dc21   98-11113

                                     CIP

Cover photo: © FPG International
Editor: Kevin M. Davis
Production Editor: Julie Peters
Text Design and Project Management: Elm Street Publishing Services, Inc.
Cover Designer: Rod Harris
Cover Design Coordinator: Karrie M. Converse
Production Manager: Laura Messerly
Director of Marketing: Kevin Flanagan
Marketing Manager: Suzanne Stanton
Advertising/Marketing Coordinator: Krista Groshong

This book was set in Garamond by Carlisle Communications, Ltd.
and was printed and bound by Victor Graphics, Inc.
The cover was printed by Phoenix Color Corp.

© 1999 by Prentice-Hall, Inc.
Simon & Schuster/A Viacom Company
Upper Saddle River, New Jersey 07458

All rights reserved. No part of this book may be reproduced,
in any form or by any means, without permission
in writing from the publisher.

Printed in the United States of America

10 9 8 7 6 5 4 3 2 1

ISBN: 0-02-407370-9

Prentice-Hall International (UK) Limited, *London*
Prentice-Hall of Australia Pty. Limited, *Sydney*
Prentice-Hall Canada Inc., *Toronto*
Prentice-Hall Hispanoamericana, S.A., *Mexico*
Prentice-Hall of India Private Limited, *New Delhi*
Prentice-Hall of Japan, Inc., *Tokyo*
Simon & Schuster Asia Pte. Ltd., *Singapore*
Editora Prentice-Hall do Brasil, Ltda., *Rio de Janeiro*

For loved ones lost during
the writing of this text
Joseph Nelson Albrecht,
Melissa Nelson Schroth,
and
William J. Smith

PREFACE

Early in his presidency, John F. Kennedy established one of the most ambitious research goals in history. The goal was to land a human being on the moon and provide for a safe return to earth. To the general population, this announcement suggested only that at some future time they would awake to a headline announcing that humans had landed on the moon. This research goal meant substantially more to members of the scientific community. While private citizens were simply drawn to the outcome or overall goal of the research endeavor, physicists, chemists, and engineers questioned each of the component steps leading to the final goal of landing an astronaut on the moon.

Knowledge of these component steps or objectives was as important as knowledge of the goal itself. Can you imagine the waste and confusion that would have resulted if the scientific community rushed into the effort without a cohesive and logical plan? Their plan had to include the component research activities, the timelines, and the persons or facilities responsible. We can be certain that the early success of the space program was as much a function of the careful management of research activities as it was the development of new technology.

Though on a smaller scale, just as the space program had to be logically organized, so too does the research program of the masters or doctoral student. Students who progress quickly from proposal to defense invariably have a research plan that ensures success. They know where to begin, where to end, and what steps fall in between. They have reasonable expectations for when each step is to be initiated. Finally, they are able to account for the personnel and material resources needed to accomplish the project.

We have written *Conducting Research* as a practical guide to the research process. The major feature that sets this text apart from others is our concern for the organization and flow of the research process. We provide as much attention to managing the research process as we do to the discrete skills needed to be a competent researcher. President Kennedy's goal was to land a human on the moon. This is analogous to your overall goal for successfully proposing and defending a research project. President Kennedy's goal depended on advanced facility with metallurgy, engineering, and life science. Attainment of your research goal will be the ability to protect human subjects, conceptualize a research question, review related literature, select an experimental design, measure dependent variables, manipulate independent variables, analyze results, and prepare and defend a proposal and a final report.

This text is designed to walk you through the research process while teaching you discrete research skills. We provide sufficient detail for you to conceptualize a problem, review the literature, select a design, conduct the study, and report your findings. We do this, however, in the context of the total research program. Having read this text, you will not only know what to do but when to do it. You will know how discrete research activities form an integrated research plan.

Objectives

Our major assumption in writing this text is that, beyond learning how to read or critique the professional literature, you are going to contribute to it through formal completion of a study. This study may meet a course assignment, or serve as an honors or masters thesis or a dissertation. Therefore, the main purpose of this text is to provide you with the information you need to select a topic, question, or hypothesis for study; conceptualize a plan for gathering the data; present the plan orally and in writing; conduct the study; and present your findings orally and in writing. Our goal is to present each step of the research process in a comprehensive manner so as to meet the needs of the beginning researcher. After reading this text, we believe you will know and understand a great deal about the research process, and you will be able to use this information to plan and carry out a study with minimal assistance.

Organization of the Book

The chapters follow the steps you will actually take to conduct a research project in the social sciences, from conceptualizing the question or hypothesis to reporting your findings. There are 16 chapters organized into four major sections.

Section I: Getting Started. Section I focuses on the preliminary steps in your research project and includes three chapters. Chapter 1 defines the concept of research and many other key terms you will encounter in subsequent chapters of the text. It also describes the various types of research projects in which you may be engaged as you complete your formal education and embark on a career in your chosen field. Chapter 2 discusses the ethical and legal issues that are the foundation for all of your research efforts. Chapter 3 addresses how you can select a research topic that is novel yet "doable," i.e., reasonable in terms of financial and time commitments.

Section II: Developing the Project. Section II focuses on the nuts and bolts of your research project. Having tentatively identified a problem or question, you need to review the literature to enhance your familiarity with this topic and investigate what other work has been done. Chapter 4 describes how to conduct a review of the literature and refine a research question or hypothesis. Chapters 5, 6, and 7 describe distinct design categories that can be used to answer the research question or test the hypothesis. Chapter 5 describes quantitative designs; Chapter 6 describes single subject designs; and Chapter 7 describes qualitative research. The choice of a design or combination of designs reflects the research question. Each of these chapters discusses the purpose of the distinct design category, implications for subject selection, and the specific designs included. Chapter 8 presents detailed information on options for selecting subjects and their implications for the quality of the research project. Techniques for measuring the dependent variable are presented in Chapter 9. These techniques include standardized tests, criterion referenced tests, systematic observations, and scales and surveys. Chapter 10 addresses the development of the independent variable and how to train assistants in its delivery.

Section III: Determining How the Data Will Be Analyzed. Section III is devoted to data analysis, a topic that students typically find to be the most intimidating aspect of their research. Chapter 11 describes how raw data from any type of study can be organized. Chapter 12 corresponds to Chapter 5 in that it describes how to analyze data from quantitative study. Chapter 13 describes how to analyze data from the single subject designs, which were presented in Chapter 6. Finally, Chapter 14 describes how to analyze data from qualitative research, the focus of Chapter 7.

Section IV: Implementing and Reporting the Project. We assume that the various stages of your research project will be supervised to some degree by one or more faculty members. Therefore, you will need to work effectively with a committee and communicate your progress orally and in writing. The chapters in Section IV assist you in meeting these responsibilities. Chapter 15 describes how to prepare and defend a proposal. Having obtained permission to move forward, Chapter 16 describes how to conduct your study, report your findings in writing, and present and defend those writings orally.

Special Features

In addition to the organization and flow of the text, *Conducting Research* includes several other special features which we believe set it apart from other texts.

Writing Style. We use a very informal writing style to describe the activities necessary to plan, conduct, and report research. Although we provide all the technical information you need to engage in research, we explain this information in a style that is easily read and understood. Our intention is not to talk down to students but to write for them to understand.

The Scope, Plan, and Sequence Chart. The scope, plan, and sequence chart presented in Chapter 1 illustrates the research process. Specific activities on this chart are keyed to subsequent chapters. The chapters are presented in the order in which the activities occur through the research process. Preceding each chapter is the appropriate excerpt from the scope, plan, and sequence chart that provides additional details for each topic. These statements enumerate content objectives from the chapter. As you might expect, the content objectives are logically ordered based on their importance or timing within the research process.

Information That Cuts Across Disciplines. A majority of the chapters present information that is common to all research. Regardless of discipline or orientation to a problem, all competent researchers demonstrate ethical behavior, possess a knowledge of related literature, are concerned for reliable measurement, and provide clear and complete research reports. Readers whose backgrounds represent psychology, sociology, social work, business, marketing, nutrition, education, special education, and speech pathology will find this book useful and relevant. We also use several real-world examples to clarify our points. These examples do not represent any one area of study; rather, they cut across the social sciences.

Information on Diverse Research Methods. Differences occur in research designs and methods of analysis. For this reason, Chapters 5, 6, and 7 each describe a different research method, including quantitative designs, single subject designs, and qualitative designs. You are encouraged to learn as much as possible about each method. Only through broad-based knowledge can you make an informed decision when selecting research tools. Similarly, Chapters 12, 13, and 14 correspond to the analysis of data from quantitative, single subject, and qualitative studies. Again, while you are not likely to use the information from each chapter, this knowledge will assist you in selecting an appropriate design and method of analysis.

Further Readings. We are aware that your individual study is likely to demand a depth of knowledge in an area that cannot be accommodated through a single text. Therefore, we have identified further readings at the end of every chapter. If your study involves nonparametric methods, we expect that you will need additional information contained in nonparametric statistical texts. If you engage in a qualitative study, the writings of Denzin, Lincoln, LeCompte, and Pressley are likely to be useful. Beyond our suggestions, your advisor and members of your thesis or dissertation committee can provide readings that will guide your efforts.

Tables, Figures, and Checklists. Throughout the text, we provide figures and checklists that you can copy and use to manage or conduct your research project. For example, in Chapter 2, we include sample release forms you can use to obtain permission for subject participation. In Chapter 4, we provide a figure you can use to evaluate the scholarship of a publication and determine its relevance in your own work. In Chapter 9, we provide data sheets you can use to conduct systematic observations.

Acknowledgments

We wish to acknowledge the assistance of several of our friends and colleagues. First, Dr. James Matta provided a critical eye in reading selected sections of the manuscript. He also made substantial contributions to Chapter 4. Heather Strauch and Carol Arnold provided invaluable clerical support. Rebecca Fisher assisted with information retrieval. We also wish to acknowledge the students in our advanced research design courses for allowing us to field test text content. A strong note of thanks is extended to our editors at Merrill Education. Kevin Davis and Holly Jennings provided outstanding support throughout manuscript preparation and production.

Finally, we wish to thank the following reviewers whose thoughtful comments guided us through several revisions: David Donovan, Kean College; Jim C. Fortune, Virginia Polytechnic Institute and State University; James P. Gaffney, Xavier University; Robert Hale, Pennsylvania State University; James P. Key, Oklahoma State University; Norman G. Lederman, Oregon State University; Chester H. McCall, Pepperdine University; Betty W. Meers, University of Florida; Thomas S. Parish, Kansas State University; Doris L. Prater, University of Houston-Clear Lake; and Edward M. Reeve, Utah State University.

Patrick J. Schloss

Maureen A. Smith

BRIEF CONTENTS

CONTENTS

Section II Developing the Project

1

What Is Research?

INTRODUCTION

You are probably reading this text because you are about to embark on a research project. Depending on the requirements of either your degree program or place of employment, you may be feeling somewhat intimidated at the thought of planning and conducting research. Certainly, the definition of research suggests that there is a substantial amount of work involved. Although many definitions are available, we like the description offered by Best (1997). Research is a process through which individuals seek solutions to problems or identify cause and effect relationships between variables. Research is a formal, systematic, and intensive process directed toward the discovery and development of an organized body of knowledge. Systematic and objective analysis and recording of controlled observations establishes generalizations, principles, or theories that enable the prediction and possible control of events. While we like this definition, we acknowledge that, taken as a whole, it may contribute to a perception that planning and carrying out a research project is a major task with no end in sight. Although understandable, such an attitude can be very self-defeating.

Research projects can be more manageable when broken down into smaller units. Best's (1997) definition lends itself quite nicely to such an analysis. As illustrated in Figure 1.1, the process unfolds by developing a question; identifying a variable or behavior of interest; establishing a technique or factor believed to affect the variable; creating a method for determining if there is a relationship between variables; and developing an unbiased measurement instrument. Once the planning and development is completed, the plan is implemented and data are collected and analyzed. Finally, results are related to existing knowledge. Without losing sight of the long-term goal, breaking a project down into components enables you to remain focused and on task.

For students, completing a research project generally leads to graduation and job offers. It also leads to enhanced professional and financial satisfaction. Coursework and previous experiences may have helped you realize the tremendous impact research has had on our personal and professional lives. On a personal basis, the healthy diet we follow is the result of research in nutrition. The cars we drive and the speed at which we drive are the results of product safety research. Are you anticipating several headaches and bouts with an upset stomach over the duration of your study? The variety of over-the-counter remedies available to you is the result of medical research. Your particular preference is probably the result of careful marketing research.

Are you thinking that your research project will never have that kind of impact? You're probably right. A single research project seldom does. It is the cumulative results of many research activities that produce such an impact. As the saying goes, the journey begins with just one step.

Figure 1.1 The Scope, Plan, and Sequence Chart for Conducting Research

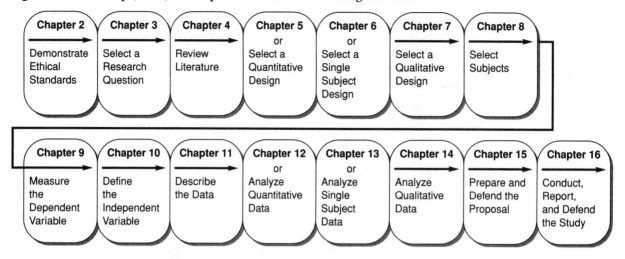

THE PURPOSE OF RESEARCH

The purpose of research can be found in its definition: to seek a solution to a problem or identify a cause and effect relationship. Each piece of well-conducted research should expand a theory or contribute to a knowledge base. This goal can be accomplished through basic or applied research; however, applied research should also improve the quality of the participants' lives.

THE IMPORTANCE OF RESEARCH

Life would be substantially different were it not for research. Again, the diet you follow, the car you drive, and the medication you take are the results of someone else's research. Without it, your life would probably be shorter, less pleasant, and substantially more hazardous.

Put quite simply, research is important because it keeps us from making incorrect decisions or behaving in ways that are nonproductive. We may be wasting valuable time and effort and depleting already limited resources. You may remember that a major car company developed and marketed a new model. It sold quite well in the United States but was not received with great success in Mexico. The reason was the name of the model. In Spanish, "Nova" sounds like "no va" which means "no go." It would be hard to think of a more inappropriate name for an automobile. Our guess is that marketing research executives at that company did not do their homework, and a substantial amount of money was lost.

We can think of many instances where the lack of well-conceived, carefully implemented research has had adverse effects. More extensive biomedical research on the use of the drug, thalidomide, may have avoided physical disabilities among children born to women who used it to avoid a miscarriage. Engineering research could have allowed designers to predict that the Verazano Narrows Bridge would oscillate to the point of destruction in high winds. Educational research could have demonstrated that many aspects of the open classroom are detrimental to student achievement.

As is suggested throughout the preceeding examples, research avoids the waste of time, money, and effort. We can select and use ideas that enable us to grow personally and professionally. By conducting research, we contribute to a knowledge base from which others benefit. Your own research will make you more enthusiastic about your work and will certainly shape the decisions you make as you practice your profession. Over time, a line of research can promote reform by leading to fundamental changes in practice (Sardo-Brown, 1995). Finally, if you are in a human service profession, research is a tool for advocacy. It can provide information that dispels myths. You have the opportunity, if not an obligation, to help the community that made your research possible. Community members can use the results of your research to examine the appropriateness of existing practices and make modifications if warranted (McLaughlin, 1995).

PUTTING YOUR RESEARCH PROJECT IN PERSPECTIVE

There will be many opportunities for you to engage in research through the degree program. As we discuss in the next sections, opportunities vary in the level of sophistication and skills required from students.

Research for Course Requirements

We have heard many undergraduate and graduate students say things such as "I have to do a research paper," or "I have to go to the library and do some research on my paper." We interpret such comments to mean the students have to write a theme paper or a term paper and are using the variety of media available at the library to assist them. We share Leedy's (1996) belief that such activities are not research. Students are merely locating existing information and transforming it into another format. By the time they complete their papers, we hope they will know something they didn't know before; however, their work does not constitute a contribution of new knowledge to their field of interest. On the other hand, you may be taking a course that requires completion of a true research project. You need to pose a research question, then develop and carry out a plan for answering the question. Your finished product should have many of the components found in research reports. Elements of your paper may include a literature review, research questions or statement of hypotheses, a description of research methods, results, and a discussion that integrates findings with the literature review. It should also contribute new knowledge to your field.

Given that most courses last about 15 weeks, though, there are limits on what can be accomplished. The study must be planned and conducted while acquiring cognate information included in the course syllabus. Usually there are other requirements for this course, and you may be taking more than one course during the semester. As a result, the research project is going to be much less ambitious than a thesis or a dissertation.

Honor's Thesis

Occasionally, a student completing an undergraduate program is demonstrating significant promise in his or her chosen field of study. Perhaps a GPA is very high, or the person is making a substantial contribution by way of service. Many college and university programs offer an honor's track to such students. They complete a carefully chosen, rigorous sequence of courses and typically produce an honor's thesis toward the end of the program. Perhaps you are in the process of completing such a paper, and it involves research. In our own experience, an honor's thesis is not in the same league as a master's thesis or a dissertation. However, it can produce challenges and evoke feelings experienced by those in the final stages of completing research requirements for advanced degrees. If you are preparing an honor's thesis, you are working closely with a faculty member whose interests you share. He or she may have suggested the research question and should be providing you with very clear direction as your thesis develops.

Master's Thesis

It is possible that the completion of a master's thesis marks the end of your role as solely a consumer of professional literature and the beginning of your role as a contributor. Although smaller in scale, a thesis has much in common with a dissertation. Both require a statement of the problem; a detailed literature review that leads to your research questions; a methods section that describes your subjects, dependent and independent variables, measurement systems, general procedures, and design; a results section that addresses each research question; and a discussion section that explains the results, identifies major limitations of the research, and offers recommendations for future work. You may be able to identify a research question independently, although it is not uncommon for a student to work closely with a faculty member to develop and answer a research question. Depending on the college or university you attend, you may need to work with faculty who provide advice and guidance throughout the study. Their final approval of your project is essential for graduation.

Dissertation

The dissertation is the culminating experience of any doctoral program and contains components similar to those in a thesis. By this point, you should have completed much coursework in your cognate area and in your research design and data analysis. The dissertation advances the level of knowledge in your field by using skills in research design and analysis. It also requires fairly sophisticated writing skills. Although you will be guided by a committee, your dissertation marks the formal beginning of your research agenda. Its completion indicates you are capable of planning and conducting important research.

We hope your dissertation is not the first time you have participated in a research endeavor. Perhaps you have worked cooperatively with university faculty or fellow students to conduct a line of research and gain valuable experience at the same time. This experience, coupled with coursework, should enable you to identify a research question independently and, with the approval of your committee, plan and carry out a strategy for answering it. It is a challenging process that requires completion of many tasks by seemingly impossible deadlines. Upon its completion, you may look back and notice that there may have been inadequacies in the literature review, in the design and analysis, and in the final document. Despite its role as a culminating activity, it is still a learning process. You will learn things that will prepare you for a career that includes scholarship and research.

Grants

As a master's or doctoral student, you may have assisted college or university faculty who have received grants from state or federal authorities, institutes, or private agencies. Money from a grant may be making it possible for you to study full time. Pending resources, many agencies make funds available for student-initiated grants. These grants can provide resources to help you finish your dissertation. Grant money of varying amounts is also available to individuals employed in applied settings, such as schools and clinics. Finally, as a faculty member, you may be interested in, or strongly encouraged by your dean to apply for, funding from external agencies. Although organized differently, a grant has many of the components found in a thesis or a dissertation.

Research for Publication

Having invested the time, energy, and money necessary to plan, conduct, and write about your research, you may feel that your work is completed. One purpose for conducting research described by McLaughlin (1995), however, is to advocate. As a researcher, you are obligated to "give something back" to the community that allowed you access to the information you were seeking. Community members in turn can use this information to examine, and, where necessary, modify existing practices. Publication of your research is an ideal way to get new information into the hands of those who can benefit from it. Whether completed for a thesis, a dissertation, or a grant, your work can be transformed into the format required for publication.

In addition, your thesis or dissertation should mark the beginning of your research rather than the end. Having demonstrated that you are capable of planning and carrying out research to finish a degree, we hope you will continue formulating and answering questions of interest to you. Many people completing advanced degrees pursue careers in higher education where publishing scholarly research is a major professional responsibility. No doubt, you have heard the phrase "publish or perish."

Whether the project you are planning marks your first foray into research or you have completed a few or several projects, your work will need to be transformed into a format suitable for publication. Fortunately, there are many similarities between a final research report and a manuscript you submit for publication. Both require careful planning and solid writing skills. Although length varies considerably, both have abstracts, an introduction or a literature review, a methods section, a results section, and a conclusion.

PURPOSE OF THE TEXT

The major purpose of this text is to outline and discuss the skills you need to conduct a research project in the sequence in which you use them. It provides you with a chronologically ordered plan for designing, proposing, conducting, reporting, and defending research. Our intention is to enable you to develop and evaluate your own program of research with minimal technical support from your advisor.

This is an ambitious task for many reasons. First, as you will note, there are many skills in the sequence. We have tried to include detailed discussions of each skill and to address the variety of research methodologies (i.e., group designs, single subject designs, qualitative research) available to answer your research questions. Each methodology has unique techniques for data analysis, with entire books and courses devoted to them. Second, we assume the majority of our readers are students completing degrees that represent a variety of fields included within the social sciences. While we believe the research process is the same across these fields, we hope you will find items among our examples, references, and recommendations for further readings that pertain to your area of interest. Third, we also believe there are major similarities in the process all students must complete to meet college or university requirements for completing a thesis or a dissertation. For example, students typically work with a committee that oversees the project. We have included several chapters to assist you through these requirements. Fourth, it is also possible that you are not a student but are engaged in, or about to embark on, a line of research. Chapters describing how to work effectively with college or university committees may not be particularly relevant for you; however, you should benefit from chapters that describe planning and conducting research and putting findings into a written report.

SUMMARY

In this chapter, we defined research, explained its purpose, and discussed its importance. We also presented you with some key terms that will be used frequently. Research can be conducted to complete a variety of requirements for a degree or for employment. Regardless of the role it plays in your education or profession, we know that conducting research can be a tedious process, particularly for the novice. Therefore, we suggested that engaging in research may be more appealing or less intimidating if the process is broken down into smaller, more manageable tasks. This text includes chapters that address each of these tasks.

Have you ever watched a professional athlete or an artist and wondered, "How do they do that?" No doubt, they were born with some innate talent. The athlete doesn't just play in a game, however, and the artist does not perform only for a crowd. These individuals get to the top of their professions and stay there because they practice and work at it. What appears so easy is actually the result of years of dedication and hard work. Remember this as you start to conduct research. Your first project may be very challenging, but all the hard work paves the way for the next project. The more you plan and conduct research, the easier the process becomes.

REFERENCES

Best, J. W. (1997). *Research in education* (8th ed.). Upper Saddle River, NJ: Merrill/Prentice Hall.

Leedy, P. D. (1996). *Practical research: Planning and design* (6th ed.). New York: Macmillan.

McLaughlin, J. A. (1995). Research as a tool for advocacy: A commentary. *Remedial and Special Education, 16,* 195–198.

Sardo-Brown, D. (1995). The action research endeavors of six classroom teachers and their perceptions of action research. *Education, 116,* 196–200.

FURTHER READINGS

Flor, R. (1991). An introduction to research and evaluation in practice. *Journal of Experimental Education, 14,* 36–39.

Fuchs, L. S., & Fuchs, D. (1993). Writing research reports for publication: Recommendations for new authors. *Remedial and Special Education, 14,* (3), 39–46.

Ghauri, P. N., Gronhaug, K., & Kristianslund, I. (1995). *Research methods in business studies: A practical guide.* Upper Saddle River, NJ: Prentice Hall.

Johnson, E. S. (1981). *Research methods in criminology and criminal justice.* Upper Saddle River, NJ: Prentice Hall.

LeCompte, M. D., & Preissle, J. (1993). *Ethnography and qualitative design in educational research* (2nd ed.). San Diego: Academic Press.

Lytle, S. L., & Cochran-Smith, M. (1992). Teacher research as a way of knowing. *Harvard Educational Review, 62,* 447–474.

Malouf, D. B., & Schiller, E. P. (1995). Practice and research in special education. *Exceptional Children, 61,* 414–424.

Manheim, J. B., & Rich, R. C. (1991). *Empirical political analysis: Research methods in political science.* New York: Longman.

May, T. (1993). *Social research: Issues, methods, and process.* Buckingham, England: Open University Process.

Reid, D. K., Robinson, S. J., & Bunsen, T. B. (1995). Empiricism and beyond: Expanding the boundaries of special education. *Remedial and Special Education, 16,* 131–141.

Sardo-Brown, D. (1991). Secondary teachers' participation in action research. *High School Journal, 75,* 48–58.

Silverman, F. H. (1997). *Research design and evaluation in speech-language pathology and audiology.* Needham Heights, MA: Allyn & Bacon.

Smith, S. W., Brownell, M. T., Simpson, R. L., & Deshler, D. (1993). Successfully completing the dissertation: Two reflections on the process. *Remedial and Special Education, 14* (3), 53–60.

Stenhouse, L. (1985). *Research as a basis for teaching.* London: Heinemann.

Straubert, H. J., & Carpenter, D. M. (1995). *Qualitative research in nursing: Advancing the humanistic imperative.* Philadelphia: J. B. Lippencott Company.

Webb, J. R. (1992). *Understanding and designing marketing research.* San Diego: Academic Press.

2

Ethical and Legal Issues

INTRODUCTION

Three major factors should help you focus your research. The first is the topic's scientific merit. A topic is judged to be appropriate if you have a thorough knowledge of the topic, are skeptical about past conclusions, and are able to conceptualize a research plan that is likely to provide insights beyond isolated facts.

The second factor is the project's "practical feasibility." A research project must fit within your budget. You must account for time, transportation, material resources, and personnel resources needed to complete the study. Thus, there is often a compromise between "ideal methodology" and "practically feasible methodology."

The third factor is the appropriateness of the project when judged on ethical grounds. Ethical considerations are somewhat less practical than administrative constraints. They may also be less scholarly than topical constraints. With regard to individual privacy and freedom, however, ethical constraints may be the most important factor. Ethical constraints ensure that The Golden Rule applies to our conduct as researchers. Specifically, we must accord research subjects the same freedom, dignity, and comfort that we would expect for ourselves in similar circumstances.

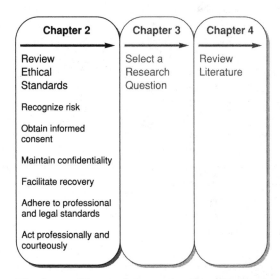

The Scope, Plan, and Sequence Chart for Conducting Research: The First Step in the Research Process

Understanding and committing to abide by The Golden Rule, however, may not ensure the ethical treatment of human subjects. Breaches in research ethics generally do not occur through the purposeful disregard for the welfare of others. Instead, research ethics may be violated through oversight or our inability to anticipate conflict situations. This chapter provides information to assist you in avoiding ethical dilemmas.

Following is a recent experience that demonstrates how oversight can lead to a breach in research ethics. As part of a human subjects review committee, we recently reviewed a research proposal for its ethical integrity. A psychology professor planned to conduct a structured interview to determine children's perceptions of discipline approaches used by their parents. The questions in the interview were highly innocuous. For example, the children would be asked if their parents impose household "chores" or if the child is allowed to select "chores" through mutual negotiation. Similarly, the children were asked if sibling disputes simply result in punishment, or if parents help them to learn ways to work through conflicts.

The investigator ensured that all statements would be held in strict confidentiality. She indicated that no names would be placed on the recording sheet, and that it would be impossible to identify individual children through their responses. Further, the children, and their parents, could decline participation in the project at any time.

We were confident that the proposal would be approved and could not imagine any risks that could result from this investigation. The clincher was that all aspects of the study were to be described to the children and their parents prior to data collection. They were told the number of questions, the general nature of questions, the purpose and expected benefits of the study, and any other factor that might assist them in deciding whether or not to participate. The children and their families were not to be deceived, coerced, or manipulated.

As others pointed out, this initial judgment about the potential for risk was terribly wrong! A two-hour debate eventually led to the unanimous rejection of the proposal. She had clearly overlooked elements of the proposal that could place the children or their families at risk. The major problem was that school personnel, including educational researchers, are legally obligated to report suspected abuse and neglect. The board judged that interview questions could elicit statements judged to raise the suspicion of abuse or neglect. Therefore, the confidentiality statement was at odds with current law requiring disclosure of abuse or neglect.

Given this oversight, the most thoughtful researcher could be forced to engage in unethical behavior. To report abuse or neglect would violate a family's right to confidentiality. It would also be contrary to the researcher's assurance that responses would not be disclosed. Failing to report abuse or neglect would violate child welfare laws and hold the researcher criminally liable. The solution, in this case, was for the researcher to disclose to the child and family members that confidentiality would not be maintained if statements by the child left a suspicion of abuse or neglect. The researcher was required to indicate that if the interview yielded information suggesting the child had been neglected or abused, the researcher would provide a report to the Department of Family Services. This disclosure eliminated the potential conflict between confidentiality and the reporting of abuse or neglect.

The importance of protecting human subjects, coupled with complexity inherent in ensuring the ethical treatment of research participants, has resulted in a substantial amount of professional discussion. The essential result of this discussion has been the development of standards by professional organizations and the Federal Government. Knowledge of these standards will help you protect human subjects participating in your research. The following section reviews the major tenets underlying the protection of human subjects as proposed in federal legislation and by professional organizations.

This chapter will assist you in identifying potential conflict situations. Both professional organizations and the legislature have established standards that minimize the risk of research on human subjects. We will review common features of these standards. We will later present specific requirements from federal law and professional organizations. Finally, we will discuss broader issues of professional conduct and courtesy.

ETHICAL STANDARDS

Recognition of Possible Risk

Risk is the possibility of damage, injury, or loss. It can involve adverse physiological, psychological, or material consequences. Risk may be a direct effect of research activity, as in the case of a subject being inadvertently shocked by an experimental apparatus. It may also be an indirect consequence of the research. For example, an employer may not give a merit raise after obtaining information about subjects' attitudes.

It is important to emphasize that all research exposes an individual to some degree of risk. Time spent away from activities during data collection can be viewed as minimal risk. Aggressive or depressive reactions that may result from experimentally induced failure may suggest a moderate level of risk. The possibility of adverse health effects while engaged in experimentally controlled physical exertion or diet may suggest higher levels of risk.

The importance of recognizing possible risks to human subjects is obvious. First, recognizing risk is the first step toward avoiding risk. You should be able to modify your experimental protocol to eliminate the potential hazard. For example, you realize that information obtained on a questionnaire may be harmful if read by others. Therefore, you use a coding procedure to protect the anonymity of subjects.

Second, recognizing risk may lead to the use of procedures that offset the potential hazard to subjects. For example, let's say you use an experimental procedure that may excite elementary students. Returning the children to a sedentary class may increase the likelihood that they will misbehave. Therefore, students may be encouraged to listen to a calming story prior to returning to class. While the risk of students becoming excited still remains, the calming story may neutralize the risk prior to students returning to the classroom setting.

Third, recognition of risk allows you, the human subject review board, and subjects themselves to judge whether benefits expected from the research outweigh potential liabilities. For example, a concern expressed by advocacy groups for persons with Acquired Immune Deficiency Syndrome is that potentially effective experimental drugs are not used in human experimentation without substantial laboratory research. Advocates claim that the benefits of putting these drugs into quicker service with critically ill humans substantially exceed the risks associated with their premature release. Ultimately, federal review panels will judge whether the risks are justified.

Informed Consent

Identifying potential risk is valuable only if subjects are fully informed of that risk. Therefore, informed consent is one of the most important ethical responsibilities. In fact, this responsibility is so strong that federal regulations require the consent of participants (or the parents/guardians of young children or persons with cognitive impairments) whenever more than minimal risk is present. This requirement will be discussed later.

In short, informed consent involves advising potential subjects, in clear and nontechnical writing, of all aspects of the project that may affect whether or not they choose to participate. Essential elements of informed consent have been described by the United States Office for Protection from Research Risks (1983b) and include the following:

1. An indication of the purpose of the research, expected duration of subjects' involvement, procedures to be followed, identification of experimental procedures, and indication that the results may be published.

2. A description of anticipated risks and benefits to the subject or society.

3. The identification of alternative procedures or treatment methods that may be used by the subject.

4. An assurance of confidentiality or conditions under which confidentiality would be breached.

5. The identification of compensation and alternate treatments that may be provided if injury, discomfort, or other hardship occurs as a result of the study.

6. The identification of whom to contact if additional questions arise or if research related injury occurs.

7. A statement that participation is fully voluntary, and that participation may be discontinued at any time (p. 9).

It is important to emphasize that informed consent occurs only when your participants fully understand the scope, plan, and purpose of the study. To ensure clear communication, we recommend that information be provided in language that reflects the communication levels of participants. Communications should not influence the individual to participate in the study through the use of coercion, deceit, or omission. Further, oral explanations should accompany the written document. Participants should have an opportunity to ask questions. Finally, the dominant language of the participant should be used both in writing and oral communication.

As emphasized earlier, informed consent requires clear and complete communication between researchers and subjects. Developmental and cognitive features limit some individuals' ability to provide informed consent. Children with normal intelligence and older individuals with developmental delays may not be able to understand the scope, plan, and purpose of your research. They may not recognize the time and effort you are requiring from them. They may not be well equipped to judge potential risks and benefits. Finally, they may feel obligated to participate when asked to do so by an authoritative researcher.

We recommend, and in some cases federal law requires, that informed consent be obtained from parents or guardians whenever young or cognitively disabled individuals are exposed to more than minimal risk. In this case, the consent letter should indicate that the parent or guardian is asked to advocate on behalf of the potential subject. In any case, the individual should be accorded the same attention and respect provided to the person actually signing the consent document.

Figure 2.1 and 2.2 illustrate two sample letters of consent. The first is written to potential participants of a study on the effectiveness of various computer-assisted instruction modules used by college students. The second is written to the parents/guardians of preschool-aged children who are asked to participate in a social skill training program. Figure 2.3 includes a template from which an informed consent letter may be developed. It includes elements of informed consent previously discussed. You may wish to add specific language appropriate to your investigation.

Confidentiality and Anonymity

Confidentiality is the assurance that information learned about a subject through the study will not be released to any other individual. As we discussed earlier, you may be legally compelled to breach confidentiality when a subject's responses suggests a "reportable offense" as in the case of child abuse. Even if you are not obligated to report an offense, research data are generally not

Agreement to Serve as a Research Subject

I consent to serve as a research subject in the project "Effect of Various Computer Assisted Instruction Module Formats on College Student Learning." The project is conducted by Mr. John Smith, a Master of Science candidate and supervised by Dr. Mort Walker. Both represent the Department of Technology Research at Boone State University.

I am aware that the project involves the following procedures: I will complete a microcomputer module designed to provide information about human variance in learning and emotion. Interactive aspects of the module will require me to provide brief responses to questions. In some cases, correct responses will result in module sections being skipped. Incorrect responses may result in additional information, drill, or practice.

Time involved in completing the module and other aspects of the study may range from 90 to 160 minutes. Interactive microcomputer modules are rarely used in University classes. Therefore, this method of instruction is considered experimental.

I understand that I will be asked to complete a 40 item criterion referenced test over material in the module. A code will be used on my test form so that my identity can be connected to the test only with the use of a key. The key will be kept in a locked file accessible only to Mr. Smith and Dr. Walker. It will be destroyed immediately following data analysis.

The major benefit of this project involves providing additional instructional resources to University professors. Effective computer-assisted instruction modules would enhance independent study and distance learning practices. They would also provide cost-effective alternatives to large lecture hall classes. Finally, they may be a useful adjunct to lab classes.

I recognize that participation in this study is voluntary. No penalty exists for refusal to participate, and I am free to withdraw consent and end my participation at any time. Content in the module is not based on objectives for any current University course, and performance is not expected to help or hinder my ability to compete for grades. If I am interested in the content, but wish not to be a participant in the study, the researcher will make the module available for my use upon completion of data collection. I am also aware that no remuneration is provided to research subjects.

I understand that this project is not expected to involve risks greater than those ordinarily found in daily life. While it is not possible to identify all risks in experiments involving human subjects, I recognize that safeguards will be taken to minimize anticipated risks.

If questions arise about the experimental procedure, the testing method, or any other aspect of the study, I am free to contact Mr. Smith or Dr. Walker.

Signature:_____Date: _____

Figure 2.1 Sample Consent Form

Consent for My Family Member to Serve as a Research Subject

I agree to permit _____ (minor child's name) _____ to be a subject in a study intended to evaluate the effectiveness of methods for teaching social skills. The study is titled "Social Skill Enhancement for Preschoolers with Developmental Delays." It is conducted by Dr. Robert Jacowski, Assistant Professor of Child Development, Walbash University.

I understand that Dr. Jacowski has identified three important social skills: interactive play, complying with authority requests, and requesting assistance from others. He will initially use observational learning methods to develop the first objective. The methods include demonstrating correct performance, prompting my family member to use the same skill, providing correction/feedback, and providing social reinforcement. Once my family member performs the first objective consistently, Dr. Jacowski will focus training on the second objective. Again, once consistent performance is obtained he will address the third objective.

My child's performance throughout the project will be evaluated through direct observation during times in which the skills are expected to occur. These may include "free play" time, lunch period, and during art activities. I understand that development of the three objectives is likely to take four weeks with direct instruction provided for two 15-minute periods a day. Feedback and reinforcement will be provided throughout the day as indicated by my family member's performance.

Records resulting from my child's performance in this project will be kept in a locked cabinet accessible only to Dr. Jacowski. I understand that he is likely to publish the research results, and the report will describe my child's learning and behavioral features and illustrate my child's performance under the program. I also understand that my child, the school, and community will not be identified by name.

This study is expected to provide a direct benefit to my child. The social skill training is an important element in the program. If effective, experimental methods will aide my family member in achieving preexisting objectives. I also recognize that, if shown to be effective, other children with developmental disabilities may benefit from these procedures.

I understand that my family member's participation in the project is fully voluntary. Refusal to participate, or withdrawing during the course of the study, will result in no penalty or loss of service for my child or family. Further, the educational staff will strive to achieve the skill training objectives using methods ordinarily employed in the preschool setting regardless of my child's status as a subject in the study.

I understand that risks involved in this study do not exceed those expected in daily life. While all potential risks can not be anticipated, I understand that all reasonable safeguards will be taken to minimize harm.

If questions arise about the experimental procedure, the observation method, or any other aspect of the study, I am free to contact Dr. Jacowski.

_____   _____
Family Member's Signature/Date   Child's Signature/Date

Figure 2.2 Sample Form Used to Obtain Parental Consent for Minors

Consent to Serve as a Research Subject

I agree to participate in the research project title _____,

directed by _____ who is affiliated with

_____.

I understand that the study involves the following experimental and assessment procedures:

_____

_____

_____

I understand that confidentiality is protected through the following conditions:

_____

_____

_____

Benefits expected to be derived by society or myself from this investigation include the following:

_____

_____

_____

I understand that participation in the study is voluntary, and that there is no penalty for refusing to participate. I may also withdraw from the project at any time without retribution.

I understand that the following risks may be incurred in the project, and the following methods will be employed by the researcher to minimize these or other risks:

_____

_____

_____

If I have questions about the research, I may contact the investigator at any time.

Signature:_____Date:_____

Figure 2.3 Template for Development of an Informed Consent Statement

protected from subpoena as are lawyer and client conversations, or husband and wife discussions. Informed consent must be structured so the participant is aware of these possibilities.

Breach of confidentiality may be the most common source of risk for social and behavioral science research projects. Surveys designed to identify consumer habits, child rearing behaviors, heterosexual values, and so on may produce information harmful to the subject if disclosed to others. For example, an instrument that reveals tax fraud, child abuse or neglect, or substance abuse may lead to criminal prosecution. In other cases, the information may diminish economic or social opportunity. For example, an instrument may document criticism of an employer, personal earnings, and extramarital relationships.

Nowhere is concern for breach of confidentiality debated more emphatically than in areas that concern sexual relations and reproductive freedom. AIDS advocates debate the consequences of breaches of confidentiality in the area of HIV status. A major argument against AIDS testing is the effect of breaches in confidentiality on an individual's insurance and employment. Advocates of reproductive freedom are concerned about the disclosure of adolescent women's medical examination results and subsequent medical decisions to family members. Concern is expressed that families may not act in a young woman's best interest if they obtain this information.

As noted earlier, anonymity is the highest standard of confidentiality. Anonymity is assured when your research methods do not allow the individual's name to be linked to his or her responses. Information provided anonymously does not present the same risk of reporting or subpoena as other data. You cannot attribute a suspected offense to a specific individual. Therefore, you are unable to breach confidentiality of the anonymous subject.

Methodological constraints may preclude the anonymous collection of data. If you are studying individual performance using multiple data sources over an extended period of time, you generally need to link data to the individual. Observational and naturalistic studies may require the identification of individual subjects. When your research involves potentially criminal or otherwise sensitive behavior, you should take extraordinary care to ensure confidentiality. Methods that include allowing subjects to use either a code number known only to them or an alias may be effective in achieving this end.

For most studies, protecting the identity of individual participants is a sufficient ethical safeguard. Invasion of privacy may also occur, however, when group data are reported. One example of a breach of confidentiality for groups of individuals was reported by Foulks (1987, 1989). The author studied alcohol abuse and treatment in an Inupiat community in Barrow, Alaska. Alcohol-related values and responses were studied in a sample of 88 community members over the age of 15. The analysis revealed that 41 percent of the population acknowledged excessive alcohol use, 50 percent indicated that alcohol caused problems in their family, and 62 percent indicated that they frequently fought when drinking. In general, the research report identified a substantial alcohol abuse problem in the community. Findings of the study were also reported in the popular press. The reaction to the study by members of the Inupiat community was very negative. While no individual was identified by name, individuals argued that their right to privacy was violated by the report of information adverse to their community. This experience emphasizes that confidentiality applies to groups of individuals as well as individual subjects.

Deception

Research designs in the social and behavioral sciences often require that you deceive subjects by providing false or incomplete information. In some cases, deception is used to provide as natural an analogue as possible to real-life situations. In others, it is used to ensure ecological validity in a natural situation. We will provide examples of each and then discuss their implications for ethical research practice.

Using Deception to Provide a Natural Analogue. The most widely discussed example of deception in an experimental analogue was reported by Milgram (1963, 1965). Milgram was concerned with the common explanation for atrocities of German soldiers. He wondered if "following orders" was a real justification for behavior that an individual would not ordinarily perform independently. Obviously, Milgram could not observe natural situations in which men under the command of an authority figure performed reprehensible behavior. Similarly, he could not create a direct experimental analogue of the natural phenomena. The only possible method for testing the strength of authority control over deviant social behavior required deception.

Forty men agreed to serve as subjects of his investigation. He told the subjects only that they were to assist in an experiment on human learning. He "randomly" assigned each of the subjects to the role of "teacher" and deceptively indicated that another subject had been selected "at random" to be a "pupil." In fact, the subject selected to be a pupil was actually a confederate who was fully informed of all aspects of the project and trained to act out the role in order to deceive the subject.

The pupil was led into a room and strapped to a chair and an electrode was attached to the his wrist. The teacher was seated at an elaborate electrical control panel. Switches were labeled with voltage levels ranging from 15 to 315. Several switches had corresponding phrases such as "Extreme-Intensity Shock," "Danger—Severe Shock," and "XXX." Teachers had seen the pupil being strapped into the chair but could not observe him from the control panel. Teachers were asked to read a randomly ordered list of word pairs under the pretense of determining the pupil's ability to match the words. A light on the control panel indicated whether or not the pupil had matched words correctly. Whenever an error was made, the teacher was required to throw one switch beginning with the lowest voltage and progressing to the highest voltage. As the intensity of the shock increased, so did the pupil's verbal and physical reaction. He screamed for mercy and pleaded for the experiment to end. Of course, there was no actual electric shock, and pupils' reactions were contrived.

The experimenter instructed the teacher to continue the procedure regardless of the reaction. Toward the end of the sequence, the pupil would kick the wall between the rooms and scream as loud as possible. Shortly thereafter, the pupil would become silent regardless of the question or voltage level. The experimenter indicated that no answer should be judged an error and the next higher shock should be applied until throwing the switch labeled "XXX" ended the teaching procedure.

Of the forty adult men who served as a teacher, all continued increasing the intensity of shocks until the pupil was kicking the wall. Even at that point, only five refused to continue. Twenty-six of the forty subjects continued to increase the voltage and shock the pupils at a maximum intensity of 450 volts.

Subjects in Milgram's experiment were deceived in several ways. First, they were not told the actual purpose of the study. Second, they were told that they were actually administering a shock as a consequence of incorrect responding. Finally, they believed that pupils were subjects selected through the same means that they were selected. The effects of the deceit on the actual subjects was extreme. All became highly nervous and agitated throughout the experiment. Several had uncontrollable nervous and muscular reactions. For many, the psychological effect of learning that they were capable of harming or killing another individual was long lasting and severe.

Deception to Ensure Ecological Validity in Natural Situations. Another widely discussed example of deception allowed a researcher to observe behavior in a natural situation without distorting subject reactions. Laud Humphreys (1970) conducted naturalistic observations of casual homosexual acts between strangers in tearooms (i.e., public rest rooms in city parks). He was intrigued that presumably heterosexual men who lived normal lives and were respected in their communities engaged in isolated homosexual acts. His observational study was designed to describe the social and psychological conditions that surrounded the homosexual activity.

Homosexual activity in tearooms generally involved three individuals: two engaging in oral sex and one participating as a lookout. Humphreys assumed the role as a lookout for the suggested purpose of gaining vicarious sexual satisfaction. Of course, his actual purpose was to record the activities. Humphreys used license plate numbers to obtain names, phone numbers, and home addresses of tearoom participants from the Department of Motor Vehicles. He visited the participants' homes in disguise and told participants that he was conducting a survey (presumably unrelated to homosexual behavior). He used information obtained through the fictitious interview to provide a more comprehensive view of tearoom participants.

In this case, deception occurred as Humphreys misled participants regarding his interests in observing the homosexual acts. Further, he misled participants regarding his purpose for conducting follow-up interviews. Effects of this example of deceit on the subjects was substantially less severe than those occurring in the preceding case. Without widespread publicity, it is unlikely that the subjects would have even known that they were research subjects. On a broader scale, however, researchers and the general public expressed concern over the general invasion of privacy.

Issues in Using Deception. Considerable disagreement exists regarding whether or not it is ever ethical to use deception. In many cases, the basis for this belief is the untested assumption that deception causes people to distrust researchers and their research findings. Despite this view, many forms of deception can be used with minimal risk to subjects. More important, the benefits of conducting a study using deception may substantially outweigh the projected risks. Diener and Crandall (1978) argued that deception may be justified in some cases; however, they suggested that the following issues be considered prior to initiating a study involving deception:

1. A judgment should be made regarding the appropriateness of deception. The major factor in this judgment involves weighing the possible detrimental effect on you or your subjects against the importance of knowledge gained through the investigation.

2. Studies involving deception should be designed so that negative effects experienced by subjects are limited to the experimental situation.

3. Deception should not be practiced when alternative research methods are available.

4. Informed consent should be used in studies involving deception any time more than minimal risk is involved. In some cases, the subjects may not be informed about the specific deceptive aspects of the study. However, they should always be aware of possible adverse effects of the study. As emphasized previously, participation in the study should always be voluntary.

5. Finally, subjects should be debriefed once their participation in the study is complete.

Recovery

Participation in a research project may produce a lasting change in your participants' lives. In some cases, these changes may be very minor. Some studies, for example, may simply provide personal insights that are new to subjects. They may learn that they are stronger, more creative, or more compassionate than other people. They may also learn that their performance is below that of others. This knowledge may change subjects' perceptions of themselves. However, it may have a minimal lasting effect on their personal adjustment.

In other cases, the changes may be substantial. As we noted earlier, participants in Milburn's study experienced major changes in the way they viewed themselves and others. These changes are likely to have a lasting impact on their relationship with authority figures and their compassion for others.

Regardless of expected lasting effects, you are obligated to assist your subjects in "recovering" to their pre-experimental state of physical, mental, and social well-being. Three methods have been suggested for this purpose; they include debriefing, dehoaxing, and desensitizing.

Debriefing. Even studies that do not involve deception may leave subjects with unanswered questions about their performance or the performance of the larger sample. The credibility of the researcher and research process is likely to be enhanced if subjects are provided a complete and accurate account of the scope, plan, purpose, and outcome of the study. Further, subjects or their family members may benefit from an analysis of their performance. Most parents are interested in knowing the child's achievement levels, motor capabilities, and career interests. Executives involved in cardiovascular fitness studies may benefit from knowing their performance level and the associated implications for diet and exercise.

Researchers using deception have a higher ethical motive for using debriefing. In a majority of studies, deception is needed only during the data collection process. Even then, it is only used because benefits exceed ethical liabilities. Once complete, there is no reason to deprive subjects of information, and we believe that you are ethically obligated to make amends for the deception. You should provide a full account of the real purpose and method of the investigation. For the sake of researcher/subject relations, you should identify the reasons that deception was required. You should highlight the societal benefit of new information obtained through the study. Finally, you should provide a perspective on the research experience that reduces feelings of manipulation, gullibility, or diminished character.

Dehoaxing. Debriefing simply informs the subject about the plan and outcome of a study. In some cases, this information is not sufficient to avoid misconception by the subject. Dehoaxing is the process of convincing subjects that what was described in the debriefing is actually true. By doing so, you can remove undesirable effects of a study.

In most cases, you can dehoax subjects by demonstrating the experimental procedure. In Milgram's experiment, for example, the control panel may have been opened at the conclusion of a trial. Subjects could then see that the switches were not connected to a power source. In a study not involving deception, subjects may be shown how reading achievement scores are determined from the experimental testing procedures. A more widely recognized achievement test may also be given to support conclusions drawn from the experimental test.

Desensitization. Debriefing and dehoaxing may not be effective in avoiding lasting harm to a subject. Regardless of how information was obtained and interpreted, some individuals may experience lasting adverse effects from the experiment. You have an ethical obligation to assist subjects in understanding and dealing effectively with new personal insights. Desensitization is a method you can use to help subjects accommodate this new information.

One desensitization method is to demonstrate to subjects that their performance resulted from idiosyncrasies in the experimental procedure and not from cognitive or personality disorders. You may highlight aspects of the study that are different from what occurs in everyday life. You may note that performance during the contrived experiment is unlikely to relate to future habits.

Another desensitization procedure involves demonstrating that the characteristic disclosed through the experiment is common to a majority of healthy children or adults. To this end, you can provide subjects with a brief and informal review of studies describing the pervasiveness of the experimental phenomena among humans.

A final desensitization procedure involves providing an educational or therapeutic intervention that is likely to support the individual's return to the pre-experimental state. For example, relaxation exercises may be provided following a study that resulted in heightened anxiety.

Similarly, subjects may become anxious when they are confronted with vocational performance deficiencies through a study. To overcome these feelings, you may provide instruction that brings the subject's skill up to an acceptable level.

Professional Standards

Policy committees of professional organizations have attempted to preempt government regulation of research by establishing ethical guidelines. *The Ethical Principles in the Conduct of Human Research with Human Participants* by the Committee on Protection of Human Participants in Research of the American Psychological Association (1982) is the set of standards most widely cited in the behavioral and social sciences. Their guidelines are paraphrased below.

A. Investigators are responsible for evaluating a study's ethical acceptability. The investigator must protect the rights of human participants and seek advice on ethics when dilemmas are not easily or clearly resolved.

B. Investigators must consider the extent to which subjects are "at risk" based on recognized standards.

C. Investigators are always responsible for maintaining ethical practices to ensure the ethical treatment of subjects by all individuals conducting the study.

D. When research has greater than minimal-risk research, the investigator must have a clear and fair agreement with all subjects that preestablishes all obligations and responsibilities. Subjects must be informed of all research procedures expected to influence his or her willingness to participate. Special safeguards are required when deception is used or when research is conducted with children or with participants who have cognitive impairments.

E. Before conducting a study involving deception, the investigator must justify the technique based on the study's potential value, determine whether alternative, nondeceptive procedures are available, and provide explanations as soon as the deception is concluded.

F. Individual's are assured freedom to decline to participate or withdraw at any time.

G. Participants must be protected from physical and mental discomfort or other adverse consequences that may be associated with the research. Procedures that may cause harm are not used unless the failure to use these procedures may result in greater harm and voluntary consent is obtained.

H. When delaying or withholding information can be justified, the investigator must monitor the research and ensure that the subject is not harmed. A full debriefing should occur as soon as possible upon the completion of the study.

I. The investigator must detect and remove all adverse consequences to subjects.

J. A subject's confidentiality must be maintained unless agreed upon in advance. When confidentiality cannot be assured, full disclosure should be made to the participant as part of the informed consent procedure. (Committee on Scientific and Professional Ethics and Conduct, 1981, pp. 633–638).

Virtually every organization concerned for the advancement of knowledge through human experimentation has published ethical guidelines. Issues and standards for each generally parallel those offered by the American Psychological Association. Differences generally involve the extent to which the mission of the organization impacts various principles. As one would guess, American Educational Research Association standards emphasize ethical research practices in schools. The Society for Research in Child Development focuses on protecting children serving as research subjects. The American Sociological Association standards address the protection of individuals and families in the community.

As a final example, the American Association for Public Opinion Research Code of Professional Ethics and Practices (1977) emphasized research issues related to self disclosure of individual beliefs, preferences, and behavior to researchers. The code is paraphrased so you can compare its standards to those of the American Psychological Association.

I. Principles of Professional Practice

    A. Exercise care in data collection and processing to assure accurate results.

    B. Exercise care in research design and analysis.

        1. Employ only research methods suited to the research problem.

        2. Do not select research methods that may bias results.

        3. Do not profess undue confidence in results and conclusions.

    C. Describe findings and methods accurately and completely.

II. Principles of Professional Responsibility to Others

    A. The Public:

        1. Cooperate with legally authorized representatives of the public by describing research methods.

        2. Maintain the right to approve the release of findings; disclose all misinterpretations.

    B. Clients or Sponsors:

        1. Hold confidential all information obtained about the client's general business except when disclosure is expressly authorized.

        2. Be mindful of limitations and accept only assignments accomplished within limitations.

    C. The Profession:

        1. Do not cite membership in the Association as evidence of professional competence.

        2. Recognize responsibility to contribute to the science of public opinion research.

    D. The Respondent:

        1. Do not practice deception, abuse, coercion, or humiliation.

        2. Protect the anonymity of respondents unless anonymity is waived. (American Association for Public Opinion Research, By-Laws, May 1977).

The National Research Act of 1974

The vast majority of researchers belong to professional organizations and abide by their professional standards. Unfortunately, a small number of researchers have ignored these standards. Subsequent public reactions have brought legislation to protect human subjects. *The National Research Act of 1974* was passed by Congress and signed into law for the purpose of protecting human subjects participating in experiments conducted by agencies supported by the United States government. The major provisions of the law are as follows:

Review of Research by an Institutional Review Board. All research conducted by staff of organizations that receive Department of Health and Human Service funds (e.g., public schools, universities, social service agencies, mental health agencies, etc.) must be reviewed by an Institutional Review Board. The review board generally consists of researchers and administrators within the organization. The principal purpose of the board is to protect participants in research studies. The board must determine whether benefits derived from the investigation outweigh the potential for harm. Further, the board must consider if alternative research methods would reduce risks while providing comparable knowledge.

Policies and procedures of institutional review boards are prescribed by federal law. We encourage you to visit the chair of your Institutional Review Board in the early stages of your research planning. He or she should provide forms needed to initiate the review process. Figure 2.4 illustrates a typical university application used in reviewing projects involving human subjects at Bloomsburg University of Pennsylvania.

Informed Consent. The National Research Act also requires that researchers obtain informed consent from research participants. As discussed earlier, subjects must be provided with sufficient information to judge whether or not to participate in the study. Essential elements identified in the law include:

1. Purpose of the research and time/effort expected of the individual.
2. Potential risks to the individual.
3. Benefits to the individual or others.
4. Alternative procedures or treatments that the individual may consider.
5. Extent to which confidentiality will be maintained.
6. Available resources to overcome harm that may result from the study.
7. Individual to contact if questions or problems arise.
8. Assurance that participation is voluntary, and an individual may withdraw at any time without prejudice (Office for Protection from Research Risks, 1983).

Levels of Review. Regulations under the National Research Act published in the Federal Register (1983) describe three levels of review based on the degree of risk associated with a study. A project may be exempt from review when subjects are exposed to minimal risks. Federal regulations establish the following criteria for exemption:

1. Research conducted in established or commonly accepted educational settings, involving normal educational practices, such as (a) research on regular and special education instructional strategies, or (b) research on the effectiveness of, or the comparison among instruction techniques, curricula, or classroom management methods.
2. Research involving the use of education tests (cognitive, diagnostic, aptitude, achievement) if information taken from these sources is recorded in such a manner that subjects cannot be identified directly or through identifiers linked to the subjects.
3. Research involving survey or interview procedures, except where all of the following conditions exist: (a) Responses are recorded in such a manner that the human subjects can be identified directly or through identifiers linked to the subjects; (b) the subject's responses, if they became known outside the research, could reasonably place the subject at risk of criminal or civil liability or be damaging to the subject's financial standing or employability; and (c) the research deals with sensitive aspects of the subject's own behavior, such as illegal conduct, drug use, sexual behavior, or use of alcohol. All

Date _____

Investigators (status: student, faculty, others)_____

_____

_____

_____

_____

_____

Department(s): _____

_____

_____

Title of Project: _____

_____

_____

_____

Funding Agency: (if any) _____

_____

_____

_____

Category of Review (circle one): See pp. 3–5

      Exemption Requested:

      Expedited Review:

      Full Review:

Figure 2.4 The Application Used in Reviewing Projects Involving Human Subjects at Bloomsburg University of Pennsylvania

FORM A

Check one response in each area.	No	Yes	Does Not Apply
1. This application involves human subjects participating in:			
a. biomedical procedures			
b. procedures to elicit information (personality tests, questionnaires, inventories, survey, observations, etc.)			
c. procedures specifically designed to directly modify the knowledge, thinking, attitudes, feelings, or other aspects of behavior of the subjects.			
2. If biomedical procedures are involved:			
a. are provisions for emergency medical care necessary?			
b. has a qualified M.D. participated in planning the project?			
c. will the study involve drugs or chemical agents (dosages), ionizing radiation (microwaves, lasers) or high intensity sound?			
3. Does this study involve giving false or misleading information to subjects or withholding information from them such that their "informed consent" is in question?			
4. Are the procedures to be used new or innovative (not established and accepted?)			
5. Will the procedures:			
a. cause any degree of discomfort, harassment, invasion of privacy, risk of physical injury, or threat to the dignity of subjects, or be otherwise potentially harmful to subjects?			

Figure 2.4 Continued

Check one response in each area.	No	Yes	Does Not Apply
b. If answer to 5 is YES, have specific provisions been made to correct any harmful or adverse conditions that may arise (Give details in Form B—see p. 10).			
6. Can the potential benefits from the conduct of this study be considered to outweigh the risks to the subject?			
7. Will any type of electrical equipment be used that will be connected to subjects? (If YES, give, in Form B, the name and qualifications of individual who will check for electrical safety and attach a signed letter).			
8. Will subjects receive any payment for participating (money, course credit, etc.)? If YES, give details in Form B.			
9. Is the project specifically designed to involve subjects who are:			
a. minors (less than 18 years of age)?			
b. pregnant women?			
c. prisoners?			
d. mentally retarded?			
e. mentally disabled (e.g., brain damaged, psychiatric patients)?			
f. physically handicapped (e.g. uses wheelchair, walker)?			
g. institutionalized?			
h. Bloomsburg University students?			

Figure 2.4 Continued

Check one response in each area.	No	Yes	Does Not Apply
10. Do procedures include obtaining parent/guardian consent and/or institutional authorization for access to subjects if minor?			
11. Are procedures for maintaining confidentiality of all subjects' data fully described?			
12. Are procedures for obtaining informed consent fully described?			
13. Will a copy of the informed consent document and explanation of the study be provided to each subject?			
14. Have copies of informed consent documentation been submitted along with the protocol (i.e., signature document with explanation of study, transmittal letter, debriefing statement or other)?			

Figure 2.4 Continued

Fill in the number of estimates:

Average amount of time required for subject's participation (hrs): _____

If questionnaire or tests are involved, the total number of items: _____

Number of volunteers (subjects) to be involved in the study: _____

Beginning date _____ and ending date _____ of involvement of human subjects.

The investigator confirms that the project or activity described in the attached Form B is planned to adhere to University policies and, if applicable, to the institutional assurance with the U.S. Department of HHS regarding the use of human subjects. The investigator agrees that major additions and changes in procedures involving human subjects that occur after review of the application will be brought to the attention of the review committee by the investigator. In addition, the committee will be notified of any unanticipated events that do or could affect the safety and well being of subjects. University review and approval is requested.

TYPED NAME   CAMPUS ADDRESS   PHONE

_____

_____

_____
(investigator)   Signature

_____
(Advisor(s) if applicable)   Signature

Figure 2.4 Continued

research involving survey or interview procedures is exempt, without exception, when the respondents are elected or appointed public officials or candidates for public office.

4. Research involving the observation (including observation by participants) of public behavior, except where all of the following conditions exist: (a) Observations are recorded in such a manner that the human subjects can be identified directly or through identifiers linked to the subject; (b) the observations recorded about the individual, if they became known outside the research, could reasonably place the subject at risk of criminal or civil liability or be damaging to the subject's financial standing or employability; and (c) the research deals with sensitive aspects of the subject's own behavior such as illegal conduct, drug use, sexual behavior, or use of alcohol.

5. Research involving the collection or study of existing data, documents, records, pathological specimens, or diagnostic specimens if these sources are publicly available or if the information is recorded by the investigator in such a manner that subjects cannot be identified directly or through identifiers linked to the subjects (Office for Protection from Research Risks, 1983a, p. 4).

Research that involves moderate risks may receive an expedited review. This review requires only one member of the institutional review board to evaluate the proposal. Almost all of the criteria for expedited review identified in federal regulations apply to biomedical research. A few exceptions include:

1. Subjects who are 18 years old or older and experimental procedures that are minimally intrusive and common to education/treatment settings. These may include weighing individuals, testing their sensory acuity, and obtaining voice recordings.

2. Normally healthy subjects who voluntarily participate in moderate exercise.

3. Perception, cognition, or other subject characteristics that are measured in a manner that does not involve the manipulation of behavior and that does not induce stress.

Full board review must occur for all research projects not addressed in the preceding standards. In general, full board review applies to any project that exposes an individual to substantial risk through physical harm, discomfort, loss of privacy, and so on. For example, studies that involve experimentally induced failure and subsequent anxiety, extreme physical exertion, or disclosure of sensitive or criminal conduct must be subjected to full board review.

The preceding information should guide you in ensuring that your research complies with professional and legal standards for the ethical treatment of human subjects. It is also important that research be conducted in a professional and courteous manner. Standards for professional and courteous conduct are discussed in the following section.

Courtesy and Professionalism

Most researchers are employed as professors or graduate students and do not have direct administrative control over research samples. They generally work in a university setting void of typical subjects. Professionals investigating educational issues and methods generally obtain research subjects through public elementary and secondary schools. Professors and graduate students interested in social welfare issues must access social service agencies. Professors and graduate students interested in studying health-related issues may seek access to clinical settings.

In each case, access to research subjects occurs only through the cooperation of program personnel. In some cases, cooperation may be limited to simply providing intact data sources (e.g., school records, social service reports, census data, or mailing lists). Others may extend to providing release time from other program activities so that subjects may participate in the study. Under the most demanding conditions, cooperation may involve assistance in selecting subjects, seeking informed consent, scheduling activities, providing technical assistance, or implementing treatment variables. We recommend that you follow several major guidelines in promoting such cooperation.

Understand the Social Structure. The first, and possibly most important guideline, involves recognizing who must provide support, what effort is required, and what consequences may result from their failure to cooperate. We recommend that all individuals be considered, not just those assigned by the program to approve research. For example, you may naively request the assistance of a building administrator for a project that will involve teachers and paraprofessionals. It may be administratively possible for the administrator to require participation by the staff; however, the project is not likely to run smoothly if they are not willing participants.

Follow Guidelines for Informed Consent on a Program-Wide Basis. Our previous discussion of informed consent applied to individual research subjects. Informed consent of cooperating personnel may be equally important. Program administrators should be aware of the benefits and risks associated with a research project. They should have all relevant information from which to judge the appropriateness of the project for subjects under their daily care. There should be no deception or coercion in discussions with the administrator.

Ultimately, the program administrator may need to defend the value of the project to family members, school boards, advisory committees, and/or the press. The administrator must have sufficient information to be an effective advocate.

Balance Inconvenience With Benefits. As with all cooperative relationships, the research activity must have payoffs for all participants. Your payoffs are generally clear (e.g., completion of degree requirements, fulfillment of professional obligations, or satisfying curiosity); however, payoffs to cooperating personnel may be less obvious. Consequently, prior to soliciting assistance, we recommend that you consider the benefits that cooperating personnel may receive.

Whenever possible, investigations should be structured so that benefits to cooperating personnel are enhanced. For example, an educational research project testing the value of one teaching method over another may have a collateral benefit of providing achievement information to students, teachers, and family members. A health-related study may provide screening data on cardiovascular fitness of company employees. A consumer study may provide product satisfaction data to a manufacturer.

Even modest benefits may be sufficient to enlist support when there is little inconvenience to cooperating personnel. Consider all aspects of the project that may require effort from cooperating personnel and then structure activities to minimize or shift this effort to you. For example, confidentiality may require that cooperating personnel code data from existing data sources. You may minimize the effort by providing a simple recording form. You may agree to escort children from existing activities to the room in which the study is conducted. Further, you may provide enrichment activities for students not participating in the study so that teachers do not have to accommodate "split" classes.

Meeting Your Commitments. Initial conversations with program staff should provide a clear outline of the research plan. You may present the research procedures and timelines that will be followed. Many activities require cooperating personnel to alter their schedules to accommodate the research activity. Consequently, it is important that you minimize inconvenience by sticking to the timelines. Advanced notice should be given as early as possible when a change in plans is unavoidable. Analysis and writing often occupy all of your time immediately following data collection, and there is a temptation to ignore cooperating personnel. It is important, however, to remember your pre-established commitments. Be certain to follow through if you agreed to specific activities or products once data were collected. For example, provide summaries of subject performance in a timely manner. Return the physical structure of program facilities to the original or agreed upon condition as soon as possible. Send "thank you" letters immediately following the involvement of cooperating personnel.

As emphasized in Chapter 1, this may not be your last project. Your reputation in fulfilling responsibilities will be a major factor in determining future acceptance. Also, others are likely to request the assistance of individuals with whom you worked. A positive experience with your project will pave the way for future positive experiences.

SUMMARY

We have emphasized standards for the ethical treatment of human subjects. These standards emanate from The Golden Rule. We should accord others the same respect and humane treatment that we would expect for ourselves under similar circumstances. Research literature, professional organizations, and federal law identify a number of standards for research ethics. Common to each of these are the following principles:

1. *You should be aware of possible physical, psychological, or social harm to human subjects that may result from participating in the research.* Apparent risks must be balanced by benefits to the individual or society. Whenever possible, you should undertake measures to avoid or minimize possible risks. Be prepared to correct harm that does result from a study.

2. *Potential subjects should provide informed consent prior to participating in the study.* Informed consent by the subject includes knowledge of the scope, plan, and purpose of the study; anticipated risks and benefits to the individual and society; alternative procedures or treatments that may be used; the manner in which confidentiality will be handled; corrective measures that will be provided if harm occurs; and individuals to be contacted if questions arise. Informed consent also implies that participation is fully voluntary and that the subject can withdraw from the study at any time without liability.

3. *Confidentiality should be maintained whenever possible.* We recommended coding responses (using a third party to collect data) and asking subjects to use an alias to protect confidentiality. The individual should be informed of conditions, such as ethical, legal, or practical constraints, under which confidentiality may be breached.

4. *Deception should not be used whenever alternative procedures are available.* When no alternative procedures are available, you must defend the use of deception to an institutional review board. The defense is generally based on the benefits to society or the individual that result from knowledge gained during the investigation.

5. *Research plans involving deception should include debriefing, dehoaxing, and/or desensitization.* These procedures are conducted to minimize lasting adverse effects of participation in the research.

We presented the *Ethical Principles in the Conduct of Human Research with Human Participants* written by the Committee on Protection of Human Participants in Research of the American Psychological Association (1982), and the *Code of Professional Ethics and Practices* written by the American Association for Public Opinion Research (1977). These policy statements highlight the ethical principles noted here. We also emphasized provisions of *The National Research Act of 1974.* This act requires that all organizations receiving funds from the Department of Health and Human Services must review research for potential risks to human subjects. You must effectively argue that the research benefits outweigh risks to human subjects, and that alternative methods for producing similar findings are not available. *The National Research Act of 1974* further requires that researchers provide informed consent when more than minimal risk is expected.

Our final discussion emphasized the role of courtesy and professionalism in human experimentation. We discussed principles that foster cooperation between you and outside agencies or programs. These principles included understanding the social structure of an organization, keeping personnel fully informed, striving to balance liabilities to the organization with benefits, and fulfilling commitments under the research plan.

REFERENCES

American Association for Public Opinion Research. (1977). *Code of professional ethics and practices.*

Committee on Scientific and Professional Ethics and Conduct. (1982). Ethical principles of psychologists. *American Psychologist, 36,* 633–638.

Diener, E. & Crandall, R. (1978). *Ethics in social and behavioral research.* Chicago: University of Chicago Press.

Foulks, E. F. (1987). Misalliances in the Barrow Alcohol Study. *American Indian and Native Alaskan Mental Health Research, 2* (3), 7–17.

Foulks, E. F. (1989). Social stratification and alcohol use in North Alaska. *Journal of Community Psychology, 15,* 349–356.

Humphreys, L. (1975). *Tearoom trade: Impersonal sex in public places.* Chicago: Aldine.

Milgram, S. (1963). Behavioral study of obedience. *Journal of Abnormal and Social Psychology, 67,* 371–378.

Milgram, S. (1965). Some conditions of obedience and disobedience to authority. *Human Relations, 18* (5), 57–76.

Office for Protection from Research Risks. *National Research Act of 1974.* Protection of Human Subjects, *Code of Federal Regulations 45 CFR 46,* Washington, DC: U.S. Government Printing Office, March 8, 1983a, p. 4, section 46.101.

Office for Protection from Research Risks. Protection of Human Subjects, *Code of Federal Regulations 45 CFR 46,* Washington, DC: U.S. Government Printing Office, March 8, 1983b, p. 9, section 46.116.

FURTHER READINGS

Anderson, G. (1990). *Fundamentals of educational research.* Bristol, PA: Falmer Press, Taylor & Francis, Inc.

Bailey, K. D. (1988). Ethical dilemmas in social problems research: A theoretical framework. *American Sociologist, 19* (2), 121–137.

Beaucham, T. L., Faden, R. R., Wallace, R. J., Jr., & Walters, L. (Eds.). (1982). *Ethical issues in social science research.* Baltimore: Johns Hopkins University Press.

Bositis, D. A. (1990). *Research Design for Political Science: Contrivance and Demonstration in Theory and Practice.* Carbondale, IL: SIU Press.

Cohen, L. & Manion, L. (1994). *Research methods in education* (4th ed.). New York: Routledge.

Crowl, T. K. (1986). *Fundamentals of research: A practical guide for educators and special educators.* Columbus, OH: Publishing Horizons, Inc.

Eisner, E. W., & Peshkin, A. (1990). *Qualitative techniques in education: The continuing debate.* New York: Teacher's College Press.

Fowler, F. J., Jr. (1993). *Applied social research methods series, Vol. 1. Survey Research Methods.* Beverly Hills, CA: Sage Publications.

Graziano, A. M., & Raulin, M. L. (1993). *Research methods: A process of inquiry.* (2nd ed.). New York: Harper and Row.

Hedge, M. N. (1987). *Clinical research in communication disorders: Principles and strategies.* Boston: Little, Brown.

Hornsby-Smith, M. (1993). Gaining access. In N. Gilbert (Ed.), *Researching social life* (pp. 52–67). Thousand Oaks, CA: Sage.

Iverson, A. M. (1994). Guardian consent for children's participation in sociometric research. *Psychology in the Schools, 31,* 108–112.

Johnson, E. S. (1981). *Research methods in criminology and criminal justice.* Upper Saddle River, NJ: Prentice Hall.

May, T. (1997). *Social research: Issues, methods, and process.* (2nd ed.). Buckingham, England: Open University Press.

Mitchell, M., & Jolley, J. (1992). *Research design explained* (2nd ed.). Fort Worth, TX: Harcourt Brace Jovanovich College Publishers.

Pope, J. L. (1993). *Political marketing research.* NY: Amacon.

Raudonis, B. M. (1992). Ethical considerations in qualitative research with hospital patients. *Qualitative Health Researcher, 2,* 238–249.

Robinson, S. E., & Gross, D. R. (1986). Counseling research: Ethics and issues. *Journal of Counseling and Development, 64,* 331–333.

Robley, L. R. (1995). The ethics of qualitative nursing research. *Journal of Professional Nursing, 11,* 45–48.

Silverman, F. H. (1997). *Research design and evaluation in speech-language pathology and audiology* (4th ed.). Needham Heights, MA: Allyn & Bacon.

Tull, D. S., & Hawkins, D. I. (1993). *Marketing research: Measurement and methods* (4th ed.). New York: Macmillan.

Wexler, S. (1990). Ethical obligations and social research. In K. L. Kempf (Ed.). *Measurement issues in criminology* (pp. 78–107). NY: Springer-Verlag.

Zikmund, W. G. (1994). *Business research methods* (4th ed.). Chicago: Dryden Press.

3

Selecting a Topic

INTRODUCTION

Probably no step in developing and conducting a research project is as important, yet difficult, as selecting a topic. We are all familiar with the adage, "A house built on a weak foundation will not stand." In a very real sense, the research topic serves as a foundation for the entire effort. Simply put, the most extensive literature review, elaborate sampling method, elegant analysis, and comprehensive conclusions are for naught if the topic is of little interest or utility to members or beneficiaries of your profession.

It is interesting to note that of Senator William Proxmire's many accomplishments, he is most widely recognized for the creation and distribution of "Golden Fleece" awards. Senator Proxmire's (1980) book details a number of federally funded research projects that address research he believes to be useless. For example, a Golden Fleece was awarded to National Institute for Mental Health grant recipient, P. L. Van den Berghe. Professor Van den Berghe's experiment involved frequenting a Peruvian brothel to obtain information about its daily

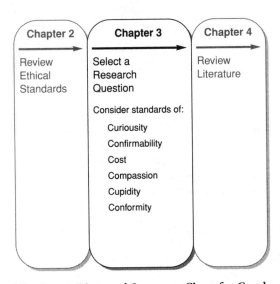

The Scope, Plan, and Sequence Chart for Conducting
Research: The Second Step in the Research Process

functioning. Another researcher obtained Department of Agriculture support for studying the effect of jogging on a treadmill in reducing stress in pregnant sows. Other noteworthy Golden Fleeces have been awarded to scientists seeking to:

1. Estimate the time required to prepare breakfast.
2. Determine the cause of cheating and lying on the tennis court.
3. Evaluate the effect of scantily clad female pedestrians on traffic flow.
4. Determine if sunfish that drink tequila are more aggressive than sunfish that drink gin.
5. Determine why prisoners wish to escape from jail.

Senator Proxmire emphasized that research sophistication and technical jargon do not ensure the importance of research conclusions. For example, he is impressed by a researcher who cites methodology that includes "target populations," "impact evaluations," "sociodemographic variables," "univariate and multivariate analyses," and "canonical correlations." He is not, however, impressed by the purpose of the research, which was to teach college students how to watch television.

There is no hard and fast rule for establishing the value of a research question, and scholars often disagree on the value of a study. There is no doubt that most scholars receiving Golden Fleece awards believed that their research was important. For example, in response to the awarding of a Golden Fleece to a researcher attempting to study the causes of romantic love, the Faculty Senate at the University of Wisconsin passed a resolution condemning Senator Proxmire. In view of these inevitable differences, one must question the basis upon which we select and defend research questions.

STANDARDS FOR PROBLEM SELECTION

Webb (1960) provided some insights for selecting an important problem. He initially described six common standards for choosing research questions. These were summarized as, " 'Am I interested,' 'Can I get the answer,' 'Will it help,' 'How much will it cost,' 'What's the payola,' and 'Is everyone else doing it?'" (p. 223). He discussed the limitations of each standard and concluded by identifying what he believed to be more important standards, specifically, knowledge, dissatisfaction, and generalizability. We believe that an understanding of all nine standards is important to evaluating the appropriateness of a research question. Therefore, each will be addressed in the following sections.

Curiosity

This criterion suggests that you address problems that are of personal interest. In doing so, you seek to gain knowledge for the sake of knowledge. A historical researcher may be urged to study African-American culture in America through discussions with a grandparent who recalls stories about her grandparents' lives on a Southern plantation. Similarly, an agronomist may question the extent to which plant production is limited by hedgerows surrounding fields. This effort may be motivated by arguments between local farmers who advocate eliminating hedges around fields and those that insist on retaining or further developing hedges.

The major value of using curiosity as a criterion for selecting a research problem is its value in motivating the researcher. Individuals with a genuine interest in a study are more likely to work diligently toward its completion. The major disadvantage is that curiosity alone may yield a topic that fails when judged against more practical standards. As noted by Webb (1960), researchers can be curious about questions that are trivial, absurd, or evil. You can imagine the reaction of your research supervisor when you argue that a problem is worth studying simply because it peaks your interest.

Confirmability

Logical positivists of the mid 1900s argued that the value of a question was best judged by the extent to which it could be answered. This criterion holds that easily defined and measured variables are more suitable for study than those that are vague and nebulous. For example, we can easily judge the probability of divorce for couples who have developed a prenuptial agreement. It would be substantially more difficult to judge marital satisfaction for couples who are effective communicators. The former question would easily pass the criterion of confirmability. The latter question may not.

Failure to develop a manageable project may be the most common problem you will face as a novice researcher. Curiosity and ambition often drive a student to select a problem that exceeds his or her resources or capabilities. The criterion of confirmability helps you develop a manageable investigation.

Use of confirmability alone may lead you to settle on a project that is best described as a "yawner." Such projects may fulfill the requirements of your master's or doctoral program; however, they are unlikely to advance knowledge in your discipline. Mature disciplines seldom offer unanswered questions that can easily be addressed with available instruments and methods. Original and valuable research often requires you to develop novel methods. Whether or not the question is confirmable can only be judged once the variables are successfully manipulated and reliably measured.

Cost

Closely related to confirmability is cost. We are often tempted to judge the value of a research question by the number of dollars required to provide an answer. This reasoning results from a false generalization that an item's cost is related to its quality. For example, most people would agree that a BMW costing $58,000 is more valuable than a Dodge costing $14,000. A refrigerator that costs $1,800 invariably has more features than one costing $900. Finally, a home worth $200,000 is likely to have more square feet, and be located in a better area of town, than a home costing $60,000.

The cost/quality generalization is not, however, applicable to research. As noted by Webb (1960), Einstein most likely used less equipment than his dentist. The cost of his lab was in no way related to the quality of his findings. One of Skinner's more interesting findings was the effect of limited schedules of reinforcement on behavioral persistence. Skinner demonstrated that the delivery of food pellets following a pigeon's pecking a keyboard key increased key pecking behavior. When his supply of food pellets began running low, he began reducing the frequency of food pellet reinforcement (e.g., one pellet every three pecks to one pellet for every fifth peck, and so on). Skinner noted that although he reduced the amount of food given for comparable levels of pecking, the pecking persisted. It is interesting to note that this important finding resulted from a lack of resources.

Compassion

Recent authors have raised questions about the extent to which a research project enhances the human condition. It is in this criterion that researchers find their heart (Wolf, 1978). Rather than concern for "statistical power," "randomized sampling," or "precision in measurement," you should question whether your research produces useful findings that ultimately enhance the quality of your participant's life.

This criterion is particularly important for applied researchers in the social and behavioral sciences. It is not sufficient to learn that a given procedure yields a statistically significant difference in the responses of human subjects. Professionals must question whether or not these differences are important to beneficiaries of the discipline. For example, one may learn that a certain treatment for depression reduces suicide attempts for an individual from three times a year to once a year. Most critics would contend that the treatment is not effective as long as there are any attempts. Less dramatically, research may indicate that a security system costing $10,000 may reduce shoplifting from an average of $3,000 a year to $1,000 a year. One would question whether this system fulfills the criterion of compassion since the cost of the system approaches the cost of the problem.

Cupidity

Cupidity is the extent to which an individual may obtain personal profit (often in the form of money or other tangibles) from engaging in a project. Cupidity is similar to compassion in that the major focus of the standard is benefit. While compassion is concerned for the payoff to the subject (or broader society), cupidity is concerned with the payoff to the researcher. As noted earlier, Senator Proxmire alluded vaguely to benefits obtained by the researcher studying Peruvian brothels. More directly, he cites a passage in a book by the same researcher that identifies possible personal benefits:

> In addition to paying part of your basic salary, grants will typically also give you an extra two months of summer salary. You can finance numerous jaunts to domestic and international conferences out of your research money without having to beg your university for it or having to justify your trip by reading a paper. And, if your research calls for going overseas, you can lead the life of an oriental potentate with an American income in a low cost-of-living country (Van den Berghe, 1970, p. 107).

Cupidity does not have to be as crass as the preceding illustration suggests. You may initially pursue research to obtain an advanced degree. Later, your research may yield promotions, tenure, and peer approval. Research may also focus on matters of deep personal interest. Alexander Graham Bell, for example, developed the telephone while studying methods to amplify sound for his hearing-impaired mother.

As with the preceding standards, cupidity used alone may not be effective in evaluating a research question. We should recognize that while a research project is good for the individual, it may not be good for others. Einstein recognized that work on the atomic bomb might produce personal rewards including money and status. He did not participate in experimentation, though, because he recognized the now-realized harm that could befall others.

Conformity

This criterion addresses the extent to which a research question is supported by the work of others. Veteran researchers acknowledge a cyclical pattern that underlies the popularity of various topics.

Research questions generally become popular because of the needs of the discipline or because of the availability of advanced technology. School improvement research is important because of evidence that children in America do not perform as well as children of other developed nations. It is reasonable for you to pursue a topic that has immediate value to society. Further, it is appropriate for you to explore adaptations of new technology to study existing problems (e.g., using more powerful telescopes to study the galaxy, microscopes to study cell tissue, and computers to assess consumer interests).

Despite the value of conformity, Webb (1960) cautioned against being over-enamored with popular topics and methods. Conforming methodology is better viewed as a means rather than an end. Using new technology is not done solely for the sake of using the technology. Rather, the technology is used because of its value in addressing existing problems. Equally important, the popularity of a topic does not necessarily confirm its value.

As noted earlier, Webb (1960) highlighted three standards that, without reservation, serve as a basis for good research questions. Knowledge and dissatisfaction are characteristics of the researcher, while generalizability is a characteristic of the problem. We will discuss each of these standards separately.

Most scholars, if not the general public, agree that knowledge is an essential prerequisite to effective research. We are all familiar with romantic accounts of uninformed individuals "stumbling" onto an important discovery. Unfortunately, these stories make for better theater than science. Breakthrough research most often results from an integration of a number of related studies and the identification of missing information. As noted by Webb (1960) "the vaunted, creative insight of the scientist occurs more frequently within a thorough knowledge of one's area than as a bolt from the blue" (p. 226).

Best (1997) emphasizes that even when lightning does strike, only the informed researcher is able to recognize its significance. Balerius Cordus, for example, is credited with the discovery of ether in the mid 1500s. While he carefully reported the intoxicating effects of the vapor, he and three centuries of science failed to establish the most important use for the chemical. It was not until 1842 that Dr. Crawford Long was called upon to assist a young man who had participated in a "sniffing party" and overdosed on the intoxicant. Noting the effect of the drug in deadening pain and slowing vital functions, Dr. Long developed ether as an anesthetic agent. The failure of scientists to apply ether as an anesthetic agent over the three centuries led to enormous human suffering in surgery.

Possessing knowledge in the area of study allows you to avoid errors of the past. Researchers familiar with the effect of experimenter attention in social science research, for example, may recognize that such attention may produce a beneficial effect regardless of the nature of the experimental treatment. (This is referred to as the *Hawthorn effect*.) Research design must control for the Hawthorn effect in order to isolate the effect of the treatment. Similarly, veteran researchers recognize that individuals are likely to react differently when they are being assessed or observed. (This is known as the reactive effect.) Consequently, the research procedures must acclimate the subject to the observer or employ covert measurement procedures. Failing to do this may result in invalid conclusions.

Finally, knowledge about an area of study may avoid embarrassment that may result from the "heralded" discovery of a phenomena well known by those familiar with the discipline. Well-informed researchers are able to systematically build upon discoveries of other researchers without retracing their efforts. This view places us at odds with academicians who function as if a prerequisite of originality is forgetting what is already known.

The second characteristic of a good research question is dissatisfaction. Countervailing forces must be present to ensure the integrity of popular ideas. Ideas surviving the scrutiny of dissatisfied researchers generally deserve high status in the discipline. Thoughts falling to skeptics and critics should be replaced with more viable ideas.

Probably one of the most celebrated examples of the value of criticism involved the presumed discovery of the N-Ray. Shortly after W. K. Rontgen discovered X rays, the distinguished French physicist, René Blondlot, claimed to discover another form of radiation. He labeled it the N-Ray after the University of Nancy. Blondlot's initial research generated a flurry of activity in wide-ranging disciplines. Physicists conducted experiments to demonstrate the physical properties of the N-Ray. Physiologists studied the effects of the ray on health and human performance. Finally, psychologists explored the value of the ray in enhancing human perception and learning.

Hundreds of research reports over several years attributed a variety of physical properties to the ray. Materials opaque to light were transparent to the ray (e.g., wood, gold, paper, iron, etc.). An aluminum lens could focus and bend the ray. Sources of N-Rays included electric-discharge tubes, certain types of gas burners, heated metals, the sun, and nerves and muscles in the human body.

Dissatisfied with the quality of experimentation and what he believed to be unwarranted hysteria over the alleged discovery, R. W. Wood, professor of physics at Johns Hopkins University, challenged researchers' claims. Professor Wood conducted a number of experiments testing the existence of the N-Ray. For example, unknown to Blondlot, Wood removed an aluminum prism from an experimental apparatus intended to refract N-Rays. Despite its absence, Blondlot still concluded that the apparatus refracted N-Rays. In another case, Wood subjected the experimenter's analysis of N-Rays to checks by two independent observers. The result was an inability of the observers to agree on the appearance or nonappearance of N-Rays.

Prompted by the work of Wood, the French journal, *Revue Scientifique,* suggested an experiment that would resolve the N-Ray controversy. They asked that Blondlot be given two equally weighted sealed wood containers, one containing lead and the other containing tempered steel (an alleged source of N-Rays). Were Blondlot able to use N-Ray detection devices to identify which box contained tempered steel, the scientific community could reasonably conclude the N-Rays did exist. Blondlot declined to participate. He argued that each person should form his or her own personal opinion about N-Rays.

Clearly, hard mentality can cause personal opinion to favor conclusions that may not be substantiated by rigorous scrutiny. Dissatisfied researchers serve as a countervailing force to ensure the validity of findings.

The final standard for an effective research question, generalizability, is the extent to which results can be applied to other experiments or to daily life. Baer, Wolf, and Risley (1968) argued that a field will advance best if research publications provide precise technological descriptions of the phenomena under study. Equally important is the relevance of the description to broader principles and practices. They suggested that describing the exact sequence of events leading to a shift in discrimination from colors to forms for a young child is useful. However, relating this observation to learning principles such as fading, discrimination training, or concept formation may be more important for the discipline.

Effective research questions provide insights well beyond isolated facts. They help us integrate new information in order to understand complex phenomena. It is interesting to know that children and primates who randomly select stocks often end up with results similar to those of highly skilled market analysts. The science (and conceptual system) of stock market forecasting is advanced further, however, when this knowledge is related to the "efficient market hypothesis." Given this generalizable application, one may recognize that all stock prices continually adjust to information available to investors. Since all expert stock pickers generally have access to this information, all stocks are priced equitably. Consequently, since all stocks are priced "fairly," an expert has no advantage over a novice who randomly selects stocks.

Webb (1960) suggested the following standards for evaluating the generality of a research finding: "In how many and what kind of specific circumstances will be relationships or rules that hold in this experiment hold in such other instances? If the answer to this is only in instances almost exactly replicable of this particular circumstance, the rules that we obtain are likely to be of little consequence. If, however, the rule applies to what apparently is a vast heterogeneity of events in time and space, in varieties of species and surroundings, this rule is likely to have great value" (p. 227).

ALTERNATIVE VIEW

As noted earlier, Webb (1960) offered a systematic and positivistic view underlying the selection of a research problem. Not all scholars agree with these principles, however. One of the most productive dissenters was B. F. Skinner (1959) who identified several "unformalized principles of scientific

1. Am I curious about this question? _____

I recognize that research projects often require substantial time and effort. Without substantial curiosity, I may lose interest in the project prior to completion.

2. Can I answer the question? _____

I have selected a research question that can be answered objectively with reliable instruments. My experimental procedures can be implemented with precision. I am able to rule out threats to the accuracy of my conclusions.

3. Can I afford to conduct the project? _____

There is a good possibility that I will complete the research project. I have sufficient resources (e.g., time, skill, money, technical assistance, etc.) to carry out the project. Impediments to my success have been accounted for, and I have a reasonable plan to overcome them.

4. Will the results of my research project benefit society? _____

My project will offer insights that aid others. Successful results go beyond simply rejecting a null hypothesis at some level of statistical significance. They also include demonstrating differences that may be judged socially significant.

5. Will I benefit from the project? _____

Completion of the research project will produce the personal benefits that I expect. These may include attainment of a degree, prestige in my discipline, professional advancement, and so on.

6. Does my research question conform to the interests and activities of other scholars?

_____

My research question builds upon previous questions addressed by other scholars. There is a reasonable body of literature supporting my effort. This literature can be used to introduce and establish the importance of my topic. It can also be used to interpret my conclusions.

7. Do I have a thorough knowledge of the literature underlying my inquiry?

_____

I have read all available professional literature on the topic of my investigation. I understand the background of the problem, am aware of previous efforts in this area, and have reviewed methodology related to my investigation.

8. Am I skeptical about current knowledge relating to my research question?

_____

Having carefully studied the problem, I am not fully satisfied with current explanations. My study should resolve questions that remain.

9. Will the results of my investigation provide insights beyond isolated facts?

_____

The results of my study can be generalized to the understanding of broader or more complex phenomena. The outcome of my work may have general value to others interested in my topic.

Figure 3.1 Evaluation of Topic Selection

practice" in his book *Cumulative Record.* These principles include dropping other research activities to study interesting questions that you may run into, employing the easiest and most efficient method to study a phenomena, and being prepared to take advantage of luck or serendipity.

Skinner argued as follows: ". . . I (never) behaved in the manner of Man Thinking as described by John Stuart Mill or John Dewey or in reconstruction of scientific behavior by other philosophers of science. I never faced a problem which was more than the eternal problem of finding order. I never attacked a problem by constructing a Hypothesis. I never deducted Theorems or submitted them to Experimental Check. So far as I can see, I had no preconceived Model of behavior—certainly not a physiological or mentalistic one and, I believe, not a conceptual one. If I engaged in Experimental Design at all, it was simply to complete or extend some evidence of order already observed" (p. 88–89).

You may find it difficult to sell a thesis or dissertation committee on a research proposal supported by Skinner's position. However, Skinner's views are useful in rounding out the standards discussed earlier. You should recognize that apologies need not be made for selecting inexpensive and efficient methods. Further, flexibility should be built into research designs so that unexpected outcomes can be pursued. Finally, a student's interests should weigh heavily in the final selection of a research topic.

SUMMARY

We have reviewed a number of standards for selecting a research topic. Some relate to the characteristics of the researcher; others relate to the characteristics of the problem itself. The checklist presented in Figure 3.1 may help you evaluate your topic.

REFERENCES

Baer, D., Wolf, M., & Risley, T. (1968). Some current dimensions of applied behavior analysis. *Journal of Applied Behavior Analysis, 1,* 91–97.

Best, J. W. (1997). *Research in education* (8th ed.). Upper Saddle River, NJ: Merrill/Prentice Hall.

Proxmire, W. (1980). *The fleecing of America.* Boston: Houghton Mifflin.

Skinner, B. F. (1959). *Cumulative record.* New York: Appleton, Century, and Croft.

Van den Berghe, P. L. (1970). *Academic gamesmanship.* New York: Abelard-Schuman.

Webb, W. B. (1961). The choice of the problem. *American Psychologist, 16,* 223–227.

Wolf, M. M. (1978). Social validity: The case for subjective evaluation or how applied behavior analysis is finding its heart. *Journal of Applied Behavior Analysis, 11,* 203–214.

FURTHER READINGS

Anderson, G. (1990). *Fundamentals of educational research.* Bristol, PA: Falmer Press, Taylor and Francis, Inc.

Cardinet, J. & All-al, L. (1983). Estimation of generalizability parameters. *New Directions for Testing and Measurement, 18,* 17–48.

Finney, J. (1991). On further development of the concept of social validity. *Journal of Applied Behavior Analysis, 24*(2), 245–249.

Gillmore, G. M. (1983). Generalizability theory: Applications to program evaluation. *New Directions for Testing and Measurement, 18,* 3–16.

Mitchell, M., & Jolley, J. (1992). *Research design explained* (2nd ed.). Fort Worth, TX: Harcourt Brace Jovanovich College.

Renzeth, C. M. & Lee, R. M. (1993). *Researching sensitive topics.* Newbury Park, CA: Sage.

Ross, S., & Morrison, G. (1992). Getting started as a researcher: Designing and conducting research studies in instructional technology. *TechTrends, 37*(3), 19–22.

Stainback, S., & Stainback, W. (1988). *Understanding and conducting qualitative research.* Reston, VA: Council for Exceptional Children.

Storey, K., & Horner, R. (1991). An evaluative review of social validation research involving persons with handicaps. *Journal of Special Education, 25*(3), 352–401.

Swanson, H. L. (1993). Selecting a research program in special education: Some advice and generalizations from published research. *Remedial and Special Education, 14*(3), 7–20.

4

Reviewing the Literature

INTRODUCTION

The purpose of conducting research is to contribute new information to a discipline. You will be at a distinct disadvantage, however, if you are not thoroughly familiar with the information that is already available about your topic. Just because the idea seems new or innovative to you doesn't mean that your topic hasn't already been addressed definitively by other investigators.

The best method for supporting the value of your topic is through an extensive review of "the body of research information related to the research problem" (Wiersma, 1995, p. 45). Be forewarned that conducting a literature review is a challenge. It requires hours of careful reading and attention to detail.

This chapter provides a rationale for conducting a literature review. We also describe specific steps you can follow to complete this stage of the research process and identify effective resources.

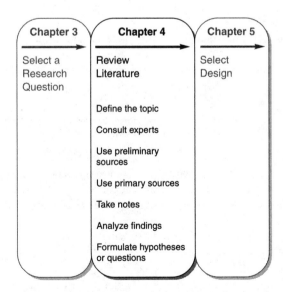

Chapter 3	Chapter 4	Chapter 5
Select a Research Question	Review Literature	Select Design
	Define the topic	
	Consult experts	
	Use preliminary sources	
	Use primary sources	
	Take notes	
	Analyze findings	
	Formulate hypotheses or questions	

The Scope, Plan, and Sequence Chart for Conducting Research: The Third Step in the Research Process

PURPOSE OF REVIEWING THE LITERATURE

Perhaps by now you have obtained a copy of the thesis or dissertation standards from the graduate office at your university. One of the first things you see on the list of required items is a literature review. Because you have written term papers, you may think that you are fairly well prepared for this aspect of the research process. While previous experience helps, conducting a thesis or dissertation literature review will take you to a whole new level. You will be spending many hours in the library, perching on a stool in front of a computer screen, sitting in study carrels poring over books and journals, and waiting in line for the photocopy machines. There had better be a good reason for all this work! Actually, there are several.

In addition to meeting graduate school requirements, a thorough review allows you to verify that you have chosen an appropriate topic. It would be exciting to learn that your topic is entirely new. It is more likely, however, that you will discover your work on this topic will expand information currently available. Either way, *your* topic should have the potential for making a difference to theory or practice. It is also possible that you may learn that your topic is neither new nor a contribution to existing information. As difficult as it may be, we suggest you select another topic. It is a waste of precious time, energy, and resources to investigate a topic already studied extensively by other investigators unless you can bring new and interesting information to light by doing so.

A literature review can help you define and refine dependent and independent variables, select a research design for evaluating the relationships between them, and identify formal and informal techniques for measuring them. We will address this information in subsequent chapters. Seeing how other investigators have handled these issues will be extremely valuable as you move forward in your own work. Modifying or directly using techniques, instruments, or materials with proven track records reduces your workload and allows you to focus on other problems.

A literature review can help you gauge the feasibility of pursuing the topic. You will be able to determine if you have the skills necessary to conduct the research and answer your question. For example, can you select, develop, and administer measurement devices? Are you comfortable with the design and statistical procedures that may be necessary? You can also consider the time commitment and amount of financial resources necessary to conduct your study.

When you summarize your literature review in writing, you will be able to familiarize committee members and other interested readers with the background necessary for understanding how your topic emerged. You can establish the importance of your topic and justify the effort you will expend to conduct the study (Crowl, 1993). On a related note, a literature review provides a logical rationale for the hypotheses you are stating or the questions you are posing. You can show how your study can bridge the gap between what is known and unknown in your area of interest.

METHODS FOR CONDUCTING A LITERATURE REVIEW

The literature review that you include in your proposal and final report sets the stage for new data. It addresses theories and studies specifically related to the data you hope to present. In your literature review, you will need to (a) describe theoretical constructs that explain the phenomenon in which you are interested, (b) review and critique previous work, and (c) show how your work will be a logical extension of previous efforts.

You can conduct a literature review either manually or with the assistance of a computer. While you may occasionally engage in a manual search, we strongly recommend that the majority of your efforts to locate relevant material be conducted with the assistance of electronic information retrieval systems. You can locate greater amounts of current resources more quickly and at minimum expense.

Borg, Gall, and Gall (1993) identified several steps for conducting a literature review. We will list and discuss them separately and expand upon some in subsequent sections.

1. *Define the topic as clearly and precisely as you can.* You may have already read a little bit of information about your topic. Use what you know to develop a rough statement of your hypothesis or question.

2. *Contact the experts.* No doubt there are people at your university or in your community who have expertise in areas directly and indirectly related to your topic. Contact them and make an appointment to meet at a mutually convenient time and place. During your meeting, the expert can share his or her perspective on your topic, help you focus your statement, recommend specific print resources, and direct you to other experts in the field. Obviously, you will also want to take advantage of people whom you have selected to serve on your thesis or dissertation committee.

   Another way of meeting the experts is to subscribe to a discussion list in your discipline. One of the advantages of the Internet is that it allows rapid exchange of information and multiple pathways of interaction among professionals. Most professionals are glad to steer a beginner in the right direction and will usually respond to a specific request for aid. In addition, many discussion lists archive their postings, and the archives can be searched for "threads" on a specific topic.

   The experts at your university may be able to tell you about specific useful discussion lists or you can find sites on the World Wide Web that provide discussion lists by subject area with subscription information. You might try http://www.liszt.com or http://tile.net/lists/ as a starting point. You could also use a search engine such as AltaVista or Yahoo to find other sites. Before you post to a discussion list, though, it is generally a good idea to read the postings for a week or two to get a feeling for the general nature of the discussions and the tone of the postings. Some discussion lists are much more formal than others.

3. *Review secondary sources of information.* These sources, such as books and review articles, give a general picture of the work that has already been completed on your topic. You can consult *Books in Print* or the catalog at the library, look for Annual Reviews in your subject area, or use titles recommended previously by the experts. You need not spend hours reading these books just yet. Scanning selected sections is sufficient preparation for the next step.

4. *Select relevant preliminary sources.* These sources help you locate primary sources and additional secondary sources related to your topic. We will present more information on these resources shortly.

5. *Select key words.* These key words can be used to describe or label your topic. Ideas for key words come from examining your topic, listing synonyms and closely related words, and consulting the thesaurus or dictionary of key words that accompanies preliminary sources. For example, if your topic were related to HIV, you would select words and phrases such as AIDS, Acquired Immune Deficiency Disorder, sexually transmitted diseases, and communicable diseases.

6. *Use these keywords to look up information.* You can then find information in the preliminary sources you have selected.

7. *Prepare a bibliography.* If you are using a computer, simply choose the print option. The computer will generate a hard copy of the citations in which you are interested. If you are conducting a manual search, you will need to copy citations by hand.

8. *Obtain, examine, and analyze primary sources, keeping detailed notes.*

USING A VARIETY OF SOURCES

The phrases "preliminary sources," "primary sources," and "secondary sources" refer to distinct sets of materials that affect the comprehensiveness of your literature review.

Preliminary Sources

Preliminary sources include the abstracts and indexes listed in Table 4.1. They are available in both print and computerized formats and offer access to thousands of publications that may be useful to you, including books, articles, and other documents. University libraries offer computerized access to reference materials. We mentioned the advantages of this technology earlier, but there are also some disadvantages you should know about. Databases differ in how they are ac-

Table 4.1   Abstracting and Indexing Services

Preliminary sources include several abstracts and available indexes. These can be very helpful in identifying primary and secondary sources of information for your literature review.

Name	Description
Psychological Abstracts	Published monthly and covers every major journal in the world in psychology and related fields. It includes a thesaurus of index terms. The institutional affiliation of the first author is provided. You need to know at least one term frequently used to describe the area of interest.
PsychLIT	Summarizes literature from 1,400 journals related to psychology.
Educational Resources Information Center	Screens, organizes, and disseminates literature related to educational practices or issues. There is a dictionary of descriptors and two monthly guides to its contents. The first is the *Current Index to Journals in Education (CIJE)*, which includes journals related to the field of education. The second is *Resources in Education (RIE)*, which focuses on nonjournal sources of information such as dissertations and reports on government funded projects.
Dissertation Abstracts International	Focuses exclusively on dissertations.
Social Sciences Citation Index (SSCI)	Identifies and groups together all newly published articles that have referenced the same, earlier publication. It includes areas related to the social sciences and is useful when certain researchers are associated with a topic.
Sociofile	Contains information on approximately 1,500 journals in sociology and related fields.
Education Index	Covers many of the same sources as *CIJE*. It is an index of titles and citations arranged according to topic headings and author headings. It does not contain abstracts.
Reader's Guide to Periodic Literature	Indexes articles of a popular and general nature according to subject and author.
Business Periodical Index	Covers over 100 periodicals in business, accounting, labor and management, marketing, public administration, and related fields.
Exceptional Child Education Resources	Contains resources solely about special education.

cessed and in key words used to locate materials. Also, you may not be able to use them to access information published prior to a certain year. In this situation, you will have to conduct a manual search using the print version of the preliminary source.

There are several bibliographic databases on the Internet, and these may be available to you through either the World Wide Web or your library. CARL Uncover, FirstSearch, ERIC, and Expanded Academic Index are several of the larger on-line indexes but there are many others. Most of these databases can be searched by author, title, or key word. Some offer full text or abstracts on line while others offer FAX or photocopy services. Using these databases can help you rapidly build your bibliography, but they usually have to be supplemented by other sources.

Procedures for searching a database are very similar to those for conducting a general literature review. Begin by meeting with experts and reviewing selected secondary literature. Next, consider what topics may relate to your research. Do you prefer to identify a particular author or collaborative team of authors? Are you more concerned with a specific population, a procedure, or testing instrument? Once this step is complete, select key terms to be used in the search. Many databases include a thesaurus of descriptors useful in retrieving literature. Following this step, develop a written plan for your search. Computer databases allow you to access topics associated with just one keyword. For example, you could use "hyperactivity" to identify journal articles on this topic. As illustrated in Figure 4.1 , you can use connectors to change the scope of your search.

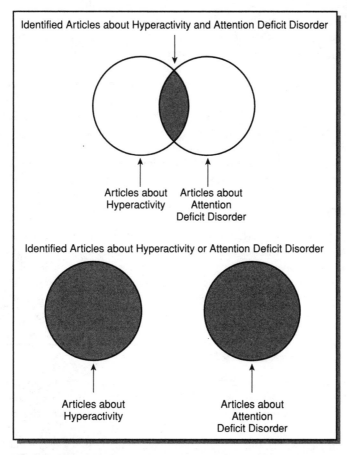

Figure 4.1 A Venn Diagram Showing How Connector Words Change the Scope of Your Study

To narrow your focus, use "and" to connect two or more keywords. For example, "cardiovascular fitness and aerobic activity" will identify materials that address both topics. If you want to broaden your search, use "or" to connect two or more keywords. This is particularly helpful when two or more words are used interchangeably to label a topic in which you are interested. You can also limit your search to a specific range of years in which studies were conducted.

Another extremely convenient way to build your bibliography is to locate a resource page on the World Wide Web with a well-developed bibliography. These are frequently maintained by an expert in the discipline or by national professional organizations as a service to other researchers and will usually include all but the most recent references. The best ways to find these resource pages is through a discussion list, by following links from other Web pages, or by using a search engine.

Your literature search will yield both *primary* and *secondary* sources. Primary sources refer to publications written by the people who actually conducted the study or developed the original argument. In a manner of speaking, the report comes directly to you from the researcher or theoritician. Primary sources include reports published in the professional literature, research reports given at professional meetings, conference proceedings, research documents prepared for funding agencies, and scholarly books and monographs that contain one or more unabridged reports.

Obviously, it is a good idea to be familiar with the research being reported in your own field of interest. You probably subscribe to several journals or receive them as part of a membership package from professional organizations. You should review journals that you have in your own professional library, but don't expect to be aware of all the subtle aspects of your topic afterwards. Journals in your own professional library may not present a complete picture for two reasons. First, due to financial constraints, it is highly unlikely that you personally receive every journal relevant to your field. Second, personal opinions of theory and practice in your field may influence your choice of journals; others representing different perspectives may be absent from your shelf. Nonetheless, those journals probably contain information that would be useful to you; therefore, neglecting them may introduce an element of bias into your literature review.

There are a variety of journals for every discipline within the social sciences. Knowledge of journals in your discipline will greatly expedite your search. Table 4.2 identifies some of the major journals according to the disciplines they represent. If you are unable to locate an article you think may be relevant, request it through the interlibrary loan department in your university library. It may take a few weeks to get a response, but the service is usually free to students.

Secondary Sources

Secondary sources include articles written by someone other than the person who conducted the study. Examples include books and review articles published in the journals. They can give you a quick review of several concepts related to your topic. Unfortunately, authors of secondary sources may have omitted key information in the interest of brevity, or they may have selectively included topics in their books based on their own perspectives. Obviously, it is better to use primary sources because secondary sources reflect someone else's interpretation of the original work.

THE WORLD WIDE WEB AS A RESEARCH TOOL

The World Wide Web is a wealth of information (and misinformation) and it can be a valuable resource for the development of your research topic and your bibliography. In order to get the most out of this resource you need a strategy for extracting information from the Web. Surfing the Web (going from one page to the next interesting link, to the next, etc.) is a fine way to waste an afternoon (or a week), but unless you are exceptionally lucky it is not a good way to research a topic. To research a topic efficiently you must use a **search engine**.

Table 4.2 Empirical Journals Within the Social Sciences

The following list is just a few of the journals that may be helpful to people conducting research in the social and behavioral sciences.

Education

Adolescence

Arithmetic Teacher

Child Development

Educational Research Quarterly

Elementary School Journal

Psychology

American Journal of Psychology

American Psychologist

Educational and Psychological Measurements

Journal of Applied Psychology

Psychology in the Schools

Guidance and Counseling

American Vocational Journal

Elementary School Guidance and Counseling

Measurement and Evaluation in Guidance

School Counselor

Vocational Guidance Quarterly

Reading

Elementary English

Journal of Reading

Reading Improvement

Reading Research Quarterly

Reading Teacher

Criminology

Crime and Delinquency

Journal of Offender Rehabilitation

Social and Legal Studies

International Journal of Criminology and Penology

Mass Communication

Critical Studies in Mass Communication

Journal of Communication

Research on Language and Social Interactions

Business

Accounting and Business Research

Journal of Business

Journal of Business Finance

Journal of Business Research

Quarterly Review of Economics and Finance

Nutrition

American Journal of Clinical Nutrition

Journal of Applied Nutrition

Journal of Nutrition

Journal of Nutrition Education

Nutrition Research

Sociology

American Journal of Sociology

American Sociological Review

Critical Sociology

International Journal of Sociology

Journal of Sociology and Social Welfare

Health and Physical Education

Health Education Quarterly

Journal of Health, Physical Education, and Recreation

Journal of School Health

Qualitative Health Research

Research for Exercise and Sport

Special Education

Exceptional Children

Journal for the Association of Persons with Severe and Profound Handicaps

Journal of Special Education

Mental Retardation

Remedial and Special Education

Speech/Language Pathology and Audiology

Brain and Language

Journal of Speech and Hearing Research

Language and Speech

Language, Speech and Hearing Services in the Schools

Seminars in Speech and Language

Topics in Language Disorders

Nursing

Clinical Nursing Research

Journal of Professional Nursing

Nursing Research

Nursing Science Quarterly

Research in Nursing and Health

Political Science

American Political Science Review

Comparative Political Studies

Journal of Politics

Political Research Quarterly

Review of Politics

Marketing

Journal of Marketing

Journal of Marketing Research

Industrial Marketing Research

International Journal of Research in Marketing

Research in Marketing

Social Work

Clinical Social Work Journal

Journal of Social Service Research

Research on Social Work Practice

Social Work Research

Search Engines

There are a large number of search engines on the Web, but they come in basically two types—**directories** (Yahoo, Galaxy, Argus, Magellan, and others) and **key word indexes** (AltaVista, Excite, InfoSeek, Lycos, and others). There are also some hybrid types and even some complex combinations. Fortunately, we do not have to understand how all of these search engines work to use them. Most will accept a few key words and then (after checking their directory or key word index or whatever) they will provide you with a list of addresses (URLs) of sites that may be of interest to you. Right below the address there is frequently a short summary or the first few sentences of the web site to help you decide if that site is of interest. The list is usually hot (linked) so that you can simply click on an address to take a look at that web page.

It is important to use a variety of search engines in your exploration of your topic on the Web. Different search engines may give you radically different results, even if you use the same key words. In order to ensure the best recovery you should do two or three searches with different search engines. A good plan of action is to do a search, examine the first 20 or 30 addresses, bookmark (save the addresses) of the interesting sites, and then do the same search with a different search engine.

Reliability

With the Web, as with any source of information including journal articles and books, you must evaluate the reliability of the information you are retrieving. Anyone with access to a computer (and that means just about everybody these days) can put a site on the Web. Further, there is no control over what goes into the site. The information that you extract from the Web has not been peer reviewed and generally does not have the status of a journal article or book. (Although there are some on-line or electronic journals that are, in fact, peer reviewed.) It is important that you carefully evaluate the reliability of the information that you retrieve. You should consider the source of the information, and in evaluating reliability you should determine whether it is factually based or whether it is opinion disguised as fact. The Web provides a wondrous source of information, but some of it is misinformation; let the user beware.

Databases

Databases are simply compilations of information on a subject, arranged in some orderly way, and with provisions for data retrieval in some logical manner. By now everybody knows how to find an address or telephone number on the Internet (try http://www.555-1212.com/whte_us.htm), but there is also a wealth of information available that is very useful for researchers. You can find the number of children living below the poverty line or other population information by searching the 1990 Census Data (http://venus.census.gov/cdrom/lookup). You can find the names and addresses of contributors to congressional campaigns on the Federal Election Commission home page (http://www.tray.com) or the latest patent information on the IBM Patent Server (http://patent.womplex.ibm.com/). You can find a catalogue of the holdings of the University of California-Berkeley Museum of Vertebrate Zoology (http://www.mip.berkeley.edu/mvz/) or biographical data (http://www.ancestry.com/ancestry/). You can find bibliographies and citation lists on many subjects, and you can do literature searches (try http://wdev.carl.org:80/) on any subject. In fact, there is so much information available that finding it is sometimes a formidable task.

How do you get organized? There are several approaches to finding material on the Web. One is to bookmark Web pages that provide links to other useful web sites. For example, the web page, "Government and Government-Related Information by Subject" (http://sunsite.unc.edu/reference/docs/subject.html) provides links to government databases. Everything from business and economics data to zip codes is linked to this site, and it is a valuable resource for many researchers. Another useful site is the University of Southern California's NETSource (http://www.usc.edu/dept/webster/source.htm). The page is intended for development researchers, but it provides links to many useful databases including business information, genealogy, newspaper and magazine archives, and legal research.

Finding "summary" sites like these is not easy. As we mention elsewhere, one of the better ways is to join one or more discussion lists in your academic area and bookmark useful sites as they come up in the discussions. There are hundreds of these discussion lists available. Try looking at the Publicly Accessible Mailing Lists page http://www.neosoft.com/Internet/paml/indexes.html) for a list that fits your needs. Some lists are more active than others, so be selective or be prepared to wade through a lot of messages.

Finally, of course, you can use a search engine to find useful sites. However you approach your search for information on the World Wide Web, you will find it to be a valuable source on most topics.

REVIEWING THE LITERATURE

It may not be necessary to photocopy all the materials you locate, but you should take good notes. Your notes should help you organize information in a manner that facilitates your ability to recall and use it in the future. We cannot tell you the number of times a student has said, "Now, where have I seen that before?" or "It was in some article I read, but I don't remember where I saw it." Even more frustrating is when the student is compiling the reference list for the final report and is unable to locate key information such as the author's initials, or the date, volume, or number of a journal article.

Your notes may include any of the following: direct quotations (using proper punctuation marks and including page numbers); paraphrasing of an author's thoughts; summaries of key concepts in the article; and/or your own reactions to the content of the article. Table 4.3 includes tips for taking notes suggested by Best (1993). Regardless of how good your note-taking skills are, you will still need to photocopy articles and book chapters that you believe are critical and that you will probably refer to frequently during your study.

Table 4.3   Taking Notes

Best (1997) suggested the following methods for taking notes.

1. Quickly scan the entire article before taking any notes.

2. Use index cards because they can be sorted according to your needs and are easily stored. Carry a stack of cards with you when you go to the library. If you are using a computer, you should have a separate disk or designate a separate folder on your hard drive for bibliographic information.

3. Assign headings to each card for convenient filing.

4. List the complete citation on the card. You may want to include the call number for a book.

5. Include only one article on each card. For lengthy articles use two or more cards. Use paper clips or rubber bands to keep them together.

6. Take your time when writing notes to enhance legibility.

7. Keep cards in a safe container, such as an index file or an expandable envelope. If you are using a computer, be sure to make frequent backup copies of your bibliographic information and store the backup in a safe place.

It is important to analyze manuscripts you collect to decide if the conclusions and implications can be taken seriously (Crowl, 1993). For empirical papers, we recommend a standard recording form to assist with this process. This format should identify important features of the study and their implications for your work. Figure 4.2 presents a form useful for taking notes and analyzing studies.

Instead of taking your notes on paper, you may want to enter them directly into a computer, using either a word processor or a bibliography program to organize them. There are several good bibliography programs available (e.g., EndNotes, ProCite, Papyrus), and they can greatly simplify the creation and management of a large bibliography. Most bibliography programs will generate your literature cited section for you in any format required. This means you can produce a literature cited section to meet the format requirements of any journal without a lot of work. Most will also allow you to specify key words to associate with a reference and to make notes on content that are linked to the reference. These features make managing a large bibliography a less daunting task.

While the results of many studies may contribute to your confidence in the topic, you should expect to find others that contradict your expectations. It is common for several studies on the same topic to contradict each other. Examine conflicting studies carefully. Can you locate factors that could have contributed to the contradictions, such as differences in sampling or testing, or subtle differences in the independent variable or how it was implemented? After your review, you may determine that a study may have been poorly executed. You don't have to eliminate it as a resource; just be aware of its flaws. As you analyze each study, put it within the context of others you have read. Is there a pattern emerging across findings? Are there major contradictions? How can you account for them?

You should identify implications of each study for the research you want to conduct. Did any of the authors use instructional procedures or materials that would be helpful to you? Did they encounter any pitfalls that you had not considered? How did they resolve these problems? Did they make recommendations for future work that have implications for what you are planning to do? Their results should shape your thinking about the results you anticipate during your study.

Probably the most common question students ask is, "How do I know when I am done with my literature review?" There are several steps to follow before you can judge your review complete. We recommend that your literature review include a variety of sources, which reduces the possibility that you are overlooking an important piece of information. In addition, you should examine the references included in each primary source you read. That source may include citations you did not uncover during your search of the databases. At some point, you will present a written literature review. After reading it, members of your committee may recommend other sources. You should locate and evaluate these items. Finally, remember that new contributions to the professional literature appear monthly. While you are in the middle of your study, you should check recent publications for new studies that are pertinent to your work.

STATING A RESEARCH QUESTION OR HYPOTHESIS

You began your literature review with a fairly good idea of the topic you wanted to pursue in your study. A solid review of the literature should help you refine your topic into a definitive question or hypothesis. You should check with your committee members to see which format they prefer. Regardless of format, we strongly recommend that you limit the number of research questions or hypotheses to one or two. You want to contribute new knowledge to your field; however, the results of your thesis or dissertation do not have to resolve long-standing burning issues. Keeping your project narrow in scope will facilitate timely completion.

Author: _____

Title: _____

Journal: _____

Year/Volume/Number/Pages:_____

Questions/Hypothesis: _____

_____

_____

Subjects
    Description _____

    Sampling Procedure _____

Dependent Variables _____

Dependent Measures _____

Independent Variables _____

Procedures_____

_____

_____

Reliability of Dependent and Independent Variables _____

Design
    Did it control for extraneous variables? _____

Analysis
    Statistical procedures_____

_____

Results _____

_____

_____

Critique/Limitations
    Faults _____

    Recommendations for future research _____

    Implications for my study _____

References
    Potentially Useful Citations _____

_____

_____

Figure 4.2 A Coding Sheet for Evaluating Databased Studies

Research Questions

You can simply phrase your topic in a question format. A research question asks about the relationship between two or more variables. If you are conducting a survey on welfare reform, you can ask, "Will the preference for welfare reform vary according to level of income of the respondents?" If you are testing a new medication, you can ask, "Will users of Drug X report fewer headaches than nonusers?" If you have developed a new training program, you can ask, "Will participants increase the frequency of socially skillful behaviors?"

Stating a Hypothesis

As stated in Chapter 1, a hypothesis is a formal statement you use to predict a single research outcome. It is an educated guess that explains a phenomenon. Generally, it defines or proposes the relationship between dependent and independent variables. The purpose of your study is to test the hypothesis, but to do so, you must formulate it carefully.

In general, a well-written hypothesis includes four components. The first identifies the experimental group (e.g., 40 youths who were randomly selected from the Wasach Basin Council to participate in orientation exercises). The second describes the experimental procedure (e.g., a program of six 40-minute orienteering activities). The third identifies the expected outcome (enhanced performance on an orienteering test). The final is the control group (e.g., 40 youths who were randomly selected from the Wasach Basin Boy Scout Council for general enrichment activities). In the null form, this hypothesis would read as follows: "There will be no difference between 40 youths who were randomly selected from the Wasach Basin Council to participate in orientation exercises and 40 youths who were randomly selected from the Wasach Basin Boy Scout Council for general enrichment as demonstrated by performance on an orienteering test."

There are four types of hypotheses: *null, correlative, directional,* and *causal* (Johnson & Joslyn, 1994). You use a *null hypothesis* to indicate that there is no relationship between the independent or treatment variable and dependent or subject performance variables. Usually, the null hypothesis is the opposite of the hypothesis you are trying to confirm. For example, a null hypothesis can state, "There will be no difference between the number of headaches reported by users of Drug X and nonusers." The data from your study will allow you to reject or retain the null hypothesis. Rejecting the null hypothesis means that there is indeed a relationship between the independent and dependent variables. For example, uses of Drug X report fewer headaches.

A *correlative hypothesis* indicates there is a relationship between the independent and dependent variables, although the exact nature of the relationship is not specified. For example, such a hypothesis can state, "There is a relationship between the strength of desire for welfare reform and the income of respondents." Data analysis will tell you whether high or low income respondents are more concerned about welfare reform.

A *directional hypothesis* requires that you specify the direction of the relationship between the independent and dependent variables. For example, you can state the following hypothesis: "High school students with high GPAs will earn higher GPAs in college than high school students with low GPAs." This statement describes a direct relationship; however, you can suggest there is an inverse relationship between independent and dependent variables. For example, you can hypothesize, "The older a person becomes, the more his or her health declines."

Finally, a *causal hypothesis* is one in which changes in one variable causes changes in another. A major causal hypothesis with which we are all familiar is that cigarette smoking causes lung cancer. A causal hypothesis is a very bold claim; however, it is difficult to confirm definitively.

There are standards for evaluating the quality of a hypothesis, regardless of the type you choose (Johnson & Joslyn, 1991). They include the following:

1. *A hypothesis should be an empirical statement.* It is an educated guess about the relationship between independent and dependent variables, based on a solid review of the literature. A hypothesis should not describe what should be true.

2. *A hypothesis should be generalizable.* It should explain a general phenomenon rather than a specific occurrence. A narrow hypothesis states, "A game can increase social skill development." A more general hypothesis states, "An activity that includes modeling, rehearsal, feedback, and reinforcement will increase social skill development."

3. *A hypothesis should be plausible.* You should have a logical rationale for believing the data from your study which will allow you to retain or reject a hypothesis.

4. *A hypothesis should be specific.* Independent and dependent variables should be carefully defined.

5. *A hypothesis should be testable.* You should be able to collect the data you need to indicate whether it should be retained or rejected.

SUMMARY

A literature review is an examination of "the body of research information related to the research problem" (Wiersma, 1995, p. 45). Although it takes a substantial amount of time and effort, conducting a literature review is essential to the research process. A solid literature review allows you to (a) verify that you have chosen an appropriate topic, (b) define and refine aspects of your own study, (c) begin to estimate the resources your own study will require, and (d) establish the importance of your topic and justify the effort you will expend.

In this chapter, we described how to conduct a literature review. We identified steps in the process and key sources such as preliminary, primary, and secondary sources. We discussed how to use these sources to select materials you will include in your review. We highlighted the importance of taking good notes and systematically analyzing what you are reading. Finally, we discussed how to state a research hypothesis.

You need to define your problem as clearly as possible and continue to refine it as you conduct your literature review. Drawing on published sources keeps you from reinventing the wheel. Using the ideas we have presented in this chapter will help you identify and examine what is already known and build upon it through your own research.

REFERENCES

Best, J. W. (1997). *Research in education* (8th ed.). Englewood Cliffs, NJ: Prentice Hall.

Borg, W. R., Gall. J. P., & Gall, M. D. (1992). *Applying educational research: A practical guide* (3rd ed.). New York: Longman.

Crowl, T. K. (1993). *Fundamentals of educational research.* Madison, WI: Brown & Benchmark.

Glesne, C., & Peshkin, E. (1991). *Becoming qualitative researchers: An introduction.* New York: Longman.

Johnson, J. B., & Joslyn, R. A. (1994). *Political science research methods* (3rd ed.). Washington, DC: CQ Press.

Wiersma, W. (1995). *Research methods in education: An introduction* (6th ed.). Needham Heights, MA: Allyn & Bacon.

FURTHER READINGS

Anderson, G. (1990). *Fundamentals of educational research.* Bristol, PA: Falmer Press, Taylor and Francis, Inc.

Beasley, D. (1988). *How to use a research library.* New York: Oxford.

Cooper, H. M. (1989). *Integrating research: A guide to literature reviews.* Newbury Park: Sage.

Ghauri, P. N., Gronhaug, K., & Kristianslund, I. (1995). *Research methods in business studies: A practical guide.* New York: Prentice Hall.

Johnson, E. S. (1981). *Research methods in criminology and criminal justice.* Englewood Cliffs, NJ: Prentice Hall.

Leedy, P. D. (1996). *Practical research: Planning and design* (6th ed.). New York: Macmillan.

Manheim, J. B., & Rich, R. C. (1994). *Empirical political analysis: Research methods in political science.* New York: Longman.

McMillan, J. H. (1996). *Educational research: Fundamentals for the consumer.* New York: HarperCollins Publishers.

Nielson, M. E., & Reilly, P. L. (1985). A guide to understanding and evaluating research articles. *Gifted Child Quarterly, 29*(2), 90–92.

Rudestam, K. E., & Newton, R. R. (1992). *Surviving your dissertation: A comprehensive guide to content and process.* Newbury Park: Sage.

Shermis, M. D., Stemmer, P. M., Berger, C. F., & Anderson, G. E. (1991). *Using microcomputers in social science research.* Needham Heights, MA: Allyn & Bacon.

Silverman, F. H. (1997). *Research design and evaluation in speech-language pathology and audiology.* (4th ed.). Englewood Cliffs, NJ: Prentice Hall.

5

Quantitative Research Approaches for Large Groups

INTRODUCTION

Having reviewed the literature and established your research question or hypothesis, you next turn your attention to the choice of a research design. *Research design* is an objective and complete description of methodology employed by the researcher. The quality and appropriateness of a design is judged by the confidence one can have that the results support the researcher's conclusions. Careful selection of a design, in combination with appropriate measurement and analysis, provides readers and critics with increased confidence that your conclusions are "believable."

Several design options are available for working with large groups. The choice of which option to use depends on the question being asked or the hypothesis being tested, and the characteristics of the sample being studied. In this chapter, we will describe four major categories of quantitative designs suitable for use with large groups. These categories include *true experimental designs, quasi-experimental designs, correlational methods,* and *surveys.* Subsequent chapters discuss small group and qualitative research designs.

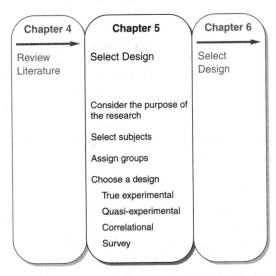

The Scope, Plan, and Sequence Chart for Conducting Research: The Fourth Step in the Research Process

The Purpose of Your Research

The design selected depends on the purpose of the research. Questions may focus on whether the scores on the dependent variables obtained by two or more groups of subjects differ due to the presence or absence of the independent variable. To answer this question, a researcher can use either a true experimental design or a quasi-experimental design. A true experimental design requires that subjects be randomly selected and assigned to groups. If random selection and assignment are not possible because of ethical or other considerations, a quasi-experimental design may be used.

You may be interested in how the same group of people perform on two different characteristics that occur naturally and cannot be manipulated. This type of question is best addressed by a correlational study. Finally, you can conduct a survey if you are interested in individuals' feelings, motivations, beliefs, or attitudes. Prior to talking about design options, we will review procedures for selecting subjects.

SUBJECT SELECTION

Probability Sampling

There are many methods for choosing subjects to participate in a study. (This will be explained further in Chapter 8.) The method affects the design. In fact, the major difference between true experimental designs and quasi-experimental designs is the manner in which subjects are selected. A true experimental design involves probability sampling which ensures that every person within the population has some specified probability of being included in the study. Quasi-experimental designs generally involve studying "intact" groups (e.g., Mr. Jones's third grade class, members of the local Rotary Club, residents of a particular skilled nursing center).

The ideal method for obtaining subjects for a true experimental design is through *simple random sampling.* Simple random sampling occurs when all members of a population have an equal chance to be included in a study. Similarly, random assignment to groups means that each subject has an equal chance of being placed in any treatment condition. Random selection of subjects and random assignment to groups allow you to assume that your participants are equivalent before implementing the independent variable. Any differences detected after the study can then be attributed to exposure to the independent variable.

Random selection and assignment of subjects increase the representativeness of the sample, making it easier to generalize results to the population at large. Unfortunately, random selection and assignment are difficult to accomplish. Therefore, *systematic sampling procedures* may be used, in which every *n*th person on a total list is selected for inclusion in the study. Another choice is *stratified random sampling,* which requires the researcher to divide the population into subgroups for subsequent comparison. Finally, *multistage sampling* can be used. Here, a researcher may be interested in surveying clients receiving direct services from nonprofit social service agencies in your county. The researcher can identify all nonprofit agencies, list all of their clients, and then select one tenth of the clients at each agency.

Nonprobability Sampling

You may not have the luxury of selecting your subjects at random; frequently, they are already assigned to intact groups. Nonprobability samples are easier to get, but because they are not random, results are likely to be less accurate and believable. They include *accident samples* in which people are studied because they are available. You are probably very familiar with this sampling procedure. No doubt while shopping at the mall you have been approached by someone conducting surveys as part of a product testing program. *Purposive or judgmental sampling* is another nonprobability sampling technique. This sample is selected on the basis of one's knowledge of the population, its characteristics, and the research questions.

Group Assignment

Once subjects are chosen, they must be randomly assigned to treatment groups. It is possible that individual subjects will vary considerably on several extraneous characteristics such as intelligence, motivation, and previous experience. Placing all such subjects into one group could affect performance on measures of the dependent variable; however, the only thing you want to affect the dependent variable is the independent variable. By randomly assigning subjects to groups, you can neutralize the effects extraneous variables may have on overall performance.

The number of groups to be used should be established before the experiment begins. Using a simple example with one treatment group and one control group, subjects can be assigned to either group by using a table of random numbers or computer generated random numbers. Ignoring all other numbers, write down the order in which 1 and 2 appear in the table or from the computer program. For example, the sequence may be 1, 2, 1, 1, 2, 1, 2, 2. The first subject is assigned to the first group, the second subject is assigned to the second group, the third and fourth subjects are assigned to the first group, the fifth subject is assigned to the second group, the sixth subject is assigned to the first group, and the seventh and eighth subjects are assigned to the second group. It is better to have equal numbers of subjects in each group.

It is possible that, despite random selection and assignment, subjects vary from one group to the next on a key characteristic. For example, a researcher may be working on a new treatment for anxiety disorders. Even though subjects were randomly selected and assigned, subjects in Group 1 may have higher levels of anxiety before the experiment than those in Group 2. The researcher may decide to match or group subjects on the basis of their similarity on a particular characteristic. A pretest can be administered to detect various levels of the characteristic. Subjects with similar scores are assigned randomly to groups; thus, the number of subjects at each level of the characteristic is comparable across groups.

Threats to Internal Validity

Internal validity is the technical term that describes the extent to which the results of a study are supported by the methodology. A well-controlled study is said to have high internal validity and "believable" conclusions. A poorly controlled study has limited internal validity limiting the confidence that you can place in the results. *Threats to internal validity* are events that can reduce confidence in research findings. Well-controlled studies eliminate specific threats.

Campbell and Stanley (1963), in what may be the most frequently cited monograph on research design, identified eight major threats to the internal validity. To varying degrees, experimental and quasi-experimental designs control for threats to internal validity. The threats are as follows:

History	An event occurring between pre and posttests, other than the independent variable.
Maturation	A change that occurs because a participant has grown older or gained more experience.
Instrumentation	A change that occurs because the testing procedures are unreliable or have been altered unintentionally.
Testing	A change that occurs because the test has sensitized the participants to the nature of the research.
Regression	The tendency of a very low score or a very high score to move toward the mean.

Selection	Group differences that occur because of sampling problems.
Mortality	Participants drop out of the investigation.
Treatment Diffusion	Inadvertently exposing participants to the independent variable when standard conditions should prevail.

TRUE EXPERIMENTAL DESIGNS

A true experimental design consists of a study in which you are able to manipulate the independent variable. It gives you the strongest possible basis for drawing inferences. A true experimental design has three major characteristics. First, subjects must be randomly assigned to experimental and control groups. Second, there must be measurements of a dependent variable. Third, there must be an independent variable.

The independent variable is an experience or activity that you systematically manipulate. For example, you may be interested in contrasting the lung capacity (dependent variable) for individuals who are randomly selected for an aerobic exercise and sedentary regimen (independent variable), the academic achievement (dependent variable) of students randomly selected for a tutorial program over those who simply attend study hall (independent variable), or the verbal problem-solving performance (dependent variable) of students who are selected through random assignment to read a book a week or watch television (independent variable).

Purpose

Each design enables you to compare the performance of subjects who received the independent variable to the performance of subjects who did not. You assume the independent variable had an effect if the performance of the former group exceeds the performance of the latter group.

Design Options

There are many design options available when conducting a true experiment. The following list of designs was organized by Campbell and Stanley (1963).

The pretest-posttest control group design with random assignment. This design requires the random selection of subjects from the population and random assignment into two groups. Subjects in both groups are tested before and after treatment; however, subjects in only one group are exposed to the independent variable. For example, you may be interested in the effects of daily exercise on patients with high blood pressure. Blood pressure readings for both groups of patients are recorded. You then instruct the subjects in one group to follow a carefully planned exercise regimen. The others are to continue their normal routines. Later, you measure blood pressure for subjects in both groups. If it is lower for subjects in the experimental group, then your exercise program had an effect.

This design controls for history and maturation, the most common threats to internal validity. However, among its weaknesses is the fact that it does not control for testing. A pretest can sensitize subjects to the nature of the intervention. Also, if gain scores from pretest to posttest are used as a dependent variable, regression may be an additional threat to internal validity. A subject who performs poorly on the pretest is likely to do better on the posttest by regression alone. Conversely, a subject who performs well on the pretest may do relatively worse on the posttest by regression alone.

The posttest-only control group design with random assignment. When a very large sample is available, two randomly selected groups can be assumed to be equivalent. Consequently, subjects do not take a pretest to establish equivalence. Subjects in the experimental group are exposed to the independent variable, while subjects in the control group follow their normal routine. Subjects are tested in both groups. Among its advantages is the control of threats to internal validity, including testing and regression. This allows the study to be completed more quickly and at less expense. Among its weaknesses is the inability to detect differences in subjects' levels of functioning before implementation of the independent variable.

Solomon four group design with random assignment. The Solomon four group design is a combination of the two previously discussed designs. It is intended to control for testing as a threat to internal validity. You need the following four groups of randomly assigned subjects.

1. The first group is pretested, exposed to the independent variable, then posttested. Using our previous example, subjects in Group A have their blood pressure tested, then follow the exercise program, then later have their blood pressure tested again.

2. The second group is similar except it is not exposed to the independent variable. Subjects of Group B have their blood pressure taken at separate intervals, but they do not participate in the exercise program between testing.

3. The third group is not pretested, but it is exposed to the independent variable before being posttested. Subjects in Group C have their blood pressure checked only after they participate.

4. The fourth group is neither pretested nor exposed to the independent variable, but it is posttested. Subjects in Group D have their blood pressure tested at the end of the study.

This design does an excellent job of controlling for threats to internal validity. Of course, it is more expensive and time-consuming to use, but it makes up for these drawbacks through its elegance and power.

Factorial designs with random assignment. The designs we have discussed previously involve only one independent variable. Factorial designs allow you to investigate two or more variables (i.e., factors) in one study. There are two or more conditions (i.e., levels) within each variable. For example, you could be interested in two different methods for treating men and women with anxiety disorders. As illustrated in Figure 5.1, you have a 2 × 2 factorial design. Theoretically, you can use any number of independent variables containing any number of levels.

As with all true experimental designs, subjects in factorial designs must be randomly sampled from the population. Equally important, they must be randomly assigned to conditions. Random assignment ensures that differences between groups are limited to the independent variable and are not characteristics associated with the sample.

A major reason for using a factorial design is that you are interested in interactions, that is, the combined effects of all the variables in your study. For example, is Treatment A better for men or women, or is it equally effective regardless of gender? Although factorial designs offer the opportunity to assess the effects of separate variables and any interactions, they do require you to include more groups, thereby increasing the cost of your study.

Analysis

In Chapter 12, we present techniques for analyzing data from true experimental designs to compare the performance of experimental and control groups on the dependent variable. You have many options. For example, you can use a *t* test for independent measures for a posttest-only design. If more than two groups are involved, you can use a one-way analysis of variance.

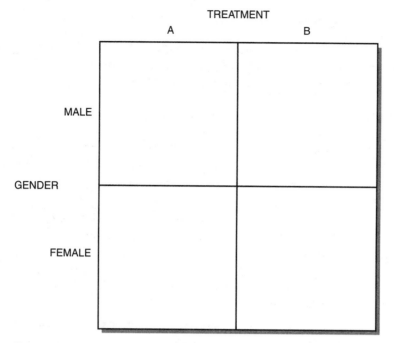

Figure 5.1 An Illustration of a Factorial Design

Advantages and Limitations

We have already discussed specific advantages associated with each design. The overall advantage in randomly selecting subjects and randomly assigning subjects is the reduction of threats to internal validity that are often present when "intact" groups are used. This feature allows for confidence when making claims of a cause and effect relationship between independent and dependent variables. It also provides a strong basis for making inferences about the characteristics of a population.

We have also discussed specific disadvantages associated with each experimental design. Generally speaking, the main advantage of true experimental designs are also their primary limitations. The requirement for random selection from the population and random assignment into groups excludes them from use for a vast number of important research questions. For ethical reasons, individuals with health problems cannot be randomly assigned to a control group with a treatment that is presumed to be inferior to the experimental procedure. Some populations are sufficiently dispersed and small that obtaining a random sample of any size would be impractical. Imagine the cost of treating a random sample of visually impaired second graders knowing that fewer than 1,000 second graders throughout the United States are visually impaired.

QUASI-EXPERIMENTAL DESIGNS

As we have indicated, it is often extremely difficult to design and implement a true experiment for some research questions. Although you can specify independent and dependent variables, you may not be able to select your sample at random from the population or randomly assign subjects to an experimental or control condition. Therefore, a variety of quasi-experimental designs are available to approximate conditions of a true experimental design.

Purpose

Quasi-experimental designs do not involve random assignment of subjects to groups. This feature necessarily makes them weaker than true experimental designs because there is less control over threats to internal validity.

Design Options

A large number of quasi-experimental designs have been employed by researchers in the social and behavioral sciences. Generally, the designs involve groups that were established prior to, and independent of, the study. Studies that compare intact classes in a school district, patients on separate wards, or employees in various divisions of a company are generally conducted with quasi-experimental designs.

Pretest-posttest control group design without random assignment. This design is also referred to as the *nonequivalent control group design* and the *untreated control group design*. This design is similar to the pretest-posttest control group design with random assignment we discussed earlier. The difference is that you have two intact groups of subjects, that is, groups already formed or selected on the basis of something other than random assignment. Subjects in both groups are pretested, one group is exposed to the independent variable, and all subjects are posttested. A common example of this design is a study comparing migrant workers employed by one farm with migrant workers employed by another. Employees of the first farm are not randomly assigned to a treatment condition; rather, the decision is made by the researcher to treat the group as a whole. This design may control for threats to internal validity such as history and maturation; however, it does not control for selection and testing.

Posttest-only control group design without random assignment. As in true experimental designs, both experimental and control groups are used. Only the subjects in the experimental condition are exposed to the independent variable; then subjects in both groups are tested. Again, the difference is that subjects were not randomly assigned to groups in the first place. However, because pretesting did not occur, the researcher has no way of knowing if subjects differed across several dimensions prior to implementation of the independent variable. Therefore, it may be difficult to attribute changes in the dependent variable to exposure to the independent variable.

Times-series design. Only one group of subjects is needed in this design. Several measurements of the dependent variable are applied at regular intervals; then the independent variable is introduced. Afterward, several regularly scheduled measurements are again obtained. The effect of the independent variable is indicated by a difference in the measurements conducted before and after its introduction. For example, water usage is measured on several different occasions in a specific city. Then a public service campaign focusing on water conservation is initiated. Afterward, water usage is again measured on several different occasions. A decrease can be attributed to the public service campaign.

Although this design offers the advantage of requiring only one group, it does not control for history as a threat to internal validity. It is possible that changes in the dependent variable could be attributed to an event other than the independent variable which happened at the same time. For example, a decrease in water usage could have happened because higher billing rates went into effect around the time the public service campaign began.

Equivalent time-samples design. This design is similar to the times-series design except that additional applications of the independent variable are included at random intervals. You can measure the dependent variable on one occasion, implement the independent variable, measure on three more occasions, implement the independent variable a second time, measure on two more occasions, implement for the third time, then measure on two final occasions. For example, you could use an equivalent time-samples design to study the effects of time-out on aggressive behavior in children.

1. Count the number of aggressive episodes for one week.
2. Use time-out for one week, continuing to record aggressive behavior.
3. Remove time-out and measure aggression for each of the next three weeks.
4. Use time-out again for a week, continuing to record aggressive behavior.
5. Remove time-out and measure aggression for each of the next two weeks.
6. Use time-out for the third time for one week, continuing to record aggressive behavior.
7. Remove time-out and measure aggression for each of the next two weeks.

While this design reduces history, its internal validity is threatened by maturation, instrumentation, testing, and mortality.

Data Analysis

Again, we refer you to Chapter 12, where we present techniques for analyzing data from quasi-experimental designs.

Advantages and Limitations

We have already discussed the advantages and limitations associated with each quasi-experimental design. In general, you use them because you are unable to randomly select subjects and assign them to groups. While they do make it possible to draw some conclusions about the relationship between the dependent and independent variables, your ability to generalize the findings to a larger population is limited.

CORRELATIONAL METHODS

Purpose

The purpose of correlation studies is to allow comparisons of the same group of people with two different characteristics. Correlational studies identify the relationship between two variables. Once the relationship is established, one characteristic can be used to predict another. Correlation research has affected all of us; examine one of the criteria colleges and universities use to select next year's freshmen from among high school seniors applying for admission. Correlational research has documented a strong positive relationship between high school performance and a college GPA. Specifically, students who did better in high school earned higher GPAs during their college careers. Armed with this information, admissions officers can use the average of high school grades and predict with some accuracy who among the applicants will do well in college.

The defining characteristic in correlation research is the absence of an independent variable. The variables you are interested in occur naturally in your subjects and cannot be manipulated. For example, the gender, health, socioeconomic background, or achievement of subjects cannot be controlled. Rather than introduce an independent variable, you examine the relationship between two existing variables. Keppel, Saufley, and Tokunga (1992) suggest you label the variables as Variable X and Variable Y.

Stating a Hypothesis About Relationships

For correlational studies, the research hypothesis depends on what was learned through the literature review. You may suspect that there is some relationship between variables, but you may not be sure of the direction. In this case, the hypothesis is stated in a nondirectional format. For example, if you were interested in maternal alcohol consumption during pregnancy and what affect that might have on newborns, you would state, "There is a significant relationship between maternal alcohol consumption and the incidence of handicapping conditions in babies." On the other hand, the literature review may suggest the nature of the relationship between the variables. Then your hypothesis can be stated in a directional form, for example, "There is a significant positive relationship between maternal alcohol consumption and the incidence of handicapping conditions in babies." A directional hypothesis can also be stated to indicate a negative relationship. For example, if you were studying the relationship between a history of spousal abuse and self-esteem, your directional hypothesis could state, "There is a significant negative relationship between history of spousal abuse and self-esteem."

Data Collection and Analysis

Data collection. Having identified the subjects, their performance on two characteristics must be measured. It is important to find or develop a valid way to measure the Variable X and Variable Y. Chapter 9 will describe how to select or develop measurement procedures.

Analysis. The method for analyzing the direction and strength of the relationship between Variables X and Y is by calculating a correlation coefficient. Perhaps the most commonly used correlation coefficient is the Pearson product-moment correlation, which is represented by the symbol r. It ranges in value from -1 to $+1$. The closer the coefficient is to either -1 or $+1$, the stronger the relationship between your variables and the more likely the relationship is to be significant. A weak relationship is expressed by coefficients that are near zero. This relationship can also be displayed visually on a scattergram or a scatterplot. Each point on a scattergram is determined by a participant's score on both measures.

A perfect correlation is represented by either a -1 or a $+1$. Data plotted on the scattergram form a straight line. In a perfect positive correlation, the person who scored the highest on one measure also scored the highest on the second measure, the person who scored the second highest on the first measure scored the second highest on the second measure, and so on until you reach the person who scored the lowest on both measures. A perfect negative correlation is the inverse. The person who scored the highest on the first measure scored the lowest on the second measure. You rarely see perfect correlations; however, you do hope there will be a high correlation in either direction because it enhances your ability to make predictions.

A positive correlation indicates that as one variable increases, so does the other. For example, your results may indicate a high positive relationship between income and job satisfaction. The more people are paid, the more satisfied they are with their jobs. This relationship is illustrated in the scattergram presented in Figure 5.2. A negative correlation indicates an inverse relationship, that is, as one variable increases, the other decreases. For example, a low golf score is better than a high golf score. We assume people who have played the sport longer have a lower golf score. This relationship is illustrated in the scattergram presented in Figure 5.3. It is also possible that you will find zero or no correlation. For example, you may find there is no relationship between reading skills and artistic abilities. This relationship is illustrated in the scattergram presented in Figure 5.4.

There are other measures of correlation. Your choice is influenced by the nature of the variables you are studying. In the examples we have used so far, all the measures produced scores that could be ranked in order because they were continuous or linear. However, not all the variables

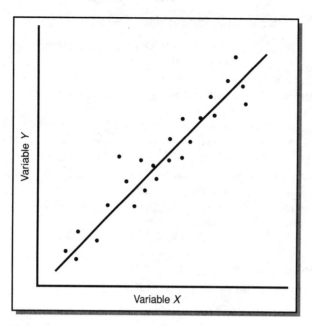

Figure 5.2 A Scatterplot Illustrating a Positive Correlation

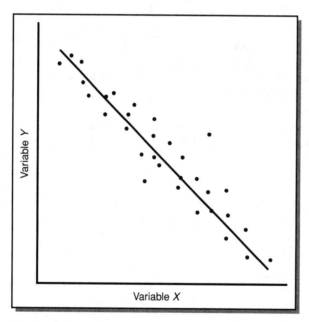

Figure 5.3 A Scatterplot Illustrating a Negative Correlation

in which you are interested may be ranked. For example, there is nothing inherently better about one gender than the other. Rather than ranking gender, male and female can be classified into a dichotomy. Similarly, there is nothing inherently better about one geographical location over another; therefore, it is meaningless to rate north as 1, south as 2, east as 3, and west as 4. Variables such as these are called *nominal* or *categorical variables.* In addition, you may be interested in

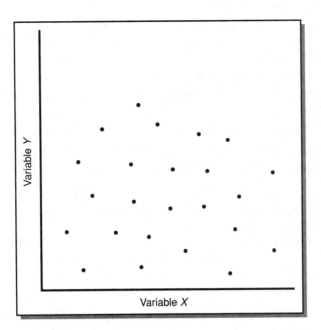

Figure 5.4 A Scatterplot Illustrating No Relationship

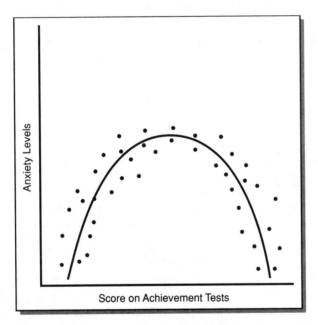

Figure 5.5 A Scatterplot Illustrating a Curvilinear Relationship

examining a relationship that is curvilinear. Crowl (1993) illustrated a curvilinear relationship using anxiety. We present it in Figure 5.5. People with very high or very low levels of anxiety do not perform well on achievement tests. People with moderate levels of anxiety do tend to perform well. The point is that the unique features of your data may require use of different measures of correlation. We list these options in Table 5.1

A correlation coefficient is more meaningful if you use it to determine how much variability your two variables have in common. More specifically, you want to know how much of the variability of the first variable is accounted for by the variability in the second variable. This measure of variability is called *variance* and can be determined by squaring the correlation coefficient (r^2). Cohen (1988) suggested the following approach for classifying the extent of a relationship measured by correlational research.

1. A small relationship is one in which r^2 is .01 ($r = +.10$ or $-.10$).
2. A medium relationship is one in which r^2 is .09 ($r = +.30$ or $-.30$).
3. A large relationship is one in which r^2 is .25 ($r = +.50$ or $-.50$).

For example, your results may indicate a $-.8$ correlation between golf scores and years of play. Squaring this value indicates that 64 percent of the variance in golf scores can be accounted for by years of play.

Finally, a correlation coefficient can be tested in many ways, including an ANOVA, to determine whether it is statistically significant. If it is, you can conclude that the correlation was unlikely to occur by chance.

Advantage

Correlational research allows you to measure the degree of a relationship between two or more variables rather than just determine whether a relationship exists.

Limitations

Although you have specified that there is a relationship between the variables, you have not demonstrated a causal relationship. You don't know if Variable X is affecting Variable Y, Variable Y is affecting Variable X, or if both variables are being affected by a third, unknown variable.

Table 5.1   Measures of Correlation

Name	Symbol	Characteristic of Variables
Product Moment	r	Both are continuous.
Rank Order	ρ	Both are ranked.
Point-Biserial	r_{pbis}	One is continuous and one is nominal with two values.
Biserial	r_{bis}	Both are continuous, but one has been artificially broken down into nominal values.
Phi	ϕ	Both are nominal and each has two values.
Contingency	C	Both are nominal and each has more than two values.
Tetrachoric	r_t	Both are continuous, but each has been artificially broken down into two nominal values.
Eta	η	Both are continuous and are used to detect curvilinear relationships.

Purpose

The purpose of a survey is to collect information directly from a sample of individuals. This information may include a number of variables, a few of which are abilities; attitudes; and personal backgrounds. The information is then used to estimate the characteristics of the larger population (Crowl, 1993). A survey usually takes one of three forms. A questionnaire can be designed for a person to complete either independently or with assistance. Surveys can also be conducted over the phone. Finally, a personal interview format can be used. As is the case for correlation research, variables are not manipulated during a survey, so the results cannot be used to make causal statements.

Developing Your Survey Instrument

Source of items. Specific items included on a survey are derived from the research question or hypothesis. Of course, the literature review should be used in the development of the research question or hypothesis. During the review, you may have been able to identify and locate survey instruments related to your area of interest. In addition, information in Chapter 9 may help you. Examining commercially available material or the work of others and discussing ideas for items with fellow students, colleagues, or faculty members can provide valuable information.

Question format. Two types of questions may be used: open-ended and closed. An example of an open-ended question is, "What are your hobbies?" Such items allow you to obtain responses you had not anticipated. Respondents are more likely to provide more accurate information about their attitudes, opinions, and preferences. Unfortunately, a person may respond to an open-ended question with an answer that is not useful. An example of a closed question is, "What are your hobbies? Select from the following list."

People are more likely to respond to closed items. There are a variety of response formats for closed items. Respondents can be asked to agree or disagree with an item. However, such items should be used with caution. For example, do people disagree with the statement, "The quality of my medical care was fair" because they thought their care was excellent or because they thought it was poor? You can also use a nominal scale for items such as gender or a categorical scale in which they rank their educational level. On a related note, a comparative scale in which respondents rank a series of items according to their preferences may be effective. For example, employers can be asked to rank a list of management techniques from most to least preferred. Some items, such as total household income, may call for an interval number in which the numbers have real meaning. Other items require a ratio scale that has a true zero. Examples include the number of pounds lost on a special diet, cigarettes smoked, or ounces of a soft drink consumed. Finally, a graphic scale can be used. Responses are presented visually on a continuum with major points marked "strongly disagree," "neutral," and "strongly agree."

Regardless of whether you choose open-ended or closed items, there are guidelines you should follow when developing specific survey questions. They include the following:

1. Include directions for completing the items.
2. Use questions that represent only one thought.
3. Phrase questions so that they have the same meaning to all respondents.
4. Use standard English.
5. Avoid words or phases that suggest bias, such as "dope addict" or "welfare families."
6. Arrange questions so easy items appear first, and items that require more thought appear later.

7. Be very clear when using items that will allow a person either to skip a series of subsequent items or branch over to a series of follow up items.

8. Pilot questions with select individuals who are similar to the eventual sample.

Response methods. There are three methods for obtaining responses to surveys. Each has implications in terms of cost and the accuracy and completeness of the data.

First, survey instruments can be mailed. This is appropriate for large geographically dispersed samples being assessed across a small number of variables. The costs associated with mail surveys includes printing an attractively formatted questionnaire; stuffing envelopes; affixing postage; including prepaid envelopes; and sending out reminders, follow-up letters, and a second mailing. Hopefully, these expenditures will be rewarded with a good return. The more surveys that are returned, the more complete your data will be and the greater the confidence in results and conclusions. Unfortunately, it is common for researchers to receive a number of incomplete or improperly scored responses that are of little use.

The other two response methods are phone interviews and personal interviews. These methods are appropriate for small samples and several variables. Training of the interviewers is essential. They should be pleasant but neutral so that responses are not unwittingly influenced. For personal interviews, dress in a manner similar to that of the people being interviewed. For both phone and personal interviews, develop an interview protocol and make sure any assistants are well versed in its use. A protocol should include standardized questions that all interviewers will use, scripted introductions and words of encouragement, a method for recording responses, probing questions that can be used for follow up, and items the respondents are likely to ask with instructions on how to answer. Finally, you may want to ask the respondent's permission to audiotape the interview.

There are expenses associated with phone and personal interviews. Interviewers must be paid for the time they spend in training and in data collection. There are costs associated with printing a sufficient number of forms for recording respondents' answers. Obviously, phone interviews mean phone bills. Personal interviewers may have travel expenses. The benefit of conducting interviews is that the percentage of completed surveys will be higher.

Data Collection and Analysis

Data collection. Depending on the nature of your research question, surveys can be conducted in several ways. They can be cross-sectional. For example, you can survey recent graduates of a nursing program during their first year of employment to see if their professional preparation enables them to meet all the demands of their jobs. A trend survey can be conducted by contacting the nursing classes of 1995, 1996, and 1997 and posing the same questions. Group members will vary, but all are responding to the same items. A cohort survey can be conducted by surveying different people at different times. For example, a researcher can survey the different nurses once every five years. Finally, a panel survey can be used. Here, the same people are surveyed at specific intervals over a long period of time.

A major challenge with survey research is ensuring an adequate return rate. People might not get a mailed survey, may refuse to provide the data, or may be unable to respond because of illness or language differences. To increase your return rate for mailed surveys, send it out with a cover letter. This letter should be professional, personalized, and attractive. It should explain the purpose of your research, emphasize its importance and usefulness, and offer the opportunity to examine the results. Always include a prepaid envelope or have your survey printed in the form of a self-mailing questionnaire. A follow-up letter or reminder postcard can be sent 10 business days after the first survey was mailed. Send another letter after 10 more days and include another copy of the questionnaire and a prepaid envelope.

To increase the number of surveys completed during phone or personal interviews, send out a letter that advises people of an upcoming call or visit and informs them of the purpose and importance of the research. Hire interviewers who have flexible schedules that enable them to make numerous calls or visits at different times of the day.

Obviously, the higher your return rate, the better. Without a follow-up, you can expect about a 30 percent return rate. Babbie (1992) suggests that a 50 percent return rate is adequate, at least 60 percent is good, and 70 percent is very good.

Analyzing responses. Survey data can be analyzed in a variety of ways. You can present descriptive statistics about information such as gender, age, income level, and educational background. You can also report results using more sophisticated statistical techniques we present in Chapter 12.

Advantages

Despite the expenses associated with their use, surveys are economical. They make it possible for you to collect data from large samples and ultimately describe characteristics of a large population. They are also highly standardized; that is, the same question is asked of all respondents.

Limitations

Standardized questions can also be limiting. By trying to devise items that are minimally appropriate for a large number of people, you may miss what is important to some. In addition, responses can be artificial because, frankly, your respondents can lie. Surveys are self-reports of what people say they think or do. You have no way of knowing if the information they are providing is accurate; thus, the validity of your study may be undermined. Finally, surveys measure public opinions. They do not measure truth. One may be tempted to determine ecological policy based on a survey. The results would indicate the popularity of a policy, not how the policy would actually affect the environment. True or quasi-experimental research would be required for this purpose.

Summary

In this chapter, we described designs for use with large numbers of people. The first category was true experimental designs, which you can use if you have the luxury of being able to select your sample from the population and assign subjects randomly to groups. While ideal, few of us are able to meet this requirement; therefore, we use quasi-experimental designs. Both true experimental designs and quasi-experimental designs allow you to study the effects of variables you manipulate. Other methods, such as correlational designs and surveys, do not require you to manipulate a variable.

For each design category, we discussed the purpose; described how to select subjects, and collect and analyze data; and identified advantages and limitations. For more information and other examples, we refer you to the list of further readings.

We discussed only four of the design options you have. In fact, given your research question or the characteristics of your sample, these designs may be inappropriate. The next chapter will describe designs suitable for use with smaller groups of subjects.

REFERENCES

Babbie, E. (1995).*The practice of social research* (7th ed.). Belmont, CA: Wadsworth.

Campbell, D. & Stanley, J. (1963). *Experimental and quasi-experimental designs for research*. Chicago: Rand McNally

Cohen, J. (1988). *Statistical power analysis* (2nd ed.). Hillsdale, NJ: Erlbaum.

Crowl, T. K. (1993). *Fundamentals of educational research*. Madison, WI: Brown & Benchmark.

Keppel, G., Saufley, W. H., & Tokunga, H. (1992). *Introduction to design and analysis: A student's handbook* (4th ed.). NY: W. H. Freeman and Company.

FURTHER READINGS

General Information on Designs

Bositis, D. A. (1990). *Research design for political science: Contrivance and demonstration in theory and practice*. Carbondale, IL: SIU Press.

Churchill, G. A. (1991). *Basic marketing research* (2nd ed.). Fort Worth, TX: Dryden Press-Harcourt Brace Jovanovich College Publisher.

Cohen, L., & Manion, L. (1994). *Research methods in education* (4th ed.). New York: Routledge.

Cook, T. D., & Campbell, D. T. (1979). *Quasi-experimentation: Design and analysis issues for field settings*. Boston: Houghton Mifflin.

Fowler, F. J. (1993). *Survey research methods* (2nd ed.). Newbury Park, CA: Sage.

Ghauri, P. N., Gronhaug, K., & Kristianslund, I. (1995). *Research methods business studies: A practical guide*. Upper Saddle River, NJ: Merrill/Prentice Hall.

Graziano, A. M., & Raulin, M. L. (1996). *Research methods: A process of inquiry*. (3rd ed.). New York: Harper and Row.

Hedge, M. N. (1987). *Clinical research in communication disorders: Principles and strategies*. Boston: Little, Brown.

Johnson, J. B. & Joslyn, R. A. (1994). *Political science research methods* (3rd ed.). Washington, DC: CQ Press.

Kazdin, A. E. (1998). *Research design in clinical psychology* (3rd ed.). Needham Heights, MA: Allyn & Bacon.

Kinnear, T. C., & Taylor, J. R. (1995). *Marketing research: An applied approach* (5th ed.). New York: McGraw-Hill, Inc.

Leedy, P. D. (1996). *Practical research: Planning and design* (6th ed.). Upper Saddle River, NJ: Merrill/Prentice Hall.

Manheim, J. B. & Rich, R. C. (1994). *Empirical political analysis: Research methods in political science* (4th ed.). New York: Longman.

May, T. (1997). *Social research: Issues, methods, and process* (2nd ed.). Buckingham, England: Open University Press.

Mitchell, M., & Jolley, J. (1992). *Research design explained* (2nd ed.). Fort Worth, TX: Harcourt Brace Jovanovich College Publishers.

Mueller, D. (1991). *An interactive guide to educational research: A modular approach*. Needham Heights, MA: Allyn & Bacon.

Newell, R. (1993). *Questionnaires*. In N. Gilbert (Ed.), *Researching social life* (pp. 94–115). Thousand Oaks, CA: Sage.

Polit, D. F. & Hungler, B. P. (1995) *Nursing research: Principles and methods* (5th ed.). Philadelphia: J. B. Lippencott.

Pope, J. L. (1993). *Practical marketing research*. New York: Amacon.

Silverman, F. H. (1997). *Research design and evaluation in speech-language pathology and audiology* (4th ed.) Needham Heights, MA: Allyn & Bacon.

Tull, D. S., & Hawkins, D. I. (1993). *Marketing research: Measurement and methods* (4th ed.). Upper Saddle River, NJ: Merrill/Prentice Hall.

Webb, J. R. (1992). *Understanding and designing marketing research*. San Diego: Academic Press.

Zikmund, W. G. (1994). *Business research methods* (4th ed.). Chicago: Dryden Press.

Examples of Quasi-Experimental Studies.

Areni, C. S., & Kim, D. (1994). The influence of in-store lighting on consumers' examination of merchandise in a wine store. *International Journal of Research in Marketing, 11,* 107–115.

Grewel, D., & Baker, J. (1994). Do retail store environmental factors affect consumers' price acceptability? An empirical examination. *International Journal of Research in Marketing, 11,* 107–115.

Graves, R., Openshaw, D. R., & Adams, G. R. (1992). Adolescent sex offenders and social skills training. *International Journal of Offender Therapy and Comparative Criminology, 36,* 139–153.

Haley, W. E., Wadley, V. G., West, C. A., & Vetzel, L. L. (1994). How caregiving stressors change with severity of dementia. *Seminar in Speech and Language, 15,* 195–205.

Hussey, L. C. (1994). Minimizing effects of low literacy on medication knowledge and compliance among the elderly. *Clinical Nursing Research, 3,* 132–145.

Nichols, L. A. S., & Schmidt, M. K. (1995). The impact of videotapes in educating grocery store shoppers about fat and cholesterol. *Journal of Nutrition Education, 27,* 5–10.

Singh, S. N., Mishra, S., Bendapudi, N., & Linville, D. (1994). Enhancing memory of television commercials through message spacing. *Journal of Marketing Research, 31,* 384–392.

Smith-Hanrahan, C., & Deblois, D. (1995). Postpartum early discharge: Impact on maternal fatigue and functional ability. *Clinical Nursing Research, 4,* 50–66.

Spitzer, M., Beuckers, J., Beyer, S., Maier, S., & Hermle, L. (1994). Contextual insensitivity in thought-disordered schizophrenic patients: Evidence from pauses in spontaneous speech. *Language and Speech, 37,* 171–185.

Examples of Surveys

Abramowitz, A. I. (1995). It's abortion, Stupid: Policy voting in the 1992 presidential election. *Journal of Politics, 57,* 176–186.

Bergman, L. (1992). Dating violence among high school students. *Social Work, 37,* 21–27.

Cromwell, P., & McElrath, J. (1994). Buying stolen property: An opportunity perspective. *Journal of Research in Crime and Delinquency, 31,* 295–310.

Giles, H., Fox, S., & Smith, E. (1993). Patronizing the elderly: Intergenerative evaluations. *Research on Language and Social Interactions, 26,* 129–150.

Guttmacher, S., Lieberman, L., Ward, D., Radosh, A., Rafferty, Y., & Freudenberg, N. (1995). Parents' attitudes and beliefs about HIV/AIDS prevention with condom availability in New York City Public High Schools. *Journal of School Health, 65,* 101–106.

Kiechhefer, G. M. & Spitzer, A. (1995). School age children's understanding of the relationship between their behavior and their asthma management. *Clinical Nursing Research, 4,* 149–167.

Kren, L., & Kerr, J. L. (1993). The effect of behavior monitoring and uncertainty on the use of performance-contingent compensation. *Accounting and Business Research, 23,* 159–168.

Lennon, M. C., & Rosenfield, S. (1994). Relative fairness and the division of housework: The importance of options. *American Journal of Sociology, 100,* 506–531.

Mohr, L. S., & Bitner, M. J. (1995). The role of employee effort in satisfaction with service transactions. *Journal of Business Research, 32,* 239–252.

Polloway, E. A., Epstein, M. H., Bursuck, W. D., Roderiquez, T. W., McConeghy, J. L., & Jayanthi, M. (1994). Classroom grading: A national survey of policies. *Remedial and Special Education, 15,* 162–170.

Richardson, L. E., & Freeman, P. K. (1995). Gender differences in constituency services among state legislators. *Political Research Quarterly, 48,* 169–179.

Sierfert, C. F., Frye, J. L., Belknap, D. C., & Anderson, D. C. (1995). A nursing survey to determine the characteristics of medication administration through internal feeding catheters. *Clinical Nursing Research, 4,* 290–305

Sims, R. I. (1995). The severity of academic dishonesty: A comparison of faculty and student views. *Psychology in the Schools, 22,* 233–238.

Taylor, S. (1994). Waiting for service: The relationship between delays and evaluation of service. *Journal of Marketing, 58,* 56–69.

Umberson, D., & Chen, M. D. (1994). Effects of a parent's death on adult children: Relationship salience and reaction to loss. *American Sociological Review, 59,* 152–168.

Winborne, D. G. (1992). Address unknown: An exploration of the educational and social attitudes of homeless adolescents. *High School Journal, 75,* 144–149.

Young J. R. & Hite, S. J. (1995). The status of teacher preservice preparation for parent involvement: A national study. *Education, 115,* 153–158.

Examples of Correlation Studies

Berry, R. A., & Murphy, J. F. (1995). Well being of caregivers of spouses with Parkinson's disease. *Clinical Nursing Research, 4,* 373–386.

Brown, D. S. (1995). Hospital discharge preparation for homeward bound elderly. *Clinical Nursing Research, 4,* 181–194.

Eckhardt, L., Woodruff, S. I., & Elden, J. P. (1994). A longitudinal analysis of adolescent smoking and its correlates. *Journal of School Health, 64,* 67–72.

Liberton, M., Silverman, M., & Blount, W. R. (1992). Predicting probation success for the first time offender. *International Journal of Offender Therapy and Comparative Criminology, 36,* 335–347.

Power, T. G., & Woolger, C. (1994). Parenting practices and age-group swimming: A correlational study. *Research Quarterly for Exercise and Sport, 65,* 59–66.

Stout, K. D., & Buffum, W. E. (1993). The commitment of social workers to affirmative action. *Journal of Sociological and Social Welfare, 20* (2), 123–135.

6

Single Subject Designs

INTRODUCTION

An individual's interest in specific research questions plays a key role in the selection of a research design. In Chapter 5 we discussed several designs that are appropriate for studying large numbers of people. However, not every problem lends itself to these designs. For example, you may be interested in testing the effectiveness of an intervention for a small number of students with multiple disabilities residing in your community. The fact that there are only a few students who could potentially benefit from this intervention makes your findings no less important than the statistical or social significance of an intervention involving dozens or hundreds of people. A small number of participants, however, is no excuse to relax standards for scientific rigor. Fortunately, we do not have to because single subject design methodology is available. These designs and their variations are perfect for use with small numbers of people.

Several terms have been used to describe single subject designs, including single case designs, intrasubject-replication designs, $N = 1$ research, and intensive designs. A single subject design refers to a process rather than the actual number of participants. The unique feature of each single subject design is that it allows you to focus on the performance of one person or a

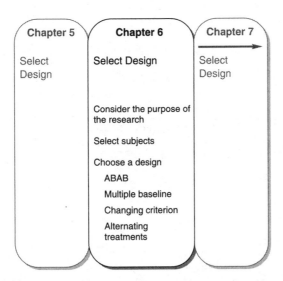

The Scope, Plan, and Sequence Chart for Conducting Research:
The Fourth Step in the Research Process

small number of persons over time. Each participant serves as his or her own control. If an investigation involves five participants, the data describe five complete experiments, or one experiment with four replications.

Single subject designs have been used by investigators representing many disciplines including special education, speech language pathology, psychology, rehabilitation, social work, and counseling (Kazdin, 1982). Despite its popularity, single subject design methodology is viewed by some as a departure from other research, particularly group designs. In reality, much of the more traditional research is based on careful investigation of one person rather than comparisons between groups of individuals. For example, Pavlov's breakthroughs in the area of respondent conditioning were based primarily on studying one or a few subjects at a time. Single subject design methodology has gained popularity because of limitations associated with group designs. Among these problems are ethical objections to withholding treatment from a no-treatment group. A second problem relates to the difficulties associated with locating a large number of individuals with similar characteristics. Even if a sufficient number of people can be located, the cost of involving them in your project could be prohibitive. Third, group designs in which results are averaged may obscure individual outcomes. People in social service professions may work directly with individuals who vary widely in personal characteristics, education, and backgrounds. Conclusions about average group performance may not match the professional's main concern, which is the effect of a treatment on an individual (Kazdin, 1982).

In this chapter, we discuss four single subject designs. We describe how to use each, and what the variations and advantages and disadvantages are.

The Purpose of Your Research

The purpose of single subject design is to establish the effects of an intervention on a single individual or a small group of individuals. An independent variable, such as a training program, is presented in different settings or with different people. Depending on the design, the program may even be withdrawn for a short time, then reapplied. Data analysis should indicate that any change in behavior or performance is the result of the intervention and not the result of chance or other factors. As with group designs, single subject designs can establish functional and causal relationships.

Selecting Subjects

Not only do single subject designs differ from quantitative designs in the number of subjects involved, but they also differ in how subjects are selected for inclusion in the study. In Chapter 8, we discuss how to sample subjects randomly and assign them to groups. Such procedures are not appropriate for studies involving single subject designs. These designs are applied in nature; their purpose is to directly improve a product or a process that enhances the participants' quality of life (Best, 1997). It is not uncommon for a single individual or a small group of individuals to demonstrate a problem or experience a skill deficit. Your independent variable is developed to address this need. You do not need to select subjects randomly; you probably already have a very clear idea of who your subjects should be. Participation in your study is dictated by need rather than by luck of the draw.

DESIGN OPTIONS

The ABAB (Reversal) Design

The most basic and commonly used single subject design is the ABAB design or the reversal design. It is also referred to as a withdrawal design, an equivalent time-samples design, an interrupted time series with multiple replications design, a within series elements design, or an operant design. When using the ABAB design, you compare your participant's performance across several conditions or phases. The first A phase is a baseline. Data are collected on the participant's current level of performance before implementing a treatment variable. During the first B phase, the treatment is applied and data continue to be collected. Ideally, a performance change should be recorded. This change alone is not enough to establish a functional relationship, as it may be the result of chance events. Therefore, the treatment is discontinued during a second A phase. This reversal or return to baseline should be characterized by a return of the dependent variable to the level in the earlier A phase. At this point, a functional relationship is established. Reimplementation of the independent variable during the final B phase should be accompanied by a positive change in the dependent variable. Conclusions about the relationship between the dependent and independent variables are then further strengthened.

Using the ABAB design. Correct use of the ABAB design requires adherence to a series of steps.

1. Clearly define the dependent and the independent variables.

2. Develop a system for recording your participant's level of performance. The systematic observation methods discussed in Chapter 9 are used frequently for this purpose.

3. Use an observation system to gather baseline data for three to five days, or until data are stable or going in undesired (contratherapeutic) direction. The best way to see the trend is to graph the data. As illustrated in Figure 6.1, behavior strength is recorded on the y axis and baseline and treatment sessions are recorded on the x axis. Three to five days of data collection should provide enough information to decide whether to implement your independent variable. For example, if you want to increase your participant's performance, his or her baseline data should be either low and stable or decreasing. If you want to decrease your participant's behavior, your baseline data should be either high and stable or increasing.

4. Implement the independent or treatment variable and continue until the participant's performance improves and stabilizes. Graph the data and examine the trend.

5. One A phase and one B phase are not sufficient for deciding that chance behavior changes are not the result of the treatment. At this point, a believable demonstration of cause and effect has not been produced. Therefore, withdraw the independent variable and continue collecting data until performance is stable. Ideally, the data path in this second A phase should reverse so that it is similar to the data path in the first baseline.

6. During the second B phase, reintroduce the independent variable. The data path should improve as it did during the first B phase. Such an outcome further verifies the functional relationship between implementation of the independent variable and changes in the dependent variable.

An illustration. Let's say Ms. Dugan is a physical therapist whose elementary school client, Susan, is refusing to participate for the full length of her forty-minute treatment session. She selects as her dependent variable the number of minutes Susan is on task. Using duration recording, Ms. Dugan notes that Susan is on task 10, 2, and 8 minutes, respectively, over three baseline sessions. As the independent variable, Ms. Dugan has decided to reward Susan with a "Dugan Dollar" for every 10 minutes she is engaged in therapy. Ten Dugan dollars will earn Susan the right to an extra art lesson with Ms. Leonard. Ms. Dugan explains the program to Susan and starts using it on the fourth day. Her data over the next four days of the B phase indicate Susan is on task for 20, 25, 29, and 30 minutes, respectively. Susan's behavior has changed in the desired direction. To be sure that the intervention program is the only reason for the improvement, Ms. Dugan stops

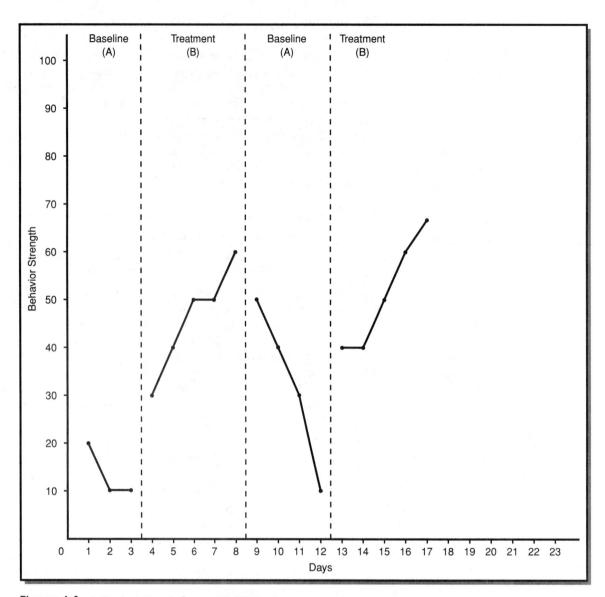

Figure 6.1 A Typical Graph for an ABAB Design

using Dugan dollars on the eighth day. Her data during the second A phase indicate that Susan is spending less time on task (18, 15, and 9 minutes). This reversal establishes a functional relationship between use of Dugan Dollars and an increase in time engaged in therapy. This relationship is strengthened further during the second B phase in which the use of Dugan Dollars is accompanied by an increase in on task behavior.

Advantages and disadvantages. There are three advantages associated with using an ABAB design (Kazdin, 1982; Tawney & Gast, 1984). First, it is very easy to use. Second, the replication or repetition of basic phases allows you to establish a functional relationship between independent and dependent variables. Third, an ABAB design is very flexible. At a minimum, the ABAB design must include three phases or you will not be able to draw conclusions regarding the functional relationship; however, there are numerous variations on this design. Though not as strong, an ABA design allows you to establish a functional relationship. Because the design ends on a baseline phase, it is generally used because of subject attrition during the course of a study. You can also use an ABAB design where A and B are separate treatments rather than baseline and treatment. This variation offers the advantages of always having some sort of treatment available. For example, you can measure the effects of medication or medication plus exercise on high blood pressure. A third variation is ABAC where the C phase is either a different intervention or a modification of the intervention presented in B. The modification is necessary because the original intervention was not as effective as the researcher thought it would be. For example, A is a baseline measure of noncompliance; B consists of the delivery of praise and tokens; C consists of praise, tokens, and time-out. A fourth variation, BAB, is used either when the severity of the problem (such as self-abuse) warrants immediate intervention or when preliminary observations indicate that a behavior is performed at zero levels. In this instance, baseline data serve no purpose.

Unfortunately, there are disadvantages to using an ABAB design (Kazdin, 1982; Tawney & Gast, 1984). First is the ethical concern over the withdrawal of treatment. In our illustration, it would not be surprising if Ms. Dugan were reluctant to stop using Dugan Dollars. Susan was on task longer, and the therapy was producing benefits. You should think about the potential impact of withdrawing the intervention before choosing this design, particularly if the dependent variable addresses a serious behavior. For example, you may not want to use an ABAB design to evaluate the effects of medication on seizure activity. Allowing an individual's behavior to get worse is not in his or her best interests.

Another disadvantage to the ABAB design is that not all behaviors can be reversed easily; that is, not all behaviors will be unlearned and will return to baseline when the intervention is removed. For example, Mr. Watkins may be interested in evaluating the effect of a new reading program on sight word recognition. Use of the new program may in fact increase sight word recognition during phase B; however, discontinuing the program during the second A phase does not mean students will forget how to read words they have just mastered. If a behavior doesn't reverse, then you must question the strength of the functional relationship between the independent variable and the dependent variable. Fortunately, the next single subject design option overcomes these disadvantages.

Multiple Baseline Designs

A multiple baseline design gets its name from the fact there are at least three dependent variables of interest. For example, you could be interested in the effects of a special diet and exercise program on the weight of three patients. In this instance, you are using a multiple baseline across subjects design. Or you could be interested in three distinct behaviors of one person as, for example, the effects of a speech articulation program on one student's ability to pronounce vowels, diphthongs, and consonants. This situation requires a multiple baseline across behaviors design. Finally, you may be interested in whether a person uses newly acquired social skills in settings other than the classroom, such as at home, on the job, and in the community. For this project, you need a multiple baseline across settings design. The basic premise of the multiple baseline design is that you implement the intervention program with one individual, on one behavior, or in one setting at a time. The remaining individuals, behaviors, or settings are not exposed to the treatment. Once behavior stabilizes, you expose the second individual, behavior, or setting to the intervention. A functional relationship is established only when the individual, behavior, or setting under treatment improves.

Using the multiple baseline design. There is a series of steps to be followed when using a multiple baseline design.

1. Define the dependent and independent or treatment variables. Be reasonably sure the dependent variables will respond to the treatment variable while ensuring that the dependent variables in each baseline are not related, that is, they do not co-vary. For example, you may be interested in using an aggression management program with three students in your class who always fight among themselves. Exposing one student to the aggression management program may cause a decrease in aggression demonstrated by the other two students. They are not directly affected by the program; however; there is one less person with whom they can fight.

2. Develop a system for recording the dependent variable.

3. During phase A, gather baseline data for three to five days or until they are stable. Depending on the design you choose, gather baseline data for three individuals, for one individual demonstrating three behaviors, or for one individual in three settings. Again, you should graph your data using the format illustrated in Figure 6.2.

4. Examine the data paths and choose the individual, behavior, or setting that is the most stable or most in need of attention. For example, you may try your special diet and exercise program on the person who needs to lose the most weight.

5. During phase B, introduce the independent variable with the first subject, on the first behavior, or in the first setting and continue to gather data on performance. Also, continue to gather and graph data on subjects, behaviors, or settings still in baseline, since they are still in phase A. Ideally, you should see a change in the desired direction only in the subject, behavior, or setting exposed to the intervention.

6. Examine the data and choose the next subject, behavior, or setting.

7. For your next phase B, introduce the independent variable to the second subject, behavior, or setting and continue to gather data on performance. Now, two of the three subjects, behaviors, or settings are in phase B, the treatment phase. Ideally, only these two subjects, behaviors, or settings are changing or continuing to change in the desired direction. You now have evidence of a functional relationship because the dependent variable changes only when the independent variable is applied.

8. Strengthen your conclusions by introducing the independent variable to the remaining subject, behavior, or setting. Phase B is in effect across the board.

Illustrations. Mr. Anderson is a counselor with his own private practice. He has three clients who are afraid to drive across bridges spanning water. He decides to combine systematic desensitization with emotive imagery to help them and to evaluate the effectiveness of the program with a multiple baseline across subjects design. He selects two dependent measures of anxiety. The first is the clients' blood pressure as they approach a bridge in their car; the second is a self-report. During baseline, Mr. Anderson takes his clients individually to a section of town where there is a bridge spanning water. He measures blood pressure and asks the client to rate his or her anxiety using a scale. After three days, he chooses the client with the highest blood pressure who reports the greatest amount of anxiety. This client is exposed to systematic desensitization and emotive imagery. He continues to gather treatment data for the first client and baseline data for the remaining two clients. When anxiety levels are reduced for the first client, Mr. Anderson exposes a second client to the treatment, keeping the third client under baseline conditions. Finally, when the anxiety levels of the first two clients are decreasing, the third client is exposed to the treatment. Mr. Anderson can prove there is a functional relationship between the exposure to the in-

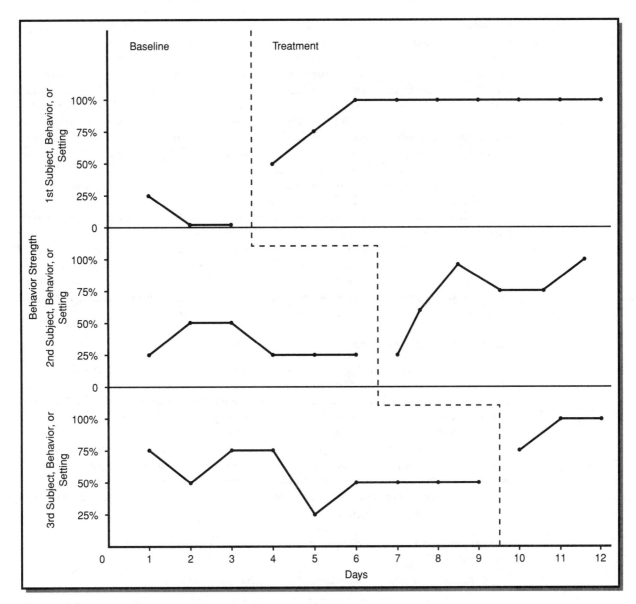

Figure 6.2 A Typical Graph for a Multiple Baseline Design

dependent variable and changes in the dependent variables if his clients demonstrate lower blood pressure and report lower anxiety only after using systematic desensitization and emotive imagery.

Advantages and disadvantages. The multiple baseline design offers nine advantages (Kazdin, 1982; Tawney & Gast, 1984). First, it is very easy to use. Second, it can be used to establish a functional relationship between independent and dependent variables. Third, unlike the ABAB design, this design does not require a reversal phase. This feature should ease ethical concerns that you, your colleagues, or your participants' parents may have over the withdrawal of treatment. Fifth, more than one dependent variable can be analyzed. Sixth, you can test a treatment on a small scale before extending its use. It is possible that an intervention will not have the effects you had hoped for, so you can stop using it before investing more resources. Seventh, using the multiple baseline across subjects design allows you to note individual variation in treatment effectiveness. Eighth, using the multiple baseline across behaviors design is less demanding for a participant as you are requesting that he or she change only one behavior at a time. Finally, a multiple baseline design is very flexible. For example, the effect of the intervention applied to the first subject, behavior, or setting may be less than you had hoped. Therefore, you can modify it so that now you have an ABC design within the multiple baseline. If the modified intervention has the desired effect, you can apply it sequentially to other baselines. Another example of the flexibility of this design is that you can use as many baselines or dependent variables as you want. Perhaps you are working with six individuals. You could implement the intervention program to two individuals at a time.

There are also some disadvantages associated with use of multiple baseline designs, though. First, although treatment is not withdrawn, it is withheld for a period of time from a subject, a behavior, or a setting. Extended baselines mean that there is a delay in treatment. On a related note, another disadvantage is that this design is not suitable if the dependent variables are serious or dangerous and must be changed quickly. For example, this design would not be appropriate if you were working with three students who demonstrate self-injurious behavior. It would not be ethical to delay treatment to the second and third students.

Changing Criterion Design

The ABAB and multiple baseline designs are appropriate for evaluating an independent variable that changes a behavior quickly; however, not all dependent variables can be changed rapidly. Another single subject design that is suitable for evaluating a slow change in an individual's behavior is the changing criterion design. Using this design requires a researcher to break a long-term goal into smaller, more manageable steps. The treatment variable, most often a criterion for reinforcement, is implemented until the individual's behavior reaches the criterion (e.g., five spelling errors a page produces free time), then the standard is raised (e.g., four spelling errors a page produces free time). Again the treatment continues until the criterion is achieved, at which time the criterion is made even more rigorous (e.g., three spelling errors a page) and so on until the overall goal is achieved (e.g., no spelling errors).

Using a changing criterion design. There is a series of steps to follow when using a changing criterion design.

1. Clearly define the dependent and independent variables.

2. Develop a system for recording the dependent variable.

3. Gather baseline data for three to five days until the data are stable or going in contratherapeutic direction. Again, it is very useful to graph your data. Figure 6.3 presents a graphing format for this design.

4. Set two criteria. The first criterion is the standard the individual is expected to meet at the end of your intervention program. This can be done by using the social comparison method (Wolf, 1978) we discuss in Chapter 13. The second criterion is the first interim level of performance. It can be the lowest point of baseline for a behavior to be decreased or the highest point of baseline for a behavior to be increased. It can be the average of your baseline data. The most stringent interim criterion is half of the baseline average.

5. Present the independent variable and continue gathering data until two out of three sessions are at or below the criterion for a dependent variable you want to decrease. If

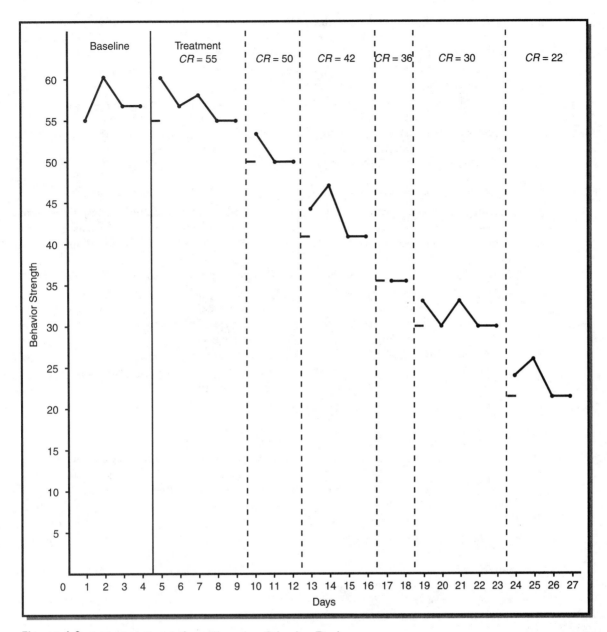

Figure 6.3 A Typical Graph for a Changing Criterion Design

you want to see an increase, the dependent variable should be at or above the criterion. This is the beginning of a functional relationship, but you can't draw any solid conclusions.

6. Select a new criterion level and repeat application of the independent variable. A new interim criterion can be adjusted if the individual experiences difficulty meeting it. There should be a steplike function of change across a minimum of four subphases. A functional relationship is demonstrated by gradual changes in the dependent variable over the course of the intervention phase.

An illustration. Eileen has decided that she wants to give up smoking. She has tried before to quit cold turkey with only limited success. This time, she decides to give up smoking gradually. For five days, she counts the number of cigarettes she smokes using frequency recording. Her data indicate that she smoked 30, 35, 29, 30, and 31 cigarettes during this time. Her long-term goal is to eliminate smoking completely; however, she chooses 29, her lowest point during baseline, as her first interim criterion. She decides that for every day she doesn't smoke more than 28 cigarettes, she will reward herself by putting three dollars toward an expensive piece of jewelry she wants. She keeps track of the number of cigarettes she smokes. After reaching this interim criterion for two out of three days, she selects a new, lower criterion. She continues until she reaches her goal of eliminating cigarette smoking completely.

Advantages and disadvantages. The first advantage, as we already mentioned, is that a changing criterion design is ideal for dependent variables that can be changed slowly. Second, you can use this design to evaluate interventions designed to increase or decrease behaviors. Third, there is less demand on the individuals for substantial change in behavior. The criterion becomes more strict only after the individual demonstrates mastery of performance at an easier level. Finally, unlike the ABAB and multiple baseline designs, you do not need to withdraw or withhold a treatment.

The first disadvantage of a changing criterion design is related to its first advantage. Because it is suitable for slow changes, it is not suitable for evaluating an intervention, which is supposed to produce quick changes. For example, a dangerous behavior must be changed quickly. Second, it is possible that there will be rapid changes in the dependent variable. An individual who quickly surpasses the interim criterion level may be under the influence of something other than the intervention program (Kazdin, 1982; Tawney & Gast, 1984).

Alternating Treatments Design

The three designs just discussed focus on one independent variable. Often, we already suspect or know that several independent variables will change a dependent variable. The question is which independent variable works best. If your research question involves comparing the effects of two independent variables on the dependent variable, you can use an alternating treatments design. This design shows which of two or more independent variables is more or most effective, or that there is no difference (i.e., they are equally effective). There are many names for this design including the multiple-treatment design, multi-element design, simultaneous treatment design, multiple schedule design, concurrent schedule design, randomization design, multi-element manipulation, and comparative intervention design. The most important feature of an alternating treatment design is that two or more treatments are alternated rapidly. Data are collected to measure the effect of each on the dependent variable. The most effective independent variable produces the greatest positive change.

Using the alternating treatments design. Follow this series of steps to use an alternating treatments design.

1. Clearly define the dependent variable and at least two independent variables. The dependent variable must occur frequently enough so that it is possible to apply the independent variable. The independent variables must be distinctly different, but each should have the potential for producing a change within the treatment session during which it is administered. Finally, the effects of each intervention cannot linger or carryover.

2. Develop a method for recording the dependent variable. In contrast to designs discussed earlier, baseline data need not be collected prior to treatment, although, as

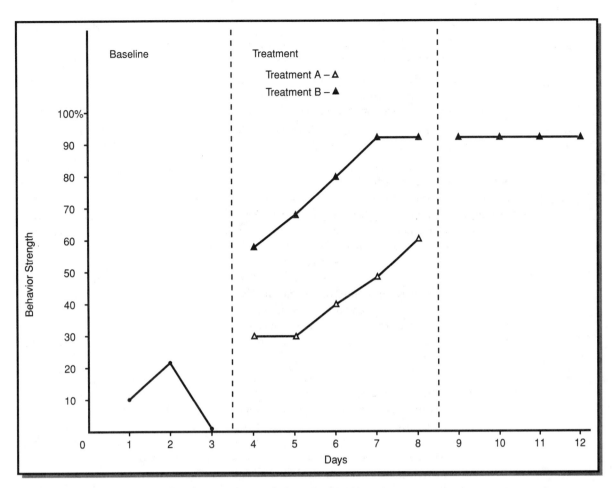

Figure 6.4 A Typical Graph for an Alternating Treatments Design

Neuman and McCormick (1995) point out, it is a good idea and is a feature in the variations.

3. Schedule the independent variables on an a priori basis. Balance them so that each intervention is administered an equal number of times. They can alternate within a single session (e.g., the first and last 20 minutes of a class), within a day (e.g., morning vs. afternoon), or from day to day. Presentation should be randomly counterbalanced to neutralize the effects of conditions other than the independent variables. Remember that the need to balance treatments means that you are limited in the number of interventions you can use during any one study. The more interventions you have, the more sessions or days you need to ensure there is a balanced presentation.

4. Present the treatments. Treatments all occur in the same phase, but they are not in effect at the same time. They have to be administered separately in some way so they can be evaluated. Continue to gather and graph data until the dependent variable stabilizes in the separate interventions. Figure 6.4 illustrates a typical graph for an alternating treatment design.

5. Determine which intervention was most effective by examining the data paths. Ideally, the data paths should not overlap. Compare the vertical distance in the data paths

to determine if one independent variable is clearly better than the other. Substantial overlap between the data paths accompanied by improvement over baseline conditions suggests the independent variables are equally effective.

6. Verify the functional relationship. The major comparison is between two or more data paths representing two or more treatments. Most times, investigators using this design were very conservative and looked for clear divergence.

7. Present only the most effective independent variable during the last phase of your study.

An illustration. Ms. Swisher has two ideas for increasing her fourth graders' spelling skills. The first is peer tutoring; the second is a cover-copy-compare method. She decides to find out which technique will produce higher spelling achievement. She chooses words from the fourth grade spelling text and randomly assigns them to the peer tutoring condition or the cover-copy-compare condition. Ms. Swisher schedules two brief spelling lessons per day, one in the morning and the other in the afternoon. Every day she randomly selects one of two index cards bearing the phrases "peer tutoring" or "cover-copy-compare." She also randomly selects one of two index cards bearing the word "morning" or "afternoon." Students work on their spelling using the designated intervention. At the end of each spelling lesson, Ms. Swisher administers a brief quiz. She averages the results for the class and graphs the data separately for each intervention. After two weeks, she examines the data paths and concludes that peer tutoring produces consistently higher scores. She continues to use peer tutoring.

Advantages and disadvantages. Obviously, the primary advantage of an alternating treatments design is that you compare two or more independent variables. Second, as we suggested earlier, you do not need to collect baseline data. Even if you do, they need not be stable. Third, the dependent variable can be treated immediately, and there is no need to withdraw or withhold the independent variable (Barlow & Hayes, 1979; Rose & Beattie, 1986).

Unfortunately, there is the potential for multiple treatment interference or a confounding effect. The effects of one treatment may be influenced by, or carried over to, other treatments. Second, this design is not appropriate for measuring the subtle differences between two treatments. Finally, you may find it cumbersome to arrange and quickly alternate the independent variables (Neuman & McCormick, 1995).

SUMMARY

In this chapter we discussed several design options suitable for evaluating the influence of an independent variable used with a single individual or a small group. These options included the ABAB design, the multiple baseline design, the changing criterion design, and the alternating treatments design. We described how each design is used, illustrated how data appear on a graph, provided an example, and discussed each design's advantages and disadvantages. Used correctly, these designs can help you answer research questions from a variety of fields that involve one person or a small number of persons. As we discussed each design, we highlighted how it can be used to establish a functional relationship between implementation of the independent variable and subsequent changes in the dependent variable. In Chapter 13, we will present additional ideas for analysis of single subject design data to increase the confidence you have in your results.

REFERENCES

Barlow, D. H., & Hayes, S. C. (1979). Alternating treatments design: One strategy for comparing the effects of two treatments in a single subject. *Journal of Applied Behavior Analysis, 12,* 199–210.

Best, J. W. (1997). *Research in education* (8th ed.). Upper Saddle River, NJ: Merrill/Prentice Hall.

Kazdin, A. E. (1982). *Single-case research designs: Methods for clinical and applied settings.* New York: Oxford University Press.

Neuman, S. B., & McCormick, S. (1995). *Single subject experimental research: Applications for literacy.* Newark, DE: International Reading Association.

Rose, T. L., & Beattie, J. R. (1986). Relative effects of teacher-directed and taped previewing on oral reading. *Learning Disability Quarterly, 9,* 193–199.

Tawney, J. W., & Gast, D. L. (1984). *Single subject research in special education.* Upper Saddle River, NJ: Merrill/Prentice Hall.

Wolf, M. M. (1978). Social validity: The case for subjective evaluation or how applied behavior analysis is finding its heart. *Journal of Applied Behavior Analysis, 11,* 203–214.

FURTHER READINGS

General Information of Single Subject Designs

Hedge, M. N. (1987). *Clinical research in communication disorders: Principles and strategies.* Boston: Little, Brown.

Kazdin, A. E. (1982). *Single-case research designs: Methods for clinical and applied settings.* New York: Oxford University Press.

Neuman, S. B., & McCormick, S. (1995). *Single subject experimental research: Applications for literacy.* Newark, DE: International Reading Association.

Silverman, F. H. (1997). *Research design and evaluation in speech-language pathology and audiology* (4th ed.). Needham Heights, MA: Allyn & Bacon.

Tawney, J. W., & Gast, D. L. (1984). *Single subject research in special education.* Upper Saddle River, NJ: Merrill/Prentice Hall.

ABAB Designs

Dugan, E., Kamps, D., Leonard, B., Watkins, N., Rheinberger, A., & Stackhus, J. (1995). Effects of cooperative learning groups during social studies for students with autism and fourth-grade peers. *Journal of Applied Behavior Analysis, 28,* 175–188.

Gardner, R., Heward, W. L., & Grossi, T. A. (1994). Effects of response cards on student participation and academic achievement: A systematic replication with inner-city students during whole-class science instruction. *Journal of Applied Behavior Analysis, 27,* 63–71.

Montee, B. B., Miltenberger, R. G., & Wittrock, D. (1995). An experimental analysis of facilitated communication. *Journal of Applied Behavior Analysis, 28,* 189–200.

Multiple Baseline Designs

Beecroft, P. C. (1993). Social skills training and cognitive restructuring for adolescents on hemodialysis, *Clinical Nursing Research, 2,* 188–211.

Bornstein, P. H., Bellack, A. S., & Herson, M. (1977). Social skills training for unassertive children: A multiple baseline analysis. *Journal of Applied Behavior Analysis, 10,* 183–195.

Cuvo, A. J. (1979). Multiple-baseline design in instructional research: Pitfalls of measurement and procedural advantages. *American Journal of Mental Deficiency, 84,* 219–228.

Danoff, B., Harris, K., & Graham, S. (1993). Incorporating strategy instruction within the writing process in the regular classroom: Effects on the writing of students with and without learning disabilities. *Journal of Reading Behavior, 25,* 295–322.

Dapcich-Miura, E., & Hovel, M. F. (1979). Contingency management of adherence to a complex medical regimen in an elderly heart patient. *Behavior Therapy, 10,* 193–201.

Horner, R. D., & Baer, D. M. (1978). Multiple-probe technique: A variation of the multiple baseline. *Journal of Applied Behavior Analysis, 11,* 189–196.

Kandel, H. J., Ayllon, T., & Rosenbaum, M. S. (1977). Flooding or systematic exposure in the treatment of extreme social withdrawal in children. *Journal of Behavior Therapy and Experimental Psychiatry, 8,* 75–81.

Kazdin, A. E., & Kopel, S. A. (1975). On resolving ambiguities of the multiple-baseline design: Problems and recommendations. *Behavior Therapy, 6,* 601–608.

Lockhart, J., & Law, M. (1994). The effectiveness of multisensory writing programme for improving cursive writing ability in children with sensori-motor difficulties. *Canadian Journal of Occupational Therapy, 61,* 206–214.

Murphy, R. J., & Bryan, A. J. (1982). Multiple baseline and multiple-probe designs: Practical alternatives for special education assessment and evaluation. *Journal of Special Education, 14,* 325–335.

Schmidt, A. M., & Meyers, R. A. (1995). Traditional and phonological treatment for teaching English fricatives and affricates to Koreans. *Journal of Speech and Hearing Research, 38,* 828–838.

Shapiro, E. S., & McCurdy, B. L. (1989). Effects of a taped-words treatment on reading proficiency. *Exceptional Children, 55,* 321–325.

Strain, P. S. & Shores, R. E. (1979). Additional comments on multiple-baseline designs in instructional research. *American Journal of Mental Deficiency, 84,* 229–234.

Changing Criterion Designs

Hartmann, D. P., & Hall, R. V. (1976). The changing criterion design. *Journal of Applied Behavior Analysis, 9,* 527–532.

Johnston, R. J., & McLaughlin, T. F. (1982). The effects of free time on assignment completion and accuracy in arithmetic: A case study. *Education and Treatment of Children, 5,* 33–40.

Schloss, P. J., Sedlak, R. A., Elliot, C., & Smothers, M. (1982). Application of the changing criterion design in special education. *Journal of Special Education, 16,* 359–367.

Smith, M. A., Schloss, P. J., & Israelite, N. K. (1986). Evaluation of a simile recognition treatment program for hearing impaired students. *Journal of Speech and Hearing Disorders, 51,* 134–139.

Alternating Treatments Design

Barlow, D. H., & Hayes, S. C. (1979). Alternating treatments designs: One strategy for comparing the effects of two treatments in a single subject. *Journal of Applied Behavior Analysis, 12,* 199–210.

Cuvo, A. J., Ashley, K. M., Marso, K. J., Zhang, B. L., & Fry, T. A. (1995). Effects of response practice variables on learning spelling and sight vocabulary. *Journal of Applied Behavior Analysis, 28,* 155–173.

Daly, E. J., & Martens, B. K. (1994). A comparison of three interventions for increasing oral reading performance: Application of the instructional hierarchy. *Journal of Applied Behavior Analysis, 27,* 459–469.

Kazdin, A. E., & Hartmann, D. P. (1978). The simultaneous treatment design. *Behavior Therapy, 9,* 912–922.

Murphy, R., Doughty, N., & Nunes, D. (1979). Multielement designs: An alternative to reversal and multiple baselines evaluation strategies. *Mental Retardation, 17,* 23–26.

Ollendeick, T. H., Matson, J. L., Esveldt-Dawson, K., & Shapiro, E S. (1980). Increasing spelling achievement: An analysis of treatment procedures utilizing an alternative treatments design. *Journal of Applied Behavior Analysis, 13,* 645–654.

Weismer, S. E., Murray-Branch, J., & Miller, J. F. (1993). Comparison of two methods for promoting productive vocabulary in late talkers. *Journal of Speech and Hearing Research, 36,* 1037–1050.

7

Qualitative Research Approaches

INTRODUCTION

Chapters 5 and 6 described research methods used with large or small groups for researchers interested in determining how people will behave under certain conditions. You can answer research questions by determining if subjects actually performed in the predicted manner. You can then generalize findings to the population from which subjects were selected. Alternately, rather than making predictions about the characteristics or behavior of a population, you may be more interested in people's lives or their perceptions. For example, one researcher may be interested in why a woman would consider being a surrogate mother or how people perceive surrogate mothers. Another researcher may be interested in social movements, such as the effect of civil rights movements on the quality of life enjoyed by African-Americans. Quantitative approaches are not

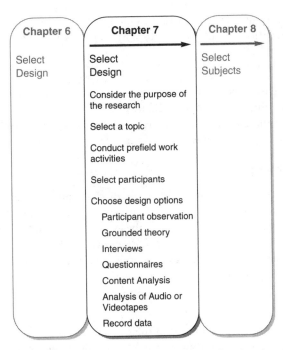

Chapter 6	Chapter 7	Chapter 8
Select Design	Select Design	Select Subjects
	Consider the purpose of the research	
	Select a topic	
	Conduct prefield work activities	
	Select participants	
	Choose design options	
	Participant observation	
	Grounded theory	
	Interviews	
	Questionnaires	
	Content Analysis	
	Analysis of Audio or Videotapes	
	Record data	

The Scope, Plan, and Sequence Chart for Conducting
Research: The Fourth Step in the Research Process

appropriate for topics such as these because they will not produce discrete numerical responses to summarize social issues.

Fortunately, another research method is available for answering these questions. It is called *qualitative research,* but it may also be referred to as ethnographic research or naturalistic inquiry. It involves observations rather than manipulations. Its problem statements, design, and analysis change during the study rather than adhere closely to prespecified conditions. Findings are summarized as text rather than statistics. Its focus is on the individuals being studied rather than concern for making generalizations to a larger population. Qualitative research was pioneered by anthropologists studying various cultural groups, but investigators in other areas of the social sciences have begun to use it, including education, sociology, history, linguistics, and psychology.

In this chapter, we will describe how to conduct a qualitative study. Although we discuss components separately, be advised that steps in conducting a qualitative study may occur simultaneously.

COMPARISON TO QUANTITATIVE METHODS

Quantitative and qualitative research methods differ in the basic assumptions upon which they are built, the role of the researcher, the purpose for which they are used, and the actual methods through which conclusions are drawn. We will discuss each of these differences.

Assumptions

Quantitative methods assume that data can be objectively and reliably drawn from a sample. These data are believed to accurately reflect reality. Further, they can be manipulated mathematically to objectively quantify differences or relationships. Qualitative research methods assume that social phenomena are complex and interactive. No single number or group of numbers can account for the variability of social interactions. Finally, we construct reality through our own perceptions. These perceptions are not subject to simple appraisals and numeric summary.

Role of the Researcher

The quantitative researcher strives to be objective, impartial, and detached from the outcome of his or her study. The qualitative researcher acknowledges that by their very nature, researchers have an interest in outcomes. They are personally involved and favor a given outcome simply by virtue of having selected a research question, assessment method, or analytic procedure.

Purpose for Conducting Research

Quantitative researchers conduct research to make predictions, produce causal statements, establish relationships, and generalize findings. Qualitative researchers conduct research to gain insight into complex social phenomena. They describe events or patterns of behavior exhibited by individuals or groups in their natural states. These descriptions increase our understanding of the ideas, feelings, beliefs, and motives related to the individuals' actions. Because social situations are unique, qualitative researchers do not seek to generalize findings from one group to another.

Methods Used

Quantitative methods involve a priori decision rules that guide the research process. The actual process generally involves demonstrating control of dependent variables by independent variables, summarizing findings through statistical techniques, and supporting the generalization of findings through sampling methods. Qualitative methods evolve during the course of the study. Methods are naturalistic and unobtrusive. Sampling is done to locate a group of interest to the researcher, not to establish a generalizable case.

TYPES OF QUALITATIVE RESEARCH

Three forms of qualitative research are generally used. *Case studies* allow you to focus on a single instance of a current phenomenon in its total context. For example, you may want to study how one teacher shifts from a direct instruction approach to a constructivist-based approach for teaching mathematics. You may want to study a couple as they prepare to adopt a child. A case study allows you to observe events as they unfold and to interview those who participate in these events. Typically, case studies involve multiple data sources, including discussions with the participants, direct observations, and analysis of written documents.

Historical Studies

Historical studies involve the interpretation of past events in light of current issues or events. The idea is that examining the past can increase our understanding of present conditions. For example, you may study the immigration patterns during the early twentieth century to understand existing immigration laws and policies. Because the phenomena has already happened, others' observations and records must be used. One approach that may be used is oral history. In this case, interview someone who immigrated during that time and who has first-hand knowledge of events. Another approach is the review of permanent products such as immigration records, newspapers, and diaries. Of course, it is important to verify the authenticity and accuracy of the documents by cross-checking against other sources of data, such as interviews and observations.

Ethnographic Studies

Ethnographic studies allow investigators to study the complex interactions of individuals within their immediate environment. As such, they focus on humans and their culture. They may involve people from different cultures, such as the Aborigine in Australia or Irish Americans in the United States. They may also involve individuals within a familiar and local culture such as a neighborhood or a school. Qualitative studies conducted in the classroom are referred to as microethnographic studies (Stainback & Stainback, 1988). They allow you to describe the details of interactions between teachers and their students.

SELECTING A RESEARCH TOPIC

In quantitative research, the dependent and independent variables are clearly identified before beginning the study. In qualitative research, however, you may have a vague notion of the problem being investigated. Crowl (1996) referred to these notions as foreshadowed problems. Erickson (1985) outlined questions you can address through qualitative research.

1. Exactly what is happening in a specific setting?
2. What do these events mean to the people who are involved?
3. Are these events organized into patterns and principles that guide everyday life?
4. How are events in this setting related to events at other system levels inside and outside the setting?
5. How does the manner in which life in this setting is organized compare with other ways of organizing life found in different places and times?

Often, researchers' ideas will come from real-world observations, dilemmas, or questions. For example, you may want to know why a crime prevention initiative is successful in one neighborhood but not in another. Is there something special about the people living in the neighborhood, social service providers, or geographic area? Perhaps you are interested in how citizens' groups affect change at local levels. Is there a technique perceived as most effective? Do tactics change as a function of the issue? Perhaps you are interested in the issue of sexual harassment of women on a college campus. Is there a discrepancy between perceptions of university officials and those of female students? Maybe you are interested in the unique challenges faced by teachers whose students have chronic illnesses. How do public school teachers perceive Do Not Resuscitate (DNR) orders that the family request be in effect, even during school hours? General questions such as these guide your early work. These questions become more narrow as specific problems, themes, or patterns emerge while you conduct your study.

Glesne and Peshkin (1991) warned that the choice of a topic should not be based on very personal issues. Individual passion for a topic may undermine a researcher's objectivity. Also, a research topic that is critical to an investigator on a personal level may have no appeal for others. Ask yourself if the topic emerged from your life history or if you are out to prove something you already know. If the answer to either question is yes, choose another topic.

PREFIELDWORK ACTIVITIES

Stainback and Stainback (1988) recommend that you engage in prefieldwork activities prior to formally beginning a study. Such activities involve a review of the literature, including professional books and journals, official reports, autobiographies, and novels. In keeping with the definition of research presented in Chapter 1, be reasonably sure your plans will produce data that go beyond existing information and contribute to our knowledge base. A thorough literature review can enhance confidence in the potential contribution of a study.

As another prefieldwork activity, you can explore research sites to identify those that are both appropriate for your needs and readily accessible. Friends, colleagues, or your own previous experience may suggest research sites. Glesne and Peshkin (1991) warn against choosing a place where you have been integrally involved. Their concern is that you may see only what you expect to see as opposed to what is really there.

Marshall and Rossman (1994) identify characteristics of the ideal site. It is one in which (a) you will have access; (b) there is a high probability that you will find a combination of processes, people, programs, and interactions related to your question; (c) you will be able to maintain a presence for as long as is necessary; and (d) data quality and credibility are reasonably assured.

Once a site is selected, you should obtain permission to conduct your study. If access to an agency or a school is needed, gatekeepers, or individuals from whom consent is required should be contacted. It helps to have a colleague on site who is familiar with important people and policies overseeing the day-to-day operations. The information presented in Chapter 2 will be useful in obtaining the necessary consent under the *National Research Act,* but we offer some additional information that is particular to obtaining consent to conduct a qualitative study. Schedule an appointment with the gatekeepers during which you will explain the topic of the study. Apprise them of the nature of qualitative work. Emphasize that specific questions may emerge and shift over the course of the study. Tell them that you will need access to people and events at the site, and describe the design for collecting and analyzing data. Again, note that although you have a design, its exact nature will change depending on the data that emerge. Explain that measures will be taken to ensure the confidentiality of participants. Guarantee that they will receive a final copy of your report.

SELECTING PEOPLE TO INCLUDE IN YOUR STUDY

You may have noticed that we did not use the term "subject" in the heading to this section. Glesne and Peshkin (1991) suggest that this word means someone who will be acted on through manipulation of variables. During qualitative work, you will be interacting with people. They prefer a phrase such as "a participant" or "a respondent" because they reflect this methodological shift.

Purposive Sampling

A sampling technique that will be discussed in Chapter 8, purposive sampling can be used to select the people you will include for a qualitative study. Briefly, purposive sampling allows you to select people on the basis of your belief that they can contribute to and expand your database rather than selecting them on the basis of predetermined criteria. Another sampling technique is called *networking* (Glesne & Peshkin, 1991). This method involves participants already selected for the study recommending other potential participants.

Having selected participants, it is important to establish rapport. Participants who trust a researcher are more likely to be candid and honest and behave normally. Examine how choices of clothing, makeup, hairstyle, taste in jewelry, manner of speech, and body language can enhance or hamper your ability to blend into the setting. Become familiar with and follow any rules governing social interaction. Get to know your participants, and identify common interests and tastes.

Early in the investigation, a few subjects may emerge as key informants, that is, people who are your main sources of information. However, don't focus exclusively on one person or a small number of people. Different people have different perspectives, and you should identify as many views as possible.

QUALITATIVE RESEARCH METHODS

Remain flexible because the design will probably change during your study. Marshall and Rossman (1989) recommend you devise a plan but reserve the right to alter it during the study as the data emerge.

Participant Observation

Participant observation is the method most commonly used in qualitative research. Immerse yourself in the setting so that you can see, hear, and experience your subjects' daily life (Marshall & Rossman, 1994). Such immersion will enable you to describe in detail the subjects who are present and the expected and unexpected events that are occurring. In classrooms, this method is referred to as *privileged observations* (Wolcott, 1988).

Participant observations can occur in varying degrees. At one extreme, you can become a full member of the community with your role as an observer concealed. This level of participant observation occurs in anthropological studies. At the other extreme, the researcher has little or no interaction with the participants. This level can occur in psychological studies. Qualitative researchers are most likely to compromise by primarily observing, but occasionally interacting.

Participant observation requires written notes, called field notes, which are dated and filed for later analysis. Initially, observations may appear loosely related; however, subsequent examination and coding of accumulated field notes may highlight concepts that will allow you to describe and explain events (Crowl, 1996). We will discuss field notes in detail later in this chapter.

Grounded Theory

We recommend frequent examination of field notes, making memos and diagrams regarding possible explanations that will guide future observations. These observations will confirm or disconfirm these explanations. This constant shift from observing and notetaking to analyzing observations is called *grounded theory*. It allows a researcher to propose a theoretical notion and check for verification (Crowl, 1996). However, use of participant observation and grounded theory may be insufficient. You may need more documentation through other sources.

Interviews

In-depth interviewing is frequently used in combination with participant observation. It offers the advantage of providing you with a large amount of information quickly (Marshall & Rossman, 1994). You can conduct several interviews over the course of a study. Generally, it is unstructured or loosely structured so that your participants can talk about items they are interested in or that they think are important. Interviews can vary from informal conversations to openended interviews to in-depth discussions with key informants. On occasion, however, you may want to conduct structured interviews on a specific topic to give you comparable data across different subjects.

To use interviews, develop a list of questions but be prepared to modify them on the basis of subjects' responses. You should avoid using yes/no questions because they typically produce one-word answers. Interviews should be scheduled in advance to ensure everyone can be there, and they should be conducted in a comfortable setting. You may want to consider using group interviews where a response from one participant can prompt a comment from another (Stainback & Stainback, 1988). Finally, with the permission of your participants, audio or videotape interviews and transcribe them into a written format.

Questionnaires

Questionnaires can be used to obtain information about a characteristic, attitude, or a belief. They can include open-ended questions or closed questions. Because they involve self-report, there is always the possibility that a respondent is not being honest.

Content Analysis

Content analysis is used to examine written records such as textbooks, novels, newspapers, music, speech transcripts, photographs, birth and death certificates, curricula, diaries, and letters. Participants can be asked to produce these documents, or the documents may be obtained from independent sources. As is true for selecting participants, careful attention must be paid in the selection of documents for analysis. You need to locate or develop a coding or classification system that will be used while going through the documents. Finally, decide which statistical procedures to use in analyzing results. Options include frequency counts and chi-square analysis, both of which are discussed in Chapter 12.

Analysis of Audio or Videotapes

As was mentioned earlier, technological devices such as tape recorders and video cameras may be used to assist with data collection. Audiotaping interviews with one or more participants is a prime example. Audiotape can also be used for recording oral histories. Video cameras are useful in both of these situations, as well as for recording staff or personnel meetings, and participants in their natural environment. These devices offer distinct advantages. First, they can reduce the need to take complete field notes on site. Second, they can be reviewed later and used as a guide for constructing extensive field notes. Third, they are particularly useful in assembling exact quotes and gathering information about characteristics such as tone of voice and use of gestures. Fourth, they can provide for a more comprehensive description of events. Finally, with careful use, technology can contribute to the reliability of results because they are permanent products.

Despite these advantages, you must still be cautious when using recording devices. Their presence may make participants more sensitive about what they say or do; therefore, they may not be acting naturally which can undermine the validity of your study. They also require careful attention to operating instructions and maintenance. Before using it, check the condition of the equipment. Be prepared by having the instruction manual, fresh batteries, and extension cords on hand.

RECORDING DATA

The primary method to record qualitative data is the use of field notes. These are very detailed, written records of what you saw and heard during observations, and your own thoughts or reactions to them. Condensed field notes should be taken on site by recording abbreviations and key words and phrases in a loose-leaf notebook, on a clipboard, or an index card. Ideally, you should use your condensed notes to develop more detailed field notes the same day you observed. The more time that elapses between making condensed notes and writing field notes, the more likely you are to forget important details. We warn you that writing field notes is a time-consuming process; plan accordingly. Complete field notes should be descriptive and analytic. They are descriptive because they include basic information such as the date, time, and place, and a description of the physical setting including a map if desired. You also identify everyone who was present during your observation and include characteristics about them such as age, gender, manner of dress, ethnic background, and use of gestures. Include detailed information about everything that occurred and include direct quotes. Field notes are analytic in that they include any reactions, confusions, hunches, insights, or interpretations you may have. Glesne and Peshkin (1992) recommend a series of guidelines to follow when writing field notes. We summarize them in Table 7.1. Sample field notes are included in Table 7.2.

Table 7.1 Maintaining Field Notes

Glesne and Peshkin (1991) offered the following recommendations for developing field notes.

1. Only write on one side of the paper. It is less confusing if you have to photocopy them or cut them up to rearrange.

2. Use big margins on both sides for coding and afterthoughts.

3. Develop your own shorthand system.

4. Do not discuss your observations until after you have written your field notes. Such conversations can alter your perceptions.

5. After completing your notes, read through them to fill in and clarify.

Table 7.2 Sample Field Notes for a Study Relating to Exaggerated Claims of Trout Fishermen

Date-May 14, 1997

Time-8:30 a.m.

Location-Susquehanna Fly Fishing Outfitters

Individuals at Location-Jim Staton (owner), Bob Simms (guide), Unnamed Customers A and B.

Observations-JS stated that he had been tearing up the whiley hatchery trout in Roaring Creek. JS stated that he caught and released 12 last evening. All were over 10 inches. He suggested a fly rod that he has on sale that is particularly effective.

BS stated that there had been a slow start to the season due to cold water temperatures (recorder's note: trout actively feed when water temperatures are in the 55° to 60° range. Water temperatures in the Creek were below 50° each day of the week preceding May 14 raising questions about JS's claim and supporting BS's conservative view).

Customer A talked about the terrific season he had last year. He had been skunked so far this year. He attributed the difference to limited stocking (recorder's note: Department of Natural Resources data indicate that stocking rates were up in Roaring Creek this year).

Customer B questioned if acid rain has degraded the creek to the point that it is not as effective in supporting trout. In any case, he claims to always catch a few fish each day. He stated that he caught six yesterday with a grey drake fly (recorder's note: the grey drake hatch is not expected for 30 days. Trout are not likely to take a fly that does not resemble current insect activity).

Date-May 15, 1997

Time-9:30 a.m.

Location-500 yards downstream from Slabtown Bridge access point to Roaring Creek

Individuals at Location-Fisherman A (grey shirt and Chicago Cubs hat)

Observations-No fish in creel, and fishing a wolly bugger through a pool. I asked how he was doing. He said he was very frustrated. He had seen a number of fish, but they were not feeding. He had not seen anyone else catch any over the past few days.

Date-May 15, 1997

Time-10:00 a.m.

Location-1000 yards downstream from Slabtown Bridge access point to Roaring Creek

Individuals at Location-Fisherman B (Camo shirt with floppy camo hat)

Observations-No fish in creel and fishing a nymph in rapid water. I asked how he was doing. He said he killed them here last week, but suspects that bait fisherman had fished out the stream in the meantime. He was going to fish another half hour and then give it up for the day.

Date-May 15, 1997

Time-10:00 a.m.

Location-1500 yards downstream from Slabtown Bridge access point to Roaring Creek

Individuals at Location-Fisherman C (beige auto repair uniform shirt, no hat)

Observations-No fish in creel and fishing a March Brown fly. I asked how he was doing.

He said he was just beginning to learn to fly fish and wasn't really good enough yet to expect to catch many. He said that he was anxious to be as skilled as his friends who talk about catching large numbers of fish. I asked if he had been out fishing with his friends. He said that he went out twice, but it was too early in the season, and the fish were not active.

STRATEGIES TO ENHANCE RELIABILITY AND VALIDITY

Reliability

Reliability is the consistency of measurement. In qualitative research, it is the extent to which observations could be replicated by another independent recorder. Qualitative researchers are not dealing with numerical data, so it is not appropriate to use the traditional procedures for ensuring reliability that will be described in Chapter 10. Alternate procedures include maintaining very detailed field notes that describe everything that occurred in an observation or during an interview. In your notes, be careful to distinguish between what actually happened during an event and your perceptions about it. Second, when possible, collect data in teams. A colleague trained in the use of qualitative procedures can provide feedback on your field notes and interview transcripts. Third, a participant in your study can review your notes or final report and provide feedback.

Validity

Validity addresses the extent to which an instrument measures what it purports to measure. You are attempting to measure perceptions and events as they occur in the natural environment; therefore, it is essential that you minimize disruptions in the natural environment. Simply by being present you have altered the natural environment; however, there are still some things that can be done to increase validity. Arrange to be in the setting for a period of time before you start formally collecting data. This gives your participants the opportunity to acclimate to your presence. Once you are no longer a novelty, participants can resume their typical patterns of behavior. Establish rapport with participants, so that they feel they can act naturally. Finally, use unobtrusive methods for recording data. If you do need to use technological equipment, have it with you during those times when you are present but not collecting data.

Another essential method for ensuring the accuracy of perceptions in qualitative research is *triangulation*. Triangulation involves confirming conclusions through more than one data source. A key informant may tell you that a garment is two centuries old. Triangulation involves checking the stitching to determine if a sewing machine was used (the sewing machine was invented in the mid-1800s). It also involves checking the fabric to determine if materials and dyes not available in the 1700s were used. Finally, you may check paintings made during the period in question to determine if the styles match.

ADVANTAGES

Studies involving quantitative research vastly outnumber studies involving qualitative research. However, this is not a reflection of its quality or its ability to make important contributions to our knowledge base. As we said at the beginning of this chapter, qualitative research allows us to discover information not available through quantitative methods. We can study a single phenomenon in great detail. Another advantage is that, although it is just as challenging to conduct, students find qualitative research relatively easier to understand than quantitative methods.

LIMITATIONS

A major criticism of qualitative research is the subjective manner in which findings are made and analyzed. The person conducting the research has substantial control over both the research design and the data analysis. Thus, the study is influenced by the researcher's perceptions. Another disadvantage is that qualitative research is very labor intensive. You are constantly collecting and analyzing data, making tentative hypotheses, then collecting and analyzing more data to confirm or disconfirm. The amount of data gathered during qualitative study is enormous, and few computer programs are available to assist with management and analysis. Thus, much of your work is done by hand.

Third, because it so easily understood, people think they can engage in qualitative research despite limited training. Certainly the quality of these studies and the accuracy of the results are then compromised.

Fourth, the purpose of qualitative research is to allow the study of one or a limited number of events in very fine detail. The qualitative researcher is seeking a deeper understanding of a specific phenomenon. This understanding only develops over time. Depending on the exact topic and available resources, it could take a year, possibly longer, to conduct a qualitative study.

Finally, there is the problem with generalizability. The unique features of individuals or settings that you study make it difficult for results to be generalized to other individuals and settings. Many authors emphasize that qualitative research is used only to describe unique social structures, and that all social structures are unique. Therefore, generalization may not be a standard by which qualitative research should be judged.

SUMMARY

Not all the research questions you have can be answered through quantitative research. Questions about people's lives, their perceptions, and social policy are best answered through verbal descriptions made possible by qualitative research approaches. Qualitative research is useful for describing events or determining patterns of behavior exhibited by individuals or groups in their natural state.

There are three types of qualitative studies, including case studies that provide information about a single current event, historical studies that describe past events, and ethnographic studies that describe cultures. Regardless of the type of qualitative research in which you are interested, the methods for selecting participants and collecting data are the same. Participants are selected by purposive sampling or by networking. Methods for collecting data include participant observation, grounded theory, interviews, questionnaires, content analysis, and analysis of audio and videotapes. Qualitative data are recorded primarily through field notes. Condensed field notes can be gathered during participant observations and expanded upon later to describe all the events that occurred and your reaction to them.

Because qualitative research results are written descriptions rather than numerical data, traditional measures of reliability and validity do not apply. To enhance reliability, we recommend careful attention to field notes, use of a team approach, and the examination of field notes and final reports by participants. To enhance validity, we recommend measures that minimize disruptions in the environment such as establishing rapport and the use of nonobtrusive recording systems.

We also discussed advantages and limitations associated with qualitative research. Advantages include the contributions it can make to our knowledge base and the ease with which these procedures are understood. Limitations include the enormous amount of work involved, the lack of computer software for managing and sorting data, and limited generalizability of results.

As a final note, it may be best to combine quantitative and qualitative designs. Researchers can use the findings of a qualitative study to generate and test hypotheses through quantitative research. Further, quantitative findings can be clarified and extended by qualitative research. For example, one study can focus on whether or not a new procedure worked (quantitative) well. The other can focus on how the procedure is perceived by those who use it.

REFERENCES

Crowl, T. K. (1996). *Fundamentals of educational research.* (2nd Ed.) Madison, WI: Brown and Benchmark Publishing.

Erickson, F. (1985). *Qualitative methods in research on teaching.* In, M. C. Wittrock (Ed.), *Handbook of research on teaching.* New York: Macmillan.

Glesne, C., & Peshkin, A. (1991). *Becoming qualitative researchers: An introduction.* New York: Longman.

Marshall, C., & Rossman, G. B. (1994). *Designing qualitative research.* (2nd Ed.) Newbury Park, CA: Sage.

Stainback, S., & Stainback, W. (1988). *Understanding and conducting qualitative research.* Reston, VA: Council for Exceptional Children.

Wolcott, H. F. (1988). *Ethnographic research in education.* In, R. M. Jaeger (Ed.) *Complementary methods for research in education* (pp. 187–210). Washington, DC: American Educational Research Association.

FURTHER READINGS

General Sources of Information About Qualitative Research

Ball, M. S., & Smith, G. W. H. (1992). *Analyzing visual data.* Newbury Park, CA: Sage.

Bositis, D. A. (1990). *Research design for political science: Contriviance and demonstration in theory and practice.* Carbondale, IL: SIU Press.

Denzin, N. K., & Lincoln, Y. S. (Eds.) (1994). *Handbook of qualitative research.* Thousand Oaks, CA: Sage Publications.

Eisner, E. W., & Peshkin, A. (1990). *Qualitative inquiry in education: The continuing debate.* New York: Teachers' College Press.

Ely, M., Anzul, M., Friedman, T., Garner, D., & Steinmetz, A. (1991). *Doing qualitative research: Circle within circles.* New York: Falmer Press.

Fielding, N. (1993). *Ethnography.* In N. Gilbert (Ed.). *Researching social life* (pp. 154–171). Thousand Oaks, CA: Sage.

Ghauri, P. N., Gronhaug, K., & Kristianslund, I. (1995). *Research methods in business studies: A practical guide.* Upper Saddle River, NJ: Merrill/Prentice Hall.

Lancy, D. F. (1993). *Qualitative research in education: An introduction to the major traditions.* New York: Longman.

LeCompte, M. D., Millrory, W. C., & Preissle, J. (1992). *The handbook of qualitative research in education.* San Diego: Academic Press.

LeCompte, M. D., & Preissle, J. (1993). *Ethnography and qualitative design in educational research* (2nd ed.). San Diego: Academic Press.

Manheim, J. B., & Rich, R. C. (1994). *Empirical political analysis: Research methods in political science.* (4th ed.). New York: Longman.

Maxwell, J. A. (1992). Understanding and validity in qualitative research. *Harvard Educational Review, 62,* 279–300.

May, T. (1992). *Social research: Issues, methods, and process.* (2nd ed.). Buckingham, England: Open University Press.

Reid, D. K., Robinson, S. J., & Bunsen, T. D. (1995). Empiricism and beyond: Expanding the boundaries of special education. *Remedial and Special Education, 16,* 131–141.

Sandelowski, M. (1995). Sample size in qualitative research. *Research in Nursing and Health, 18,* 179–183.

Seymour, D. T. (1988). *Marketing research: Qualitative methods for the marketing professional.* Chicago: Probus.

Silverman, F. H. (1997). *Research design and evaluation in speech-language pathology and audiology* (4th ed.). Needham Heights, MA: Allyn & Bacon.

Straubert, H. J., & Carpenter, D. M. (1995). *Qualitative research in nursing: Advancing the humanistic imperative.* Philadelphia: J. B. Lippencott Company.

Strauss, A., & Corbin, J. (1990). *Basics of qualitative research: Grounded theory procedures and techniques.* Newbury Park, CA: Sage.

Webb, J. R. (1992). *Understanding and designing marketing research.* San Diego: Academic Press.

Wright, R., & Bennett, T. (1990). *Exploring the offenders' perspective: Observing and interviewing criminals* (pp. 138–151). In K. L. Kempf (Ed.), *Measurement issues in criminology.* New York: Springer-Verlag.

Zikmund, W. G. (1994). *Business research methods* (4th ed.). Chicago: Dryden Press.

Examples of Qualitative Research Studies

Arnould E. J., & Wallendorf, M. (1994). Market-oriented ethnography: Interpretation building and marketing strategy formulation. *Journal of Marketing Research, 51,* 484–504.

Blum-Kulka, S. (1994). The dynamic of family dinner talk: Cultural contexts for children's passages to adult discourse. *Research on Language and Social Interaction, 27,* 1–50.

Cushman, L. F., Kalmuss, D., & Namerow, P. B. (1993). Placing an infant for adoption: The experiences of young birthmothers. *Social Work, 38,* 264–272.

Hallberg, I. R., Holst, G., Nordmark, A., & Edberg, A. (1995). Cooperation during morning care between nurses and severely demented institutionalized patients. *Clinical Nursing Research, 4,* 78–104.

James, B. (1995). Learning to consume: An ethnographic study of cultural change in Hungary. *Critical Studies in Mass Communication, 12,* 287–305.

Kagan, D. M., & Tippins, D. J. (1992). The evolution of functional lesson plans among twelve elementary and secondary student teachers. *Elementary School Journal, 92,* 477–489.

Kahn, K. F. (1993). Gender differences in campaign messages: The political advertisements of men and women candidates for the U.S. Senate. *Political Research Quarterly, 46,* 481–525.

Keaveney, S. M. (1995). Customer switching behavior in service industries: An exploratory study. *Journal of Marketing, 59,* 71–82.

Kennedy, L. W., & Baron, S. W. (1993). Routine activities and a subculture of violence: A study of violence on the street. *Journal of Research in Crime and Delinquency, 30,* 88–112.

Magill, R. S. (1993). Focus groups, program evaluation, and the poor. *Journal of Sociology and Social Welfare, 20*(1), 103–144.

Rank, M. R. (1994). A view from the inside out: Recipients' perspectives of welfare. *Journal of Sociology and Social Welfare, 21*(2), 27–47.

Rudd, J., Betts, N. M., & Birkx, J. (1993). Developing written nutrition information for adults with low literacy skills. *Journal of Nutrition, 25,* 11–16.

Salisbury, C. L., Gallucci, C., Palombaro, M. M., & Peck, C. A. (1995). Strategies that promote social relations among elementary students with and without severe disabilities in inclusive schools. *Exceptional Children, 62,* 125–137.

Steckler, A., (1992). Toward integrating qualitative and quantitive methods: An introduction. *Health Education Quarterly, 19*(1), 1–8.

Swank, E. (1993/1994). Shall we overcome? The sense of movement power among Gulf War protesters. *Critical Sociology, 20,* 31–51.

Williamson, K. M. (1993). A qualitative study on the socialization of beginning physical education teacher educators. *Research Quarterly for Exercise and Sport, 64,* 188–201.

Examples of Combined Use of Qualitative and Quantitative Research

Adams, M., & Gathercole, S. B. (1995). Phonological working memory and speech production in preschool children. *Journal of Speech and Hearing Research, 38,* 403–414.

Carey, J. W. (1993). Linking qualitative and quantitative methods: Integrating cultural factors into public health. *Qualitative Health Research, 3,* 91–111.

Conley, D. J. (1994). Adding color to a black and white picture: Using qualitative data to explain racial disproportion in the juvenile justice system. *Journal of Research in Crime and Delinquency, 31,* 135–148.

Dimond, M., Caserta, M., & Lund, D. (1994). Understanding depression in bereaved older adults. *Clinical Nursing Research, 3,* 253–268.

Goetz, E. T., Sadoski, M., Olivarez, A., Calero-Breckheimer, A., Garner, P., & Fatemi, Z. (1992). The structure of emotional response in reading a literary text: Quantitative and qualitative analysis. *Reading Research Quarterly, 27,* 361–372.

8

Selecting Subjects

INTRODUCTION

The previous chapters contained descriptions of research approaches commonly used in social and behavioral sciences. The approaches included true experimental and quasi-experimental designs, correlational research, survey research, single subject research, and qualitative research. Each method shares a common set of procedures such as selection of subjects, treatment, data collection, and analysis.

We refer to these common procedures as the "tools of research." A carpenter must use a hammer, saw, square, and tape measure to build a home. Regardless of the floor plan or style, the ultimate quality of the home will be judged by the effectiveness with which the carpenter uses these tools. Similarly, the quality of a research study will be judged by the effectiveness of the basic research tools. These quality indicators apply regardless of the specific research design. This

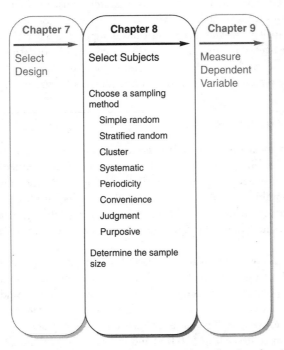

The Scope, Plan, and Sequence Chart for Conducting Research: The Fifth Step of the Research Process

chapter describes procedures for selecting subjects. Additional research tools will be discussed in the chapters that follow.

There has been an enormous proliferation of "media polls" over the past decade. It seems as if every time a major issue appears, one or more talk show hosts or news networks initiates a "call in" poll to assess public sentiment. Readers, listeners, or viewers are asked to call a 900 number and indicate their reaction to the issue. Responses are tabulated and reported back to the public through the media.

It is not surprising that various media forums ask virtually identical questions and produce substantially different results. Even the general public recognizes that the results obtained depend heavily upon the nature of the audience responding to the poll. A conservative talk-radio host is likely to produce very different responses to questions about "gay people in the military," "abortion rights," and the value of social programs than a liberal host. Readers of financial magazines are likely to express a very different view of welfare reform than individuals reading the tabloids.

The method by which people are selected has as much to do with the quality of the investigation as any other variable. To accurately report "public sentiment" on an issue, researchers would have to provide equal opportunity for all members of the public to respond to the questions. Restricting opportunity to a conservative or liberal audience biases results in favor of individuals listening to and likely to respond to either forum. (For this reason, "call-in surveys" are generally referred to as "unscientific polls.")

In the optimum case, researchers would include all members of the population to which results could be expected to be generalized. Questions of public policy, for example, would be asked of all citizens who are registered to vote. Questions about professional standards would be raised with all members of the target profession. Questions of teenage sexual attitudes and behavior would be addressed to all teenagers.

The population for many research questions is so large and inaccessible, however, that a smaller number of individuals must be studied. Also, use of an entire population does not take advantage of the efficiency of statistical inference. Researchers use only a portion of the population to make conclusions highly consistent with those that would be obtained if all individuals were studied. The validity of research generalizations is supported when this smaller number accurately represents the overall population. Generalizations must be questioned when the smaller group is a "biased" subset of the population (e.g., asking a conservative or liberal radio audience questions about public policy and generalizing the results to all citizens).

CRITICAL TERMS AND RELATIONSHIPS

The first, and possibly most important term essential to understand sampling methodology is *generalizability*. Generalizability is the relationship between results obtained from a select group of individuals and the broader group to which the results apply. A teaching effectiveness study conducted in Chicago public schools may be expected to produce findings that can be generalized to teachers and learners in all urban school systems. Generalizability, therefore, applies to the relationship between results obtained in Chicago and those expected through similar applications across the country.

The broader group to which results are expected to generalize is the *target population* or *universe*. The target population is a group of individuals that share at least one common feature. For example, the target population for a study of diet effectiveness may be middle-aged women between 20 and 50 pounds overweight. Common features that define the population include age, gender, and level of excess weight. The target population for a study of consumer preferences may be adults with a net worth exceeding $10,000 and over $20,000 in annual earnings. Common features include net worth and annual earnings.

Research focusing on the preceding target populations would involve subjects residing throughout the country. This is obviously not feasible for the typical graduate student. Consequently, research samples are frequently drawn from an accessible population. The accessible population includes a restricted set of individuals who represent the target population. An accessible population for 20- to 50-pound overweight women may be those enrolling in a diet center in a major midwestern city. An accessible population for adult consumers may be individuals shopping at a major grocery chain in the rural Southwest.

Population Validity

Population validity is the extent to which the accessible population resembles the target population in characteristics important to the study. The more similar the groups, the stronger the population validity and generalizability of findings. The greater the differences, the more limited the population validity.

In the case of the diet study, the target population is all overweight women in the United States. The accessible population is restricted by geographic region and by an interest in weight reduction (as judged by enrolling in a diet plan). Generalizations from the accessible population to the target population may be valid if measures are not influenced by these factors. For example, one would expect that purely physiological measures such as correlating respiratory rate with weight would not be biased by the sampling plan. Alternately, personality measures such as motivation to reduce weight would be biased. Women enrolling in a diet plan may have different motivational features than those in the general population.

Similarly, a study of consumer preference for spicy food over bland food may not generalize from the southwest region to other parts of the country. Conversely, a study that evaluates an individual's ability to make cost comparisons may not be affected by the region of the country from which subjects are drawn.

SAMPLING TECHNIQUES

Several strategies can be used to arrive at a sample that effectively represents the accessible or target population. These include simple random sampling, stratified random sampling, random cluster sampling, and systematic sampling. We will discuss each of these strategies separately.

Simple Random Sampling

Though sometimes the most difficult to implement, simple random sampling is generally the most effective way to obtain an unbiased representation of the target population. Simple random sampling occurs when every member of the population has an equal chance of being included in the sample. No subgroup or individual within the population has a greater chance of being selected over another. Further, selection of one subject in no way influences the likelihood that another subject will be selected (e.g., two children in the same household, all children in one class, or alternate names on a roster).

Simple random sampling is conducted by describing the target population to which generalizations will be made. If it is not possible to sample from the target population, identify an accessible population. Ensure that the accessible population does not differ from the target population in any dimension that would restrict population validity. Establish the number of subjects to be included in the sample using guidelines offered in the final section of this chapter. Finally, use a blind draw or table of random numbers procedure to select subjects from the target or accessible population.

A blind draw is conducted by placing the names of all individuals in the target or accessible population on separate equal-sized slips of paper. The slips of paper are placed in a container and mixed so as to be distributed randomly throughout the container. Without looking, the researcher selects the number of paper slips indicated by the sample size.

The table of random numbers, commonly found at the end of statistics books or manuals, is used by assigning an ordered number to each member of the target or accessible population (e.g., 000 to 479 for a sample of 480). A starting point on the table of random numbers is selected indiscriminately. Only digits for the tabled numbers that are used in the largest population number (e.g., three digits for a population of 100 to 999) are used. The researcher moves sequentially from the starting number in the table toward the final number, stopping when the desired sample size is obtained. Numbers larger than the largest population number are ignored. Members of the population with numbers that correspond to entries in the table of random numbers are included in the sample.

The following steps illustrate the use of a simple random sampling procedure:

1. The researcher selects rural midwestern elementary schools (counties with fewer than 10,000 residents and schools with fewer than 200 students) as the target population.

2. Since it is not practical to use students from all schools, an accessible population of students from all of the small rural elementary schools in a 17 county region of Southern Illinois is used.

3. Enrollment reports from the schools are collected and students numbered from 0000 to 5,976.

4. The table of random numbers begins at a random point.

5. Only five digits are used, and numbers greater than 5,976 are ignored.

6. Students with the following numbers are selected: 0009, 2333, 2344, 4522, 0032, 0423, and so on. The second number chosen was 7635. It was not included as it exceeded the population size.

7. Since a possibility exists that some students will be unable or unwilling to participate, additional subjects may be selected by continuing this process until the expected sample size is achieved.

Stratified Random Sampling

We emphasized previously that randomization increases the chances that the sample will be representative of the population. Unfortunately, it does not ensure representativeness. This is particularly true if the sample is relatively small. For example, one would expect all numbers to come up five times during 30 rolls of a "fair" die. When actually done, however, frequencies for each of the six numbers may range from two or three to seven or eight. The greater the number of rolls, the closer the numbers will approximate the expected distribution.

Researchers may not wish to trust equality of representation to chance. A survey of voter preference, for example, may be valid only if the representation of minority, white, high-socioeconomic status, low-socioeconomic status, elderly, middle-aged, and young participants mirrors the proportion found in the voting population. Given a target population exceeding a million and an expected sample of several thousand, it may not be wise to trust the proportional representation of these groups to chance.

Strata are generally based on discrete categories of individuals based on common characteristics, membership, or geographic location. Fairweather, Stearns, and Wagner (1989) used each of these variables to ensure that subjects in a national sample of school districts represented the universe of public schools:

- *Region* (*northeast, southeast, central, and west/southwest*). This classification is used by the U.S. Department of Commerce, the U.S. Bureau of Economic Analysis, and the National Assessment of Education Progress.
- *District enrollment.* Enrollment was defined as very small (fewer than 600); small (600 to 2,499); medium (2,500 to 9,999); large (10,000 to 24,999); and very large (more than 25,000).
- *District/community wealth.* This variable is the ratio of students receiving Title 1 funds to the total student population, yielding the percentage of youth in a district below the poverty level. Broken into quartiles, the wealth strata are high (1% to 4% disadvantaged youth in the population), medium (5% to 9%), low (10% to 19%), and very low (20% and over) (p. 421).

Procedures for stratified random sampling are similar to simple random sampling except that randomization occurs from within the subsets of the population as opposed to within the overall population. Stratified random sampling is conducted by describing the generalizations to the target population. An accessible population is used when the target population cannot be sampled. Strata or subgroups to be proportionately represented in the sample are identified. All members of the target or accessible population are then classified by strata. The number of subjects to be included in the overall sample and in each strata is then determined. This is generally based on the expected proportion of individuals representing these strata in the target or accessible population. Finally, a blind draw or table of random numbers is used to select subjects from each strata.

The following steps illustrate the use of a simple random sampling procedure.

1. The researcher selects mail carriers in a three-county region as the accessible population.
2. Four strata are identified including males over fifty, females over fifty, males under fifty, and females under fifty.
3. The percentage of individuals in the target population representing each strata is determined to be 30%, 16%, 42%, and 12%, respectively.
4. Based on these percentages, the optimum number representing each strata in a sample of 180 is 60, 12, 84, and 24.
5. Employee reports are used to identify the strata that each member of the target population represents.
6. Employee names within each strata are numbered from 00 upward.
7. The table of random numbers is used to select the stipulated number of individuals from each strata.

Cluster Sampling

Cluster sampling involves randomly selecting "intact" groups or clusters of individuals from a target or accessible population. Clusters are groups of population members found in one location that meet the population specifications. Typical clusters include classes of children, therapy groups, sports teams, and office staff.

Cluster sampling is generally used when the population is spread across a wide area and subject selection, without regard to location, is cost and effort prohibitive. For example, an exercise physiologist may wish to evaluate the effectiveness of aerobic exercise on the health of pregnant girls under the age of 15 and their expectant newborns. Since the prevalence of pregnancy for girls this young is relatively uncommon, selecting expectant teens from within a state would require that training sessions be conducted some distance from where a number of the children live. Transportation and training logistics would be insurmountable. Most likely, few parents would expose their child to the hardship of participating in the project.

Alternately, a greater density of expectant teens may be found in urban and low-socioeconomic status areas. Therefore, it may be more efficient to draw a sample from the case loads of a Children and Family Services office in a given urban center. In effect, the sample may be an "intact" group of pregnant teenagers served by existing programs.

Cluster sampling is conducted by describing the target population to which generalizations will be made. An accessible population is used when the target population cannot be sampled. Intact groups of individuals or clusters within the population are identified and numbered. Next, the number of subjects to be included in the overall sample and the average number of subjects in each cluster are determined. Finally, a blind draw or table of random numbers is used to select the number of clusters required to produce the expected sample size.

The following steps illustrate the use of cluster sampling.

1. The researcher selects employees of a fast food chain across the nation.
2. Clusters are designated as employees within each store.
3. The average cluster size (number of employees in each store) is 48.
4. The researcher establishes an expected sample size of 1160.
5. The researcher divides the sample size (1160) by the average cluster size (48) to produce the number of clusters to be sampled (24).
6. Stores in the population of 188 stores are numbered from 000 to 187.
7. A table of random numbers or blind draw is used to randomly select 24 stores from the population of 188.
8. Data are collected from each individual employed in the 24 cluster stores.

Systematic Sampling

This procedure is similar to random sampling except that names are selected from a roster using an objective rule rather than random draw. In the most common case, all names from the accessible population are entered into a table. Every nth subject is then selected, where n equals the interval between population members. The size of n is based on the size of the accessible population and the number of individuals to be included in the sample.

Systematic sampling does not allow every member of an accessible population to have an equal and independent chance of being selected. Once the interval rule and first individual are selected, all other choices for the sample become fixed. If names listed in the accessible population are presented in random order, the sample will be random. Contrasted with random sampling, subjects will be randomized based on order in the population table as opposed to the order of selection.

If the population list is ordered using any variable, the sample will not be random. For example, if the names on the population list are presented in the order of street address, neighbors will not be included in the sample. Similarly, if presented in alphabetical order, family members and relatives with the same last name will not be included.

Periodicity

Periodicity (rule governed order in population members) may serve to *bias* the sample or enhance its representation of the accessible population. An example of bias may occur in the way many physical education teachers select students for games. The teacher asks all students to stand in a straight line and count off by four. Ones are assigned to the first team, twos are assigned to the second, threes are assigned to the third, and fours are assigned to the fourth. No bias would occur if students stood in random order. However, students with an interest in a specific team composition may line up with "friends" separated by three individuals. Teams become imbalanced if "friends" have similar athletic characteristics.

A more insidious way in which periodicity can produce bias is illustrated in the systematic selection of students based on seating assignment. Assume that a teacher seats more capable students in the back of the class and less capable learners in the front. Also assume that there are seven rows with six students in a row. The researcher systematically samples using a seating chart as the roster of the accessible population. He or she begins with the first student and selects every sixth individual. The consequence is that all students selected are from the front seat of every row.

Acknowledgment of periodicity in the accessible population roster may enhance the representativeness of the sample in the same manner as stratification. For example, the astute teacher in our physical education class may wish to ensure that no team has a preponderance of the tall players. Given the small number of students, this may not be accomplished by random assignment. Therefore, the teacher may ask all students to stand in line in order of height (from shortest to tallest or vice versa). Counting off by fours will ensure that tall and short players are equally distributed among the teams.

Systematic sampling is conducted by describing the target population to which generalizations will be made. An accessible population is used when the entire target population cannot be sampled. Names of individuals in the accessible population are tabled in random order when stratification is not desired. Alternately, individuals are named in the order of a stratifying variable (e.g., height, intelligence, age, etc.) when an equal distribution of the variable to each group is desired. Next, the number of subjects to be included in the overall sample and the number of subjects in the accessible population is determined. The accessible population size is divided by the sample size. The quotient indicates the interval between subjects selected from the population. If two groups of the same size are to be selected, halve the interval size and place alternate individuals in separate groups.

The following steps illustrate the use of systematic sampling when stratification is not desired.

1. The researcher selects businesses listed in the yellow pages as the accessible population.
2. Business names are tabled in random order.
3. The population size of 1320 is divided by the sample size of 165 businesses yielding intervals of eight.
4. Beginning with the first, every eighth business is selected for inclusion in the study.

Note in the preceding example that if businesses were retained in alphabetical order, more than one business representing the same company but with different locations (e.g., Charlie's Fries-North; Charlie's Fries-South; and Charlie's Fries-Midtown) could not be included in the sample. This could be desirable or undesirable depending on the nature of the study.

The following steps illustrate systematic sampling with stratification based on community of residence.

1. The researcher selects insurance policy holders as the accessible population.
2. Names are placed in order of geographic region (to stratify based on residence).
3. The population size of 1728 is divided by the sample size of 24, and the resulting number (72) is divided by two to account for equal-sized experimental and control groups.
4. Alternate 36th individuals are selected for experimental or control groups beginning with the first individual. The first individual is placed in group one, the 37th individual is placed in group two, the 73rd individual is placed in group one, the 109th individual is placed in group two, and so on, until 24 individuals are chosen for each group.

Convenience Sampling

Convenience sampling generally involves selecting whatever "intact" group of individuals is available. In educational research, convenience sampling frequently involves selecting all students in a class or school. It may also include teachers in a given school district. In gerontology, it may involve selecting all residents of a nursing home or retirement community. In consumer research it may involve picking all adults who enter a store and agree to be surveyed.

A high probability of bias exists in data obtained through convenience sampling. The researcher in the preceding examples cannot be certain that students are representative of the target population. The school may be located in an area with unique demographic characteristics. The class may include students in a selective "track." The salary base may attract disproportionately higher quality educators. The nature of residents of the nursing home or retirement center may reflect the services available in the facilities. Even solicitations from individuals entering a store may produce bias. The store selected, time of day, and other variables not controlled through randomization may produce bias in the sample.

Judgment and Purposive Sampling

Judgment and purposive sampling are generally used by single subject and qualitative researchers. These scholars are generally less concerned with the "representativeness" of the sample than they are with selecting individuals that support a specific purpose.

The researcher's knowledge, or that of "expert associates," is used to select the sample in judgment sampling. For example, if you were interested in studying institutional conditions for persons who are depressed, you may ask a psychologist to identify individuals who meet the diagnostic criteria. Similarly, you may use your expertise to select clerical staff who are competent at certain job functions.

A researcher may go beyond judgment sampling and perform purposive sampling. Purposive sampling involves selecting subjects in order to complement the goals of the study. For example, you may wish to describe conditions in correctional facilities for adolescent offenders with disabilities. You may select individual subjects meeting these demographic features in order to advance the goals of the study. Alternately, a single subject research study may be developed to demonstrate methods for teaching self-catheterization skills to a preschooler with physical disabilities. The subject would be selected based on your expert judgment that the child represents a small but important group of people for whom the program may be useful.

It is important to reiterate that judgment and purposive sampling do not produce a randomly selected group of individuals who represent a broader population. Consequently, there is the question as to whether or not conclusions drawn from the sample can be generalized to others.

SAMPLE SIZE

No discussion of sampling methods would be complete without addressing what may be the most frequently asked question—how large must my sample be? Unfortunately, most discussions of sample size weigh heavily on the practical questions of how many subjects can be enlisted, and how time-consuming data collection will be. Two other considerations may be more important to the quality of the research. First, what is the optimum number of subjects needed to offer sufficient "power" against the null hypothesis? Second, how large of a sample is required to support the generalization of findings from the sample to the population? We will address each of these questions.

Practicality and Sample Size

The size of the research sample must fit within your budget. The necessary travel, supplies, postage, assessment time, and treatment time generally increase proportionately to the number of subjects included in the study. Obviously, you must reconcile the available resources with optimum design requirements.

Not all studies are equally convenient from a subject utilization standpoint. Studies focusing on human conditions that occur infrequently in the population may be particularly costly. For example, research on psychopathology in adolescents may require extensive travel on your part in order to locate sufficient numbers of students from which to sample, since government estimates suggest that fewer than one percent of school-aged children are emotionally disturbed. A researcher would need a middle school population base of 5,000 to produce 50 emotionally disturbed youngsters. This may require the full emotionally disturbed population of a major urban school district. Researchers located in rural states (e.g., Wyoming, New Mexico, North Dakota, South Dakota, or Nevada) may require the full population base of the state to accomplish the study.

Similarly, not all research methods are equally expensive. A study designed to teach social skills to juvenile offenders may involve hourly sessions several times a week that continue for several months. Even two dozen subjects require substantial time and effort. Alternately, a mail-in survey may require only a few minutes of time with a word processor and less than a dollar per item in postage.

While the study must fit within your budget, cost alone cannot be the single deciding factor in selecting sample size. Ultimately, it is possible that the most expensive study is one that fits within the researcher's budget but produces no usable findings. This is the case if the sample size is so small that significant differences cannot be obtained even when they actually exist. It is also the case when the significant differences are obtained but the sample is so small that confident generalizations cannot be made to the target population. Each of these cases merits discussion.

Sample Size and Power Against the Null Hypothesis

Sample size has a substantial impact on the power of a test to detect differences that actually exist. The larger the sample size, the more sensitive the experiment to actual differences. The smaller the sample size, the less sensitive.

Both high and low extremes in sample size can have an adverse effect on the results of a research study. An excessively small sample can result in so little power that only enormous differences between groups can be detected. In some cases, a research design may have so little power that differences of any reasonable magnitude cannot be detected. Excessively large sample sizes can produce so much power that even trivial differences are detected. Given large enough sample sizes, a specialized (and costly) reading method may be shown to be significantly better than standard educational practices. A closer look at the effect size may reveal that experimental subjects improved by only .03 of a grade level over children using traditional methods.

Statistical formulas can be used to objectively establish sample size based on the variability within the samples, the expected effect size, the number of contrasts or groups, and the significance (alpha) level. Use of these formulas is outside of the scope of this text. Several resources, including computer programs (cf. Baer & Ahern, 1988) and manuals (cf. Cohen, 1988) may be consulted for assistance in these computations.

In general, a relatively small sample size (e.g., fewer than 18 subjects in a group) can be used when other design elements indicate reasonable power. When the design elements suggest poor power, we recommend a substantially larger sample size. Essential design elements that influence the ability of a study to detect differences that actually exist are as follows:

1. Measurement precision.
2. Expected differences between groups (i.e., effect size).
3. Homogeneity of subjects within each group.
4. Number of comparisons or groups used in the study.
5. Alpha level used in the analysis.

Remember that rather than simply increasing the sample size, the preceding variables may be altered to increase power. Identifying a more precise instrument for the dependent variable, using a longer or more intense treatment (i.e., enhanced effect size), selecting a more homogeneous sample (e.g., fourth graders as opposed to elementary students), restricting the number of comparisons, and setting alpha at .05 as opposed to .01 may allow increased power without requiring the use of additional subjects.

Sample Size and Generalizability of Findings

Sample size also has a direct influence on the external validity or generalizability of results. A large and well-constructed sample is likely to mirror the results that would be obtained if the study were conducted with the entire population. Conversely, a small or biased sample is not likely to produce results that would be replicated with the population. For example, sampling the candidate preference of five voters in a small city is not likely to "predict" actual election results. Sampling one-fourth or one-half of the voters is very likely to produce an accurate reflection of the outcome.

Sample size recommendations based on the concern for external validity vary depending on the research design. Descriptive research generally requires the largest sample, since the goal of the investigation is to accurately depict the characteristics of the population. Well-controlled experimental studies generally require the smallest samples (excluding single subject and ethnographic studies).

Gay (1995) offers the following recommendations for sample size.

1. Depending on the population size, 10 to 20 percent of the population should be sampled in descriptive studies.
2. A minimum of 30 subjects should be included in the sample of correlational studies.
3. Thirty subjects per group should be included in causal-comparative studies.
4. Experimental studies with tight experimental controls should include 15 or more subjects. Thirty or more subjects may be required if less rigorous design standards are achieved.

SUMMARY

One of the most important tools in effective research is sampling methodology. A well-constructed sample allows you to make judgments about a substantially larger population without expending the time and effort needed to treat and assess the entire population. Also, in many cases, the entire population is simply not accessible. Effective sampling practices allow you to make judgments about individuals that are not accessible.

Sampling plans are devised to produce a group of individuals that reflect the accessible population (i.e., the group of individuals available to be sampled) and the even broader target population (i.e., individuals that represent the accessible population). The quality of a sample is judged by the extent to which results obtained from the sample are consistent with those that would have been obtained were the study conducted with the accessible population. The appropriateness of the accessible population is judged by its population validity or the extent to which its members mirror the target population.

Sampling bias occurs when judgments cause an inaccurate reflection of the population. Random sampling is the most effective way to reduce sampling bias. If all members of the population have an equal chance of being selected, those actually selected are likely to represent the entire group. Sampling methods based on convenience (e.g., using "intact" groups) are likely to introduce bias into the sample.

Used effectively, the sampling methods described in this chapter can minimize bias while reducing the need to study excessively large groups of individuals. We discussed several methods, including the following.

1. Simple random sampling, where every member of the population has an equal chance of being included in the sample. No individual or group of individuals has a greater chance of being selected. In addition, selection of one subject in no way influences the likelihood that another subject will be selected. Simple random sampling is the most defensible method of ensuring an unbiased sample.

2. Stratified random sampling, where randomization occurs within certain strata. Stratified random sampling ensures equal representation of specific subgroups of the population when the researcher does not wish to trust this outcome to chance.

3. Cluster sampling, in which "intact" groups of individuals (e.g., therapy groups or sports teams) are randomly selected from a target or accessible population (e.g., all therapy groups conducted by APA licensed psychologists, all sports teams within the state high school athletic association). Use of cluster sampling is advocated when the population is spread across a wide area, and subject selection without regard to location is cost and effort prohibitive.

4. Systematic sampling, where names separated by even intervals are selected from a table (e.g., selecting every nth subject). If names in the table are randomly ordered, subject selection will be fully random. Ordering names using any variable will stratify that variable. This approach can introduce bias or ensure equal representation.

We also discussed convenience sampling in which the researcher selects whatever "intact" group of individuals is available. We emphasized that a high probability of bias exists in data obtained through convenience sampling. Consequently, we recommend against its use unless extreme circumstances limit other options.

Judgment and purposive sampling were suggested to be useful for single subject and qualitative researchers. These methods are less concerned with the "representativeness" of the sample than with the appropriateness of the sample for specific demonstrative purposes. As emphasized, findings from studies using judgment and purposive sampling are not generalized with confidence to other individuals. Rather, they simply illustrate a method or trend that may be evaluated with other individuals possessing characteristics similar to individuals in the sample.

Finally, we provided guidance on the determination of the sample size. We highlighted three major concerns in establishing an appropriate sample. These included practical constraints, concern for statistical power against the null hypothesis, and concern for the generalizability of findings.

REFERENCES

Baer, L., & Ahern, D. K. (1988). StatChoice—The statistical consulting program [Computer program]. Littleton, MA: PSG Publishing.

Cohen, J. (1988). *Statistical power analysis of the behavioral sciences* (2nd ed.). Hillsdale, NJ: Lawrence Erlbaum.

Fairweather, J. S., Stearns, M. S., & Wagner, M. M. (1989). Resources students: Implications for transition. *The Journal of Special Education, 22,* 419–432.

Gay, L. R. (1995). *Educational Research: Competencies for Analysis and Application.* (5th Ed.). Upper Saddle River, NJ: Merrill/Prentice Hall.

FURTHER READINGS

Brewer, J. K., & Sindelar, P. T. (1988). Adequate sample size: A priori and post hoc considerations. *Journal of Special Education, 21,* 74–84.

Cartwright, C. A., & Cartwright, G. P. (1984). *Developing observation skills* (2nd ed.). New York: McGraw-Hill.

Churchill, G. A. (1991). *Basic marketing research* (2nd ed.). Fort Worth, TX: Dryden Press-Harcourt Brace Jovanovich College Publisher.

Crowl, T. K. (1986). *Fundamentals of research: A practical guide for educators and special educators.* Columbus, OH: Publishing Horizons, Inc.

Fowler, F. J., Jr. (1993). *Applied social research methods series: Vol. 1. (2nd ed.). Survey research methods.* Beverly Hills, CA: Sage Publications.

Ghauri, P. N., Gronhaug K., & Kristianslund, I. (1995). *Research methods in business studies: A practical guide.* Upper Saddle River, NJ: Merrill/Prentice Hall.

Haywood, H. C., & Wingenfeld, S. A. (1992). Interactive assessment as a research tool. *Journal of Special Education, 26,* 253–268.

Hillison, J. (1990). Using all the tools available to vocational education researchers. *Journal of Vocational Education Researchers, 15* (1), 1–8.

Johnson, E. S. (1981). *Research methods in criminology and criminal justice.* Upper Saddle River, NJ: Merrill/Prentice Hall.

Johnson, J. B., & Joslyn, R. A. (1994). *Political science research methods* (3rd ed.). Washington DC: CQ Press.

Kerlinger, F. N. (1985). *Foundations of behavioral research* (3rd ed.). New York: Holt, Rinehart, & Winston, Inc.

Kinnear, T. C., & Taylor, J. R. (1995). *Marketing research: An applied approach.* (5th ed.). New York: McGraw-Hill, Inc.

Manheim, J. B., & Rich, R. C. (1994). *Empirical political analysis: Research methods in political science.* (4th ed.). New York: Longman.

May, T. (1997). *Social research: Issues, methods, and process.* (2nd ed.). Buckingham, England: Open University Press.

Reid, D. H. (1991). Technological behavior analysis and societal impact: A human services perspective. *Journal of Applied Behavioral Analysis, 24* (3), 437–439.

Tull, D. S., & Hawkins, D. I. (1988). *Marketing research: Measurement and methods* (4th ed.). New York: Macmillan.

Webb, J. R. (1992). *Understanding and designing marketing research.* San Deigo: Academic Press.

Yin, R. K. (1994). *Case study research: Design and methods* (2nd ed.). Beverly Hills, CA: Sage Publications.

Zikmund, W. G. (1994). *Business research methods* (4th ed.). Chicago: Dryden Press.

9

Measurement in Quantitative and Qualitative Research

INTRODUCTION

We introduced the last chapter by discussing "tools" of research used in a majority of investigations. We suggested that a carpenter's skill in measuring, sawing, and nailing was a principal indicator of a home's quality regardless of architectural design. Similarly, regardless of experimental design, basic research tools underlie the quality of an investigation.

The previous chapter described sampling methods. We noted that an effective sampling plan served a foundation role in research. Without an unbiased sample, you do not know if your results indicate the true status of a phenomena or are just quirks inherent in the sample. People reading your work may suspect that your conclusions have more to do with the unique characteristics of the sample than with actual responses expected in the population.

This chapter provides background from which data collection instruments can be selected or developed. Four general data collection methods will be discussed, including standardized instruments commonly available through commercial publishers and applicable to a variety of

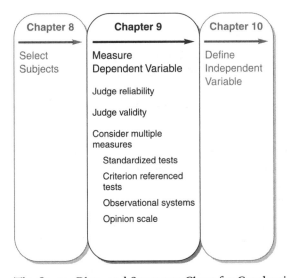

The Scope, Plan, and Sequence Chart for Conducting Research: The Sixth Step in the Research Process

research projects; criterion referenced instruments generally developed by the researcher to measure specific skills; observational systems designed by the researcher to gauge performance in natural or analog situations; and survey instruments designed to assess attitudes or opinions.

Prior to discussing these measurement systems, we will discuss general standards for effective instrumentation.

PRINCIPLES OF MEASUREMENT

All human research is based on the assumption that subjects exhibit characteristics that can be observed and measured. Observation and measurement can be direct, as when we count the number of spelling words a child writes correctly or record a youth's time in the 40-yard dash. Observation and measurement may also be indirect, as when we report the occurrence of a depression syndrome based on self-depreciating statements, or indicate one's academic potential based on aptitude test scores.

True Scores and Error Scores

Scores that result from observations contain two elements. The first element is the *true score,* the real and unchanging measure of the human characteristic. The second element is the *error score.* The error score is a positive or negative value that results from uncontrolled and unrealized variability in the measurement.

Only an omniscient being can know the actual true score and error score since all measurements include some degree of error. Exemplifying the best case, physicists measuring the mass of an element may produce confident values to the thousandth or millionth of a gram. Though present, the error score is a very small fraction of the true score. Because of the indirect and subjective nature of their measurement, behavioral and social science researchers produce scores that are subject to a substantially greater percentage of error.

Researchers must identify and minimize all possible sources of error in measurement. You may remember from our discussion in the previous chapter of "power against the null hypothesis" that precise measurement increases our ability to detect differences that actually exist. Measurement with substantial error reduces our ability to detect differences. An archery competition could be determined by each individual firing one arrow at a target. Because of substantial error inherent in the single shot (e.g., wind gusts, sighting problems, or distractions), this contest would be more likely to identify the "luckiest" archer as opposed to the best archer. The previously mentioned error sources would be distributed more equally across participants if the test were based on each contestant's average distance from the center of the target for 10 shots. We would then be more confident that the multiple shot approach provides a more accurate comparison between contestants.

We were able to identify wind conditions, sighting problems, and distractions as sources of error in the preceding example. We were similarly able to minimize these errors by providing multiple opportunities that distributed errors to all contestants. Alternately, contestants could have fired a single shot after a substantial "warm-up" and sighting period and under conditions free of wind or other distractions. The same need for identifying and minimizing error applies to instrumentation used in research. The following section includes a description of major sources of error in instruments that you may devise or select for your research. Recognizing the potential for these errors is the first step in enhancing true scores.

Nature of Error

Measurement error can be a result of the way we observe or test the individual. In the preceding example, wind and other external constraints produced errors in the observation/testing procedure. Measurement errors can also result from variability in the individual's performance. Sighting difficulties and variability resulting from not having a warm-up period exemplify this source of error. We will discuss these sources of error separately.

Observation/testing error. This source of error generally results from four major factors. First, subject performance may not be directly related to the skill or knowledge being evaluated. Minimal error would be present in a test that involved reading from the Dolch sight word list if judgments are made about sight word recognition. In this case, a direct match exists between test performance and conclusions. Conversely, a researcher may make conclusions regarding the frequency of depression in individuals with mental retardation. The depression inventory may include items such as: Are you admired by your friends for your ability to solve problems? Are you active in social groups? Do others compliment you on your abilities? Do you expect to obtain a high paying job? A close inspection of the test items suggests that the "true" measurement of depression may be obscured by items that measure cognitive limitations.

Observation and testing error may also be the result of items that are unclear to the respondent. All high school and college students are familiar with "trick" questions. These are items that are better indicators of incidental learning, test savvy, or other abilities than the knowledge or skill being assessed. The proportion of a score that represents true knowledge or skill is increased if items can produce one clear correct response while all other responses are incorrect.

Error may also be a function of the difficulty level. A test that includes very easy items will produce high scores for all subjects regardless of actual knowledge or skill differences. Similarly, a test that includes excessively difficult items will produce low scores for the most capable as well as least capable subject. In each case, the test is not able to discriminate between subjects with varying levels of proficiency.

Finally, error increases when the scope of a test is excessively broad and an insufficient sample of information is obtained for each skill or concept. A test designed to assess 20 concepts using two items each is likely to produce a substantial portion of measurement error. The true score is likely to be higher in a test that measures five concepts with eight items each. As a general rule, a test or set of observations should be short enough to allow subjects to provide reasonable effort on all items. There should be a sufficient number of items for each skill or concept to demonstrate a consistent pattern of performance.

Procedural error. A related source of error can result from the inconsistent administration, recording, scoring, and interpretation of responses. Procedural error is avoided by developing a complete and objective set of examiner procedures. These should include standards for giving directions to subjects, providing stimuli that promote responses, observing performance, recording responses, scoring responses, interpreting responses, and dealing with ambiguous situations.

Subject error. No individual performs in precisely the same manner day after day. Athletes, professionals, and students recognize that they have good and bad days. For example, a recent world record holder in the pole vault failed to place in the last Olympics. A number of winners of the prestigious Masters golf tournament have failed to qualify in their next competition.

Some traits are not subject to substantial variability. Physical characteristics including height, weight, speed, strength, and reaction time are fairly stable. Some psychological features such as intelligence are also stable. Other psychological characteristics such as interests, attitudes, and perceptions may change over relatively short periods of time.

Another common subject error involves the reaction to demand features of the observation or instrument. Reaction to demand features is illustrated by differences in the way people acted before and after the host identified himself on the old "Candid Camera" television show. People who are aware that they are being observed typically react differently than those that are engaged in "private" behavior. Similarly, children who are being tested are likely to perform more diligently or aggressively than those engaged in daily activities.

Estimates of Error

Information in the previous sections may be used to avoid or minimize error. However, all measures include some degree of error. Therefore, it is important that you estimate the amount of error present in a score so that the results can be interpreted properly.

In Chapter 1, we briefly defined two major standards that are used to judge the degree to which a score is free from error. Validity is the extent to which an instrument measures what it was expected to measure. Reliability is the consistency with which accurate results are produced. We will discuss each of these factors in detail.

Validity

As noted earlier, an instrument is valid to the extent that it measures what is purported to be measured. From your standpoint as a researcher, a valid instrument produces data that are well matched to the objectives of the study. If a study is designed to determine whether differences exist between men and women's reactions to stress, a valid instrument actually measures reactions to stress. Any portion of the measurement that relates to other features (e.g., ability to read test items, memory of critical events, reticence in self-disclosure, or reaction time and strength) is validity error.

Standards for Educational and Psychological Testing (1985) advanced by a joint committee of the American Educational Research Association, the American Psychological Association, and the National Council on Measurement in Education have connected validity judgments to the purpose of measurement. The standards emphasize that validity of an instrument depends on conclusions the researcher wishes to make. Based on these standards, an instrument cannot be judged to be intrinsically valid or invalid. Rather, the validity of the instrument is determined against each purpose for which the instrument is applied.

A test of scholastic performance may produce a highly valid indication of the current level of students' achievement in math and reading. When used as a pretest and posttest, it can produce valid conclusions regarding the effectiveness of math and reading programs. The same test may not be a valid predictor of collegiate performance. Failure of the test to measure all characteristics important to academic potential (e.g., motivation, study skills, or perseverance) diminishes the test's appropriateness or validity as an aptitude test.

The Standards for Educational and Psychological Testing (1985) suggest four major types of validity. They include content, concurrent, predictive, and construct validity. We will discuss each measure of validity with specific reference to experimental design and hypothesis testing.

Content validity. Content validity is the extent to which items match the construct being evaluated. An instrument with high content validity includes a representative sample of the skills or concepts being assessed, stimulus features comparable to those found in real situations, and response features comparable to that expected in real situations. Obviously, direct measures using natural responses in daily situations offer a greater potential for content validity than indirect or contrived measures.

Concurrent validity. This form of validity judges whether or not results obtained from the instrument concur with results obtained through a related instrument. Concurrent validity is evaluated by administering the target instruments shortly before or after administering an instrument designed to measure the same knowledge or skill. The higher the correlation coefficient (relationship) for the group of individuals, the greater the concurrent validity.

Predictive validity. This validity measure is similar to concurrent validity in that both judge the quality of an instrument against a criterion measure. They differ, however, based on the time at which the criterion measure is applied. Concurrent validity establishes a relationship between two measures of current performance. Predictive validity establishes a relationship between current performance and future performance. An instrument is said to have high predictive validity if it predicts future status as judged by a criterion measure.

Construct validity. Construct validity is concerned with the ability of an instrument to measure a characteristic or event not directly observable. Constructs common to behavioral and social science research include intelligence, locus of control, motivation, and learning characteristics. Since these variables cannot be seen or measured directly, instruments are developed to assess corresponding traits. The more consistently test results conform to expectations based on the construct, the higher the construct validity.

Construct validity is determined by identifying observable correlates of the hypothetical characteristic. For example, the construct "learned helplessness" may be shown by the following objective events: past history of unavoidable punishment, limited interpersonal skills, limited academic and vocational skills, avoidance of opportunities to succeed, and attribution of outcomes to events outside of individual control.

Construct validity is applicable only to research instruments that measure hypothetical constructs. Many applied investigations use direct measurement of knowledge or skills not intended to be related to an underlying theory. For example, a business owner may wish to evaluate whether there is an increase in sales of items moved to the front of a store. Similarly, a healthcare professional may study the effect of lighting on sleeping patterns of children. It would be unnecessary to study the construct validity of measures of sales or duration of sleep since no projection from these direct measures to underlying phenomena is intended.

Reliability

As indicated earlier in this chapter, reliability is the extent to which an instrument provides consistent results. Reliability can be judged by determining the relationship between scores of the same individuals on separate administrations of the same instrument. It can also be judged by establishing the relationship between subsets of items taken by the same individuals.

A reliable bathroom scale produces the same reading each time used, providing, of course, that sufficient time does not pass for the individual to gain or lose weight. A reliable test of vocational performance produces similar scores whether the even or odd items, first half or second half items, or items in random halves are used in scoring.

We have emphasized that both reliability and validity represent measurement error. As noted, validity is the extent to which an instrument measures what we say that it measures. Reliability is the consistency with which results are obtained for whatever is measured. A table saw that cuts between one fourth and five sixteenths right of the target line is said to be reliable. It produces consistent cuts. One may question its validity, however, since the actual cuts deviate from the target line by a fourth of an inch or more. A table saw that cuts from directly on the target line to one inch either side of the line is not reliable since the location of cuts is not consistent. Further, the target line of the table saw is also not valid since it does not provide an accurate indication of where a cut will occur. It is important to note that if an instrument is not reliable, it cannot be valid. An instrument that is unable to produce a consistent measure cannot assess what it purports to assess.

The reliability of an instrument is measured in several different ways. The most common methods include test-retest, equivalent forms, internal consistency, and interobserver agreement. We will discuss each of these methods.

Test-retest approach. This measure of reliability is also referred to as stability reliability. It is evaluated by administering the same instrument to a sample of individuals on two separate occasions. The two scores for each individual in the sample are then correlated to determine the stability of the instrument. Test scores that remain relatively constant for each individual produce a high correlation coefficient. Scores that vary result in a low correlation.

Equivalent forms. This approach, also called alternate forms reliability, involves correlating parallel forms of the same instrument. A group of individuals completes two forms of the same instrument, and a correlation coefficient is computed for the two sets of scores. A high correlation indicates consistency between the measures. Low reliability indicates variability.

Internal consistency. This is the only reliability measure that is produced through a single administration of an instrument. Internal consistency can be evaluated in several ways. In split half reliability, internal consistency is judged by correlating the score obtained on one half of a test to the score obtained on the other half. In rational equivalence reliability, the Kuder-Richardson formula, Coefficient Alpha, or Hoyt's Analysis of Variance Procedure can be used to judge the consistency of results obtained for each item with all items in the instrument.

Interobserver agreement. This approach is generally used to establish the reliability of instruments that involve direct observation and evaluation. It involves two individuals independently recording the responses of a subject. The reliability coefficient is established by determining the level of agreement between the observers.

The interobserver agreement procedure will differ based on the observational method. Some examples follow.

MEASUREMENT INSTRUMENTS

Numerous data collection instruments exist for use in research investigations. They may be widely used and extensively evaluated for reliability and validity (e.g., many commercial intelligence and achievement tests). On the other extreme, they may be used for the sole purpose of a particular investigation. In this case, the reliability and validity of the measure may be established in the course of the investigation.

The major concern when selecting a research instrument is the extent to which it is valid (and reliable) when judged against the purpose of the investigation. In some cases, you will be able to select an instrument "off the shelf." The advantage of using a commercial instrument is that much of the development, standardization, and reliability and validity testing are already completed. In other cases, the unique goals of the investigation preclude the use of existing instruments. Researchers studying consumer preferences may need to develop an inventory based directly on the choices of concern to the business.

We will now present the major instruments used in research studies. They include standardized instruments, criterion referenced tests, observational systems, and survey instruments.

Standardized Tests

Standardized tests, also referred to as norm referenced tests, are generally prepared and distributed by large commercial publishers such as The Educational Testing Service, American Guidance Service, DLM Teaching Resources, and The Psychological Corporation. Because of the uniformity of design and administration (i.e., standardization procedure), individual scores can be compared meaningfully to a sample of individuals (i.e., norm group) who have taken the test under the same conditions. A score on a standardized test may be interpreted beyond simply indicating the number of items correct or incorrect. Interpretation may include the subject's relative standing in the norm group. It may also address correlates of the subject's performance as determined by a descriptive analysis of individuals in the norm group with a similar score.

Standardized tests are adaptable to a number of areas. For example, intelligence tests are routinely used to assess mental retardation and differentially diagnose other handicapping conditions. Achievement tests are used to gauge students' progress in elementary and secondary schools across the country. Aptitude tests are used to judge employment and employment training potential for vocational rehabilitation clients. Other common classes of standardized tests include personality, vocational, language, reading, developmental, mathematics, speech and hearing, science, and motor.

Standardized instruments should be selected only after consulting the examiner's manual and confirming the appropriateness of the test for your research questions. Special attention should be given to reliability and validity data. It is important that you document the accuracy of data obtained with the instrument. It is also important for you to support the validity of the instrument given the purpose of your study. The following may be useful sources of reliability and validity data:

1. *Tests in Print IV* (1994). Published by the Buros Institute for Mental Measurement.

2. *The Twelfth Mental Measurements Yearbook* (1993). Published by the Buros Institute for Mental Measurement.

3. *A Consumer's Guide to Tests in Print* (1992). Published by PRO-ED.

You may also wish to consult major test publishers directly. The companies listed in Table 9.1 produce a majority of standardized instruments used in social and behavioral science research.

Table 9.1   Major Publishers of Standardized Tests

The following companies publish instruments that may assist you in your research.

Addison-Wesley Publishing Company, 2725 Sand Hill Road, Menlo Park, CA 94025

American College Testing Program, P.O. Box 168, Iowa City, IA 52243

American Guidance Services, Inc., Publishers Buildings, Circle Pines, ME 55014

Bobbs-Merrill Company, Inc., 4300 East 62nd Street, Indianapolis, IN 46268

College Board, 888 Seventh Avenue, New York, NY 10019

Consulting Psychologists Press, Inc., 577 College Avenue, Palo Alto, CA 94306

CTB/McGraw-Hill, Del Monte Research Park, Monterey, CA 93940

Educational Testing Service, Princeton, NJ 08540

Houghton Mifflin Company, 1 Beacon Street, Boston, MA 02107

Institute for Personality and Ability Testing, 1602 Coronado Drive, Champaign, IL 61820

National Occupational Competency Testing Institute, 45 Colvin Avenue, Albany, NY 12206

Nfer Publishing Company (formerly Ginn & Company), 2 Jennings Buildings, Thames Avenue, Windsor, Berks. SL4 1QS, England

The Psychological Corporation, 555 Academic Court, San Antonio, TX 78204

Psychometric Affiliates, P.O. Box 3167, Munster, IN 46321

Science Research Associates, Inc., 155 North Wacker Drive, Chicago, IL 60606

Sheridan Psychological Services, P.O. Box 6101, Orange, CA 92667

Western Psychological Services, 12031 Wilshire Boulevard, Los Angeles, CA 90025

Criterion Referenced Tests

Criterion referenced tests contrast a subject's performance against an objective standard. They may gauge specific academic standards (e.g., sight words recognized, science concepts articulated, math facts stated, or words correctly spelled), motor standards (e.g., speed in the 100-yard dash, strength, pounds bench pressed, seconds from a stimulus to a reaction), sensory standards (e.g., visual images recognized or sounds heard), or any other standard that can be objectively defined.

The number of criterion referenced tests prepared by commercial publishers has increased substantially over the past decade. However, most research studies that address discrete skills or abilities require unique or highly focused instruments that may not be available commercially. Therefore, we will focus the majority of our attention on how to develop criterion referenced tests for specific research purposes.

Step 1. ***Identify the skill being studied.*** As noted earlier, criterion referenced tests are used to measure discrepancies between a subject's performance and an objective standard. To be valid, the standard must be identified in clear and complete terms. Any ambiguity in the standard will produce ambiguity in interpretation. Clear and complete standards generally include three major elements. First, the standard should include a description of performance expected of the subjects. Second, the standard should include a statement of conditions under which performance is expected to occur. Finally, the standard should include a list of criteria indicating successful performance of the skill.

Step 2. ***Enumerate subskills.*** Scores that reflect performance on the overall skill may be too broad to provide useful research data. An instrument that measures dietary information can provide more discerning information if it addresses health effects of poor nutrition, calories and nutrition, minimum daily requirements, and basic food groups. An instrument measuring knowledge obtained from a science module may include two major subskills. The first would be factual and the second would be higher cognitive.

These subskills further define the scope of the instrument. Further, they provide a standard by which specific test items can be developed. In our nutrition example, the test may include an equal number of items addressing each subskill. Similarly, the science test may include 20 factual questions and 20 higher cognitive questions.

Step 3. ***Establish test specifications.*** According to Popham (1978), the essential attribute of criterion referenced tests is the clear description of a set of subskills. This description constitutes the criterion against which the test is referenced. The clarity of the description and relationship of items to that description defines the instrument's validity.

Test specifications include three general elements. The first is a statement of the overall skill and subskills measured by the instrument. As noted, this statement indicates the scope of the test so that a clear interpretation can be made of what was measured. The second includes a description of stimulus features of the instrument. Stimulus features include procedures and materials that are used to elicit subject responses. Examples may include a map of the United States, passages from a novel, or multiple choice items. The third includes a description of response features or the format through which the subject is expected to respond. This may include a written short answer, verbal report, or a demonstration of a skill.

Step 4. Develop items that represent each subskill. The characteristics of test items and response formats are dictated by the test specifications. The scope and content of items depend on the major skill and subskills assessed by the instrument. The stimulus features dictate the nature of instructions and questions, and the response features indicate the behavior expected of subjects.

As noted earlier, consistency between the test specifications and the actual items enhances the instrument's validity (i.e., extent to which the test measures what it purports to measure). Item construction and scoring procedures support the reliability of the instrument. Of course, an unreliable test is also not valid regardless of the test specifications. Therefore, development of reliable items is a critical aspect of criterion referenced test development. Table 9.2 provides examples of ambiguous and effective items. Popham's (1978) criteria for item development and use are summarized in Table 9.3. Finally, Table 9.4 includes procedures for evaluating reliability of criterion referenced tests.

Step 5. Develop a recording and scoring procedure. One of the major values of criterion referenced tests is their effectiveness in providing detailed information about student performance. Not only can a criterion referenced instrument provide an overall score, but performance on each of the subskills can be reported. For example, a test may be designed to measure the general skill of multiplication. Subskills may include the product of two one-digit numbers, the product of one and two digit numbers no carrying, and the product of one and two digit numbers with carrying. Five to 20 items for each of the subskills may produce separate scores so that the researcher can analyze overall multiplication skills (total test score) and individual performance on each of the three subskills. Another example would be the use of an error analysis scheme for scoring written language. Writing samples may be scored for content, vocabulary, syntax, and mechanical skills (i.e., capitalization, punctuation, and spelling). Again, there may be an overall score for written language as well as separate subskill scores.

Table 9.2 Examples of Ambiguous and Effective Items

Ambiguous—Knowledge of the relationship between self and family.

Effective—Ability to match family members (e.g., mother, father, brother, etc.) to relationship, given pictures of individuals and the verbal request "hand me the picture of your. . . ."

Ambiguous—Math ability.

Effective—Ability to state one-digit multiplication facts given a three-second time limit and vertical format flash card presentation.

Ambiguous—Correct use of the alphabet.

Effective—Recognition of letters A through Z given an untimed flash card presentation and verbal response.

Ambiguous—Ability to reconcile the cash drawer.

Effective—Given correct receipts, starting cash, and ending cash, ability to account for all cash proceeds. Given incorrect receipts, ability to detect discrepancies. In both cases, a calculator, coin counter, pad, and paper can be used.

Table 9.3   Guidelines for Preparing Criterion Referenced Test Questions

Binary Choice	
Characteristics:	The subject selects the correct response from two possibilities. These may include true/false, yes/no, agree/disagree, large/small, and so on.
Value:	Items are easily produced and scored.
Limitations:	A correct response can be provided 50 percent of the time by chance. They can be used only to assess skills requiring the subject to select from two discrete alternatives. Finally, binary-choice tests imply that there are always two extremes (e.g., correct or incorrect). In reality, this is seldom the case.
Application:	Limit the use binary-choice items to content that can produce dichotomous responding. Avoid negative statements, and never use double negatives. Include only one concept in each item. In the example, "Golfers are the most intelligent athletes because of the number of judgments that must be made during a round," subjects must discern whether one or both concepts are correct then decide if the relationship between the two is accurate. The researcher cannot be certain which portion of the information produced an incorrect response. This may limit the item's validity. Finally, items should remain a standard length. True items frequently contain more qualifiers; therefore, astute test takers use item length as a clue when the actual response is not known.
Multiple Choice	
Characteristics:	Multiple choice items include a stem (i.e., a question or incomplete statement), a set of foils (incorrect responses), and a correct response. The subject selects the correct response from the foils.
Value:	A range of cognitive and affective responses can be assessed with multiple choice items. They can be machine scored with minimal effort.
Limitations:	Multiple choice items are only useful in measuring a subject's ability to select from alternatives. It is uncertain whether a subject would produce a correct response if not aided by the question format.
Application:	Sufficient information should be included in each stem so that subjects are able to respond as a fill in the blank. In other words, students should be able to answer items correctly without benefit of the response alternatives. Response options should be as brief as possible with all repetitive information contained in the stem. Negative stems and double negative stem/responses should not be used. Items should be unambiguous, and one response should be clearly correct to the knowledgeable subject. All foils should be plausible. Response options should be consistent in tone, length and grammatical structure. Finally, "all" and "none of the above" alternatives should be avoided as they preclude the subject from evaluating each option and selecting the most accurate one.

Table 9.3. Continued

Matching Items	
Characteristics:	Students pair words or phrases from two parallel lists.
Value:	A substantial body of information can be tested in a relatively small space. They are also easy to construct and score objectively.
Limitations:	Matching items only assess skills that involve selecting from alternatives.
Suggestions:	Questions should be unambiguous with one and only one correct match. Words or phrases in each list should be homogeneous (e.g., matching anatomical features with function, economic principals with outcomes, etc.). A larger number of response selections should be included so that subjects cannot match the last item by default. Instructions should identify the standard on which successful matches are made.
Short Answer Items	
Characteristics:	Subjects respond to questions or incomplete statements by providing a word or phrase.
Value:	Items can measure higher cognitive skills and factual information without the assistance of response options.
Limitations:	Short answer items can be difficult to score requiring researchers to subjectively analyze each response. A specific item may have several correct responses, and some responses may be partially correct.
Applications:	The subject's response should be limited to a word or phrase. Open-ended questions likely to be answered with extensive discussion should be avoided. Items should be developed with a discrete response in mind. Qualifiers may be used to limit responses.
Essay	
Characteristics:	Essay items may be constructed using one of two formats. The restricted response format limits the scope or length of responses; the extended response format offers more flexibility in formulating answers.
Value:	Essay items can be used to evaluate higher cognitive skills. They can assess convergent processes where subjects integrate discrete information. They can also evaluate divergent processes where limited information is used to respond to broad issues. Substantial information can be obtained in a brief period of time with essay items.
Limitations:	Essay items are most prone to reliability errors in scoring than any of the preceding methods. Except in extremely well-prescribed restricted items, little advance structure is placed on the response. Consequently, researchers cannot be entirely certain that the target information will be sampled.
Applications:	Restricted questions are preferred to open-ended items because of the potential for enhanced reliability. We recommend that you develop a scoring system in advance of data collection.

Table 9.4   Procedures for Evaluating the Reliability of Criterion Referenced Tests

Test-Retest Reliability
Prior to formal data collection, identify a sample of individuals similar to the group included in the actual study. Test these individuals using the instrument. From a week to a month later, retest the sample using the same instrument. Correlate the two scores.
Alternate Forms Reliability
Develop an equivalent form of the research instrument using comparable items to measure the same skills. Identify a sample of individuals similar to the group included in the actual study. Test one half of this sample using the instrument followed by its alternate form. Test the other half using the alternate form followed by the instrument. Correlate the two scores.
Internal Consistency Reliability
Prior to formal data collection, identify a sample of individuals similar to the group included in the actual study. Test these individuals using the instrument. For each subject, tabulate the number of even and odd items that are correct. Determine the relationship between scores on even and odd items. Alternately, compute the Kuder-Richardson reliability using the K-R 20 or K-R 21 formula.

*Step 6. **Evaluate reliability and validity.*** Earlier in this chapter we highlighted the importance of establishing the reliability and validity of research instruments. The greater the true score, and smaller the error score, the more likely that your research will detect differences that actually exist. Each of the procedures used in developing a criterion referenced test (e.g., clear and complete directions, unambiguous items, consistent scoring procedures) contributes to reducing measurement error. Beyond these efforts, researchers are obligated to provide an estimate of residual error.

Content validity, concurrent validity, and predictive validity are most commonly used to determine the extent to which an instrument measures what it purports to measure. Criterion referenced tests used in research should meet three standards for content validity. First, all of the items should reflect the overall skill or subskills being assessed. Second, all of the subskills should be sampled with a reasonable number of items. Third, the stimulus and response features of the instrument should be consistent with the skill being assessed.

Concurrent validity is judged by identifying relationships between test performance and performance on other indicators. For example, a researcher may compare performance on a sight word vocabulary measure with reading achievement scores. Performance on a criterion referenced test of science knowledge may be compared to a science achievement test.

Predictive validity is judged in a similar manner to concurrent validity as a relationship is established between the experimental instrument and another measure. For predictive validity, the other measure is a future outcome that should have been predicted by the experimental instrument. A test of academic performance, for example, should predict future grade point average. A test of ability in market analysis should predict growth in an individual's portfolio. Finally, a test of technical skill should predict performance ratings by a supervisor.

In summary, Popham (1978) has offered six criteria that can be used to judge the quality of a criterion referenced instrument. While his discussion primarily addresses the use of tests for instructional decision making, the criteria are no less relevant when judging the quality of tests for research purposes:

1. Is a clear descriptive scheme presented in the test specifications? Are the overall skill and component subskills easily identified, and can results be interpreted from within these elements?

2. Are sufficient items included in the instrument to provide a reasonable sample of each subskill? Is there a clear relationship between the characteristics of each item and the subskill being measured?

3. Is the scope of the test limited to one major skill and several subskills?

4. Is the instrument reliable? Do test-retest, alternate forms, and/or split-half reliability estimates support the precision and stability of the instrument?

5. Is the instrument valid? Do test items match the skills and subskills being measured? Does test performance concur with performance on other instruments? Does it predict performance in future endeavors related to test results?

6. Has the test been demonstrated to be useful for instruction and research?

Observational Systems

Observation systems provide a direct measure of individual performance in natural situations. These situations may include classrooms, community settings, work sites, and residences. Observation systems may also measure performance in analogue settings. Analogue observations may occur during role play and other simulations of natural conditions. Examples may include grilling a hamburger patty under simulated work conditions, greeting fictitious customers in a school store, or conducting CPR on a mannequin.

As emphasized earlier, validity is the hallmark of all effective measurement systems. Direct observation of actual performance in natural settings leaves little question as to the validity of measurement. Observation systems that tabulate the number of customers entering a business, patients served by a physician, or minutes spent completing homework undoubtedly assess these outcomes.

Analogue systems are generally subject to greater validity error than observations of performance under natural conditions. For example, an analogue system may involve recording the time required to bring "victims" to safety during a simulated disaster. The analogue observation scheme cannot include the same extreme pressure and real danger inherent in an actual disaster. This omission may result in differential performance from simulation to real circumstances and diminish the accuracy of conclusions.

It is often necessary to accept this error since many natural behaviors cannot be observed for assessment/research purposes. Obviously, you cannot create real disasters to measure human performance. Also, contrived situations may be required to assess responses that occur infrequently under natural conditions. For example, we seldom have an opportunity to observe reactions to being criticized by an employer, "short changed" by a clerk, or summoned for assistance by a neighbor. Role plays or situation performance tests may be the only way to assess responses to these situations.

There are three major observational procedures used in the behavioral and social sciences. They include event recording, duration recording, and interval recording. Each method will be described along with procedures used to ensure reliability.

Event recording. This may be the most useful and least time-consuming of all the direct observation methods. Assessment is conducted by tallying episodes of the target response(s) over time. Two conditions must be met for event recording to be reliable. First, the target response must have a discrete start and stop. Examples include steps taken, balls thrown, pencils sharpened, and classes missed. Behaviors that have uncertain beginnings and endings (e.g., unhappiness, disagreements, or inattentiveness) will raise questions as to whether an event constituted one long episode or several shorter episodes.

Second, event recording is appropriate for behaviors that occur over a fairly constant duration. The number of hits in a baseball season is directly comparable from one player to another as is the number of strokes per round of golf. Conversely, one may not be able to compare the number of cross country trips, school yard fights, or projects completed, as each of these may vary substantially in length. You may indicate a two-fold increase in fights. On closer inspection, however, you may note that the duration of the fights fell from hour long assaults to three minute arguments with minimal shoving.

Aside from these two considerations, the time during which observations are made must be kept constant for frequency data to be comparable. An insurance agent may sell five policies in one week and three in another. A closer inspection of the results may indicate that the "three policy" week included only three working days due to a holiday. Therefore, it would not be accurate to conclude that she was less productive during the "three policy" week.

To control for variable observation periods, frequency of response should be converted to rate of response. The rate of response is computed by dividing the number of occurrences (frequency) by the time available for observation. In the preceding example, five sales occurred in five days (i.e., five sales divided by five days available for sales), producing a rate of one per day. Three sales occurred in three days, producing the same rate of one per day.

Similarly, a student may attend recess for 20 minutes one day and 50 minutes the next. On the first day there were two episodes of "tattling"; on the next there were six episodes. The resulting tattling rates would be .10 for the first day and .12 on the second. The following formula indicates the method for converting from frequency to rate:

$$\text{Rate} = \frac{\text{Frequency}}{\text{Time}}$$

Figure 9.1 illustrates a standard form that may be used for rate recording. If all observation times are of a constant duration, the date and frequency columns are sufficient.

Permanent product. The measurement of permanent products is similar to event recording. They differ in that, rather than measuring ongoing responses, you measure the tangible outcomes of responses. Products may include work units completed, areas cleaned, and tables set.

Permanent product recording requires that task demands be relatively constant from product to product. Houses built, for example, may differ substantially in square footage. A reduction in houses built may be attributed to an increase in size rather than a decrease in effort. Similarly, documents typed is meaningful only if document length is fairly constant. An alternative to control for varying lengths is to define the permanent product by size or complexity. For example, one may record square footage of house constructed, or document pages typed.

Figure 9.2 illustrates a form used to record permanent product data. The word "task" in the form should be defined by the products being measured.

Duration recording. This method is used to measure the amount of time an individual engages in an activity. You may seek to increase the amount of time an individual spends performing various professional responsibilities (e.g., paperwork, sales, stocking, or supplier relations). You may be interested in assessing the time required to run a mile, complete 20 push-ups, or swim 50 meters.

Date				Setting(s)	
Target Behavior					
Definition				Recorder(s)	

Time			Frequency	Rate
Start	Stop	Total		

Figure 9.1 A Sample Event Recording Form

Response latency is a variation of duration data in which the dependent measure is the amount of time from some event to a specific response. For example, one may measure the latency from traffic control signal change to stopping (or starting) a vehicle. Similarly, you may measure the time that elapses or latency from a request for assistance to initiation of assistance.

Figure 9.3 illustrates a form used to record duration data. It is modified for latency data by changing the column labels "start" and "stop" to "signal" and "response." Of course, the label "Duration" is changed to "Latency."

Date _____	Setting(s) _____
Product _____	_____
Quality Standard(s) _____	Recorder(s) _____
_____	_____
_____	_____

Task	Time			Number of Tasks Completed	Rate
	Start	Stop	Total		

Figure 9.2 A Form for Recording Permanent Product Data

Interval recording. This measure is used to monitor behaviors that do not have discrete start or stop times. It is also used to monitor responses that vary in length. Interval data are collected by dividing a longer period of time (e.g., school day, work shift, etc.) into brief intervals (e.g., 10 seconds to several minutes). In partial interval recording, responses are scored as occurring or not occurring at any time during the short time interval. In whole interval recording, an interval is scored if a response occurs continuously throughout the interval. In momentary interval recording, an interval is scored if the response is occurring at the moment the interval begins or ends. The resulting measure of behavior strength is computed as the percentage of intervals in which the behavior occurred.

	Start	Stop	Duration
1			
2			
3			
4			
5			
6			
7			
8			
9			
10			
11			
12			
13			
14			
15			

Date _____ Setting _____
Target Behavior _____ Recorder(s) _____
Definition _____
_____ Observation Time _____

Figure 9.3 A Sample Duration Recording Form

For example, a two-hour show may be divided into 120 one-minute intervals. For partial interval measurement, an observer may score each interval in which a counter person spends any amount of time waiting on customers. For whole interval measurement, an interval is checked if the counter person is waiting on customers throughout the one-minute period. For momentary interval recording, an interval is checked if the counter person is waiting on customers when the interval begins.

Interval recording can be used to score multiple responses (e.g., waiting on customers, cleaning the counter, preparing popcorn, or stocking shelves) as opposed to simple dichotomous recording (e.g., was or was not waiting on customers). In this case, each interval may be scored with a code letter signifying activities in which the counter person was engaged during the interval. These observations would be summarized by reporting the percentage of intervals in which the counter person was engaged in each activity.

Figure 9.4 illustrates a form used to record interval data. It can be modified to monitor multiple behaviors by substituting behavior codes for simple $+/-$ (occurrence/nonoccurrence) designations.

Date _____   Setting(s) _____

Target Behavior _____   Recorder(s) _____

Definition _____   _____

_____   _____

_____   Interval

                                      Length _____

Key: "−" = nonoccurence; "+" = occurrence

	1	2	3	4	5	6	7	8	9	10	% scored +
1											_____
2											_____
3											_____
4											_____
5											_____
6											_____
7											_____
8											_____
9											_____
10											_____
11											_____
12											_____
13											_____
14											_____
15											_____
16											_____
17											_____
18											_____
19											_____
20											_____

Figure 9.4 A Sample Interval Recording Form

Interobserver reliability. As we have emphasized throughout this chapter, the quality of any measurement system depends in large part on its reliability. Testing hypotheses with an unreliable dependent variable is analogous to building a house with an elastic tape measure. In the house, no two walls will be the same height. In research, no test of comparable subjects will produce similar results.

Interobserver reliability checks are conducted to test the accuracy of observational systems. Interobserver reliability is determined by assessing the degree to which two independent observers agree on the occurrence or nonoccurrence of a target behavior. High reliability (e.g., comparable judgments by independent observers) allows you to attribute variability in data to experimental effects rather than observer error.

Interobserver reliability for event and permanent product recording is established by two individuals independently tallying the frequency of response or products for subjects over the same time period. The lowest reported frequency is divided by the highest frequency to produce a reliability coefficient (i.e., rate of agreement for independent observers). For example, two research assistants may both record the number of men entering a public washroom over the same eight-hour period. One identified 74 men, the other identified 82. As illustrated here, the reliability coefficient of .90 would be computed by dividing 74 by 82.

$$\frac{74 \text{ (smaller frequency)}}{82 \text{ (larger frequency)}} = .90$$

Reliability for duration recording is established in a similar manner. The shorter duration reported by independent observers is divided by the longer duration. Reliability is computed as follows:

$$\frac{12 \text{ min. (smaller duration)}}{15 \text{ min. (larger duration)}} = .80$$

Reliability for interval recording is the ratio of intervals in which both observers scored an occurrence to intervals in which one or both observers scored an occurrence. Intervals in which neither observer scored an occurrence are excluded from the computation:

$$\frac{32 \text{ (intervals scored "+" by both observers)}}{38 \text{ (intervals scored "+" by one or more observers)}} = .84$$

Reliability checks should be made with pilot observations prior to actual data collection. Once formal data collection has begun, checks should be conducted periodically to ensure that measurement standards remain constant. In general, if high reliability is noted early in data collection (e.g., .90 or above), fewer checks are required throughout the project (e.g., every eighth observation). Reliability levels around .75 emphasize the need for frequent checks (e.g., every fourth observation). Reliability below .70 is generally considered inadequate and should trigger a refinement in your observation system.

Opinion Scale Development

The final instruments we will discuss are attitude or opinion scales. These may be the most widely used dependent variables in social and behavioral science research. They can be theory based when used to support hypotheses relating to presumed characteristics of a sample. They can also be functional when used to predict or assess practical outcomes such as anticipated market performance or consumer satisfaction. Finally, scales can be used simply to describe a sample, compare samples, or identify relationships between characteristics within a sample.

DeVellis (1991) has suggested eight major steps in scale development. These steps are summarized below.

Clearly establish what you wish to measure. The quality of a scale depends on the researcher's clear understanding of what is to be assessed. Effective scales are developed through the researcher's thorough understanding of the theoretical constructs or functional responses that are to be measured. It is also important that the scale be delimited to the precise questions addressed in the investigation. We recommend a focused inquiry into carefully defined topics as opposed to "fishing expeditions." You will find that the analysis of data from a well-focused scale will lead to clear and unambiguous conclusions. Conversely, poorly focused instruments often produce unanticipated, unexplainable, and often conflicting results.

Produce a pool of items. All items should be developed or selected with reference to a specific measurement goal. As with criterion referenced tests, we recommend that you select several items to measure each construct. Multiple appraisals of similar information are likely to produce a more reliable assessment. Because of the value of redundancy in scale development, we recommend that you develop an extensive item pool for the initial instrument. Further refinement may eliminate items that lack internal consistency.

The following features are likely to enhance the reliability of individual items.

1. Items should be unambiguous.
2. Overly long and complex items should be avoided.
3. Vocabulary level should reflect the ability of respondents.
4. Items should assess only one concept at a time.
5. Ambiguous pronoun references should be avoided.
6. Items should be worded both affirmatively and negatively.

Establish a measurement format. The format of the instrument is based on information desired and the nature of questions generated for the pool. Common questioning formats include the following:

1. *Likert-type or Summated Rating Scales* contain items that have a constant or relatively equal value/attitude loading. Respondents score each by indicating their disposition within a value range. Common anchors include agree-disagree, desirable-undesirable, and retain-reject. An example of Likert or summated scale items appears in Figure 9.5.

2. *Thurstone-type or Equal-appearing Interval Scales* assess a respondent's position within a value/attitude continuum. Each item includes a series of statements reflecting varying attitudes toward the same objective or event. Each item within the scale is constructed by collecting a number of statements with varying value loading. Independent judges sort the statements into 11 piles from low to high value loading. The distribution of the scale values assigned by each judge is plotted, and the median value of the distribution is identified. Statements for which substantial disagreement exists between judges are eliminated. The remaining statements are piloted with a sample of respondents who are asked to mark statements with which they agree. The results are judged for internal consistency, and those with high statistical values are retained. A given number of items with equally spaced scale values are retained. An example of a Thurstone-type or Equal-appearing interval scale appears in Figure 9.6.

3. *Guttman-type or Cumulative Scales* include items with a small number of increasingly difficult, complex, or value loaded statements that measure a particular attitude/value. Responding affirmatively to one item in the sequence implies a corresponding response to all of the preceding statements within the item. An example of Guttman-type or cumulative scales appears in Figure 9.7.

4. *Semantic Differential Scales* include a statement of the concept to be evaluated, a series of polar adjective pairs that serve as anchors for the scale, and a set of from five to nine (many authorities recommend seven) unidentified rating positions. An example of a semantic differential appears in Figure 9.8.

5. *Binary Option Scales* are similar to Likert-type or summated rating scales in that the item stems are weighted equally. They differ in that, as with Thurstone and Guttman scales, respondents have two polar choices for each item. Common choices include yes-no, agree-disagree, and applies to me-does not apply to me. An example of a binary option scale appears in Figure 9.9.

1. Defense spending is essential to protecting liberty.
   Strongly   ___   ___   ___   ___   ___   ___   ___   Strongly
   Agree   Disagree

2. A majority of support should go to employing defense personnel.
   Strongly   ___   ___   ___   ___   ___   ___   ___   Strongly
   Agree   Disagree

3. Women can perform effectively in both combat and noncombat roles.
   Strongly   ___   ___   ___   ___   ___   ___   ___   Strongly
   Agree   Disagree

4. High-tech defense systems will make current offensive systems obsolete.
   Strongly   ___   ___   ___   ___   ___   ___   ___   Strongly
   Agree   Disagree

5. The mandatory draft should be reinstated.
   Strongly   ___   ___   ___   ___   ___   ___   ___   Strongly
   Agree   Disagree

6. Desert Storm was an example of effective military intervention.
   Strongly   ___   ___   ___   ___   ___   ___   ___   Strongly
   Agree   Disagree

Figure 9.5 A Sample Likert or Summated Scale Items

1. University newspapers should be free to publish material considered to be offensive on any grounds.   Agree ___   Disagree ___

2. University newspapers should be free to publish all material with the exception of solicitations to engage in unlawful behavior.   Agree ___   Disagree ___

3. University newspapers should be free to publish all material that does not include morally or ethically offensive content.   Agree ___   Disagree ___

4. University newspapers should be censored only to include the most moral content.   Agree ___   Disagree ___

1. Universities should have dorm rooms that can be shared by males and females.   Agree ___   Disagree ___

2. Universities should have dorm floors with both male and female residents.   Agree ___   Disagree ___

3. Universities should have dorms with alternate male/female floors.   Agree ___   Disagree ___

4. Universities should have dorms segregated by sex.   Agree ___   Disagree ___

Figure 9.6 Thurstone-Type or Equal-Appearing Interval Scale

1. The average executive spends over 16 hours a week exercising.   Agree ____   Disagree ____

2. The average executive spends from 10 to 16 hours
    a week exercising.   Agree ____   Disagree ____

3. The average executive spends from 4 to 10 hours
    a week exercising.   Agree ____   Disagree ____

4. The average executive spends less than 4 hours
    a week exercising.   Agree ____   Disagree ____

1. The amount of alcohol consumed by the average executive
    exceeds 12 ounces a week.   Agree ____   Disagree ____

2. The amount of alcohol consumed by the average executive is
    between 8 and 12 ounces a week.   Agree ____   Disagree ____

3. The amount of alcohol consumed by the average executive is
    between 4 and 8 ounces a week.   Agree ____   Disagree ____

4. The amount of alcohol consumed by the average executive is
    less than 4 ounces a week.   Agree ____   Disagree ____

Figure 9.7 Guttman-Type or Cumulative Scale

Corvette

Fast	__ __ __ __ __ __	Slow
Stylish	__ __ __ __ __ __	Not Stylish
Dependable	__ __ __ __ __ __	Undependable
Expensive	__ __ __ __ __ __	Inexpensive
Available	__ __ __ __ __ __	Unavailable
Likely to appreciate	__ __ __ __ __ __	Not Likely to appreciate

Figure 9.8 Semantic Differential Scale

Conduct an expert review of the item pool. Items should be reviewed by one or more individuals with expertise in scale development as related to the target phenomena. The major purpose of this review is to enhance the scale's content validity. To this end, reviewers should be provided with an operational definition of the construct measured by the scale. They should then be asked to judge the relevance of each item to the construct. Further, when a scale purports to measure multiple constructs, reviewers should be able to categorize items under the separate constructs. Finally, reviewers should be invited to make anecdotal comments that aide in clarifying ambiguous items. They may also comment on additional items that may further illuminate the construct.

I work hard in school.	Agree _____	Disagree _____
I usually do my homework.	Agree _____	Disagree _____
I enjoy school.	Agree _____	Disagree _____
I like my teacher.	Agree _____	Disagree _____
I like my classmates.	Agree _____	Disagree _____
I generally obtain good grades.	Agree _____	Disagree _____
I follow school rules.	Agree _____	Disagree _____
I like extracurricular activities.	Agree _____	Disagree _____

Figure 9.9 Binary Options Scale

Develop validation items. You may wish to include items that serve as a validation check. Some items, for example, may simply check to see that the respondents were exposed to essential stimulus materials. For example, a scale may be administered to determine students' reactions to a passage about spousal abuse. Several items may simply check the respondent's comprehension of events described in the passages.

Another useful validation check is for social attractiveness. Respondents may provide answers that are socially acceptable though not accurate reflections of their attitudes. Including items that are "politically correct" but obviously incorrect when scored in the affirmative will help you check for social attractiveness errors.

Pilot the instrument with a development sample. It is important to conduct a trial of the instrument once scale items are selected. While some researchers recommend a sample of over 300 people to eliminate subject variance (Nunnally, 1994), a smaller sample may suffice if the item pool is relatively small. Large development samples are recommended over small because of the increased likelihood that a stable pattern of covariation between items will exist. A scale that is evaluated with few subjects may, by chance alone, produce an overly favorable level of internal consistency. When readministered during the actual research project, the internal consistency may decline below expectations. Also, a larger sample will more likely represent the target population.

Evaluate items based on data obtained from the sample. A number of methods are suggested for evaluating scale items.

1. Test to see that each scale item correlates highly with all other scale items. Effective items should produce results that are consistent with other items in the scale, given that all items are intended to measure the same general construct.

2. Correct items that correlate negatively with other scale items by reverse scoring. Both high positive and negative correlation are desirable as long as they are scored with reference to this value.

3. Test to see that each scale item correlates highly with performance on the total scale score or the corrected scale score (total scale score excluding the item being correlated).

4. Judge whether items on the scale produce high variance across subjects. An effective scale item will discriminate effectively between individuals in the sample.

5. Judge whether scores on items are as close to the center of the range of possible scores as possible. Value loading in Likert-type scale items, for example, should be such that the average respondent scores a three or four on a seven point scale.

6. Compute a coefficient alpha. This is the strongest indicator of the scale's overall reliability. Careful attention to the preceding judgments should eliminate items that reduce the coefficient alpha. High coefficient alpha includes that a high ratio of variance in scale scores can be attributed to true scores as opposed to error.

Establish an appropriate scale length. In general, the longer the instrument, the greater the coefficient alpha reliability. Unfortunately, longer scales may be less desirable for practical reasons. Therefore, we recommend that the number of items retained in the final instrument be long enough to produce acceptable reliability but short enough to produce acceptable return rates.

SUMMARY

All human research depends on the measurement of learning, behavioral, or attitudinal characteristics. The quality of research depends in a large part on the accuracy of this measurement. As we noted, all measurement includes a true score and an error score. All competent researchers strive to enhance the true score and minimize the error score.

The first step in minimizing error is to recognize the sources of error. We identified three major types of error. These included:

1. *Observation/testing error* often resulting from instruments that are poorly matched to the research question, unclear items, excessively difficult or easy items, and an instrument that is overly broad in scope.

2. *Procedural error* often resulting from inconsistent administration, recording, scoring, and interpretation of responses.

3. *Subject error,* also described as trait instability or natural inconsistencies in subject performance.

Regardless of our effectiveness in identifying and minimizing error, a "true" assessment of human characteristics is never produced. Therefore, it is important for us to estimate the error score. This allows readers and critics to recognize the level of confidence that may be placed in our findings. The two major standards used to judge the degree of error in a score are validity (the extent that an instrument measures what it purports to measure) and reliability (the extent to which an instrument produces consistent results). We identified four major measures of validity, including content validity, concurrent validity, predictive validity, and construct validity.

We also highlighted four major measures of reliability. These included test-retest reliability, equivalent forms reliability, internal consistency reliability, and interobserver agreement.

A wide variety of options exist for selecting or creating reliable and valid dependent variables. The easiest option is to select a *standardized instrument* developed and evaluated by commercial publishers. The major advantage of these instruments is that, because of uniformity of design and administrations, results can be compared across samples and over time. It is important, however, that the instrument produce data appropriate to the research hypotheses.

A second option is the development of *criterion referenced tests.* These instruments are typically developed for the specific purpose of the research investigation. Rather than gauging a subject's performance against a normative group as in standardized tests, performance is measured against an objective standard.

A third option is the development of an *observational system.* We identified two contexts in which observational assessment may be conducted. The first, analogue observation, involves monitoring subjects' behavior under contrived circumstances. The second is direct observation which involves observation under natural circumstances. While observation under natural conditions has the potential to produce the most valid findings, practical constraints may require the use of analogue observations.

Regardless of the context, three major observational procedures are commonly used in the behavioral and social sciences. They include *event recording, duration recording,* and *interval recording.*

The final type of instruments discussed were *attitude or opinion scales.* These may be the most widely used measures in social and behavioral science research. They can be theory based when used to assess hypothetical constructs. They can be functional when used to predict or assess practical outcomes. Finally, they can be used to describe or compare groups of individuals.

Several common questioning formats were described in the chapter, including *Likert-type* or *summative rating scales, Thurstone-type* or *equal-appearing interval scales, Guttman-type* or *cumulative scales, semantic differential scales,* and *binary option scales.*

REFERENCES

American Educational Research Association, the American Psychological Association, and the National Council on Measurement in Education. (1985). *Standards for educational and psychological testing.* Washington, DC: APA. pp. 9–18 and 19–23.

DeVellis, R. F. (1991). Scale Development: Theory and Applications: Applied Social Research Methods Series, Vol. 26. Newbury Park, CA: Sage Publications, Inc.

Duncan, O. D. (1984). *Notes on social measurement: Historical and critical.* New York: Russel Sage.

Nunnally, J. C. (1994). *Psychometric theory* (3rd ed.). New York: McGraw-Hill.

Popham, W. J. (1978). *Criterion-referenced measurement.* Upper Saddle River, NJ: Merrill/Prentice Hall.

FURTHER READINGS

Berry, K., & Mielke, P., Jr. (1992). A family of multivariate measures of association for nominal independent variables. *Educational and Psychological Measurements, 52* (1), 41–55.

Goodwin, L. D., & Goodwin, W. L. (1989). The use of power estimation in early childhood special education research. *Journal of Early Intervention, 13*(4), 365–373.

Hartwig, M. (1992). Basic statistics for the amateur scientist. *Science-Probe, 2*(2), 59–65, 126–27.

Harwell, M. R. (1988). Choosing between parametric and nonparametric tests. *Journal of Counseling and Development, 67*(1), 35–38.

Hedge, M. N. (1987). *Clinical research in communication disorders: Principles and strategies.* Boston: Little, Brown.

Johnson, E. S. (1981). *Research methods in criminology and criminal justice.* Upper Saddle River, NJ: Merrill/Prentice Hall.

Olejnik, S. F., & Algina, J. (1985). A review of nonparametric alternatives to analysis of covariance. *Evaluation Review, 9*(1), 51–83.

Penfield, D. A., & Koffler, S. L. (1986). A nonparametric K-sample test for equality of slopes. *Educational and Psychological Measurement, 46*(3), 537–542.

Rasmussen, J. L., & Dunlap, W. P. (1991). Dealing with nonnormal data: Parametric analysis of transformed data vs. nonparametric analysis. *Educational and Psychological Measurement, 51*(4), 809–820.

Sawilowsky, S. S. (1990). Nonparametric tests of interaction in experimental design. *Review of Educational Research, 60*(1), 91–126.

Zegers, F. E. (1991). Coefficients for inter-rater agreement. *Applied Psychological Measurements, 15*(4), 321–33.

10

Defining the Independent Variable in Quantitative Research

INTRODUCTION

The previous chapter gave a detailed discussion of how to measure your dependent variable. Regardless of whether you have chosen to engage in quantitative or qualitative research, the information in Chapter 9 will be useful. For example, before conducting a large group or single subject study, you need to identify the exact nature of the dependent variable and how you will measure any changes that result from exposure to the independent variable. In addition, you want to make sure that any differences in the dependent variable are in fact due to manipulations rather than problems with the measurement procedures. Similarly, if you are planning a qualitative study, the information in Chapter 9 can help prepare to gather data by interviewing, administering questionnaires, or conducting systematic observations.

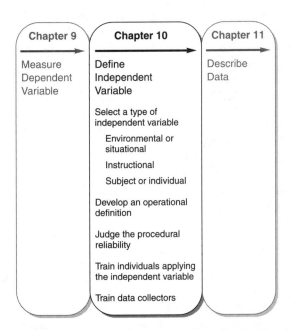

The Scope, Plan, and Sequence Chart for Conducting
Research: The Seventh Step in the Research Process

Unique to the area of quantitative research, however, is concern for the independent variable. In qualitative research, you are observing people and events in their natural settings without any attempt to manipulate. In fact, you take every precaution not to disturb the setting so as not to undermine the validity of your results. This is not the case with a quantitative study in which your primary interest is testing for a relationship between dependent and independent variables. To increase the confidence in the results of your study, you must be able to show that you addressed aspects of the independent variable with the same care and precision used to define and record the dependent variable.

We have two examples to illustrate the importance of the independent variable. Our first example is based on our own work with a multiple disabled youth. We were trying to develop an intervention program to eliminate a high level of aggression demonstrated by a student with a profound hearing impairment and a serious emotional disturbance. We were not sure how to go about doing this and decided to consult the professional literature for some ideas. After a hand and computer search, we were only able to locate one article that described an intervention involving another student with similar characteristics. We were even more dismayed when we read the description of the independent variable provided by the authors. They made one brief note to the effect that their client had participated in counseling. No other details were provided.

A second example is humorous and based on an episode of the classic "Dick Van Dyke Show." Millie asks Laura for her famous avocado dip recipe. Laura gives it to her, and Millie makes the dip. Unknown to Millie, however, was the fact that Laura had overheard Millie making some disparaging comments about Rob and her. In an unusual fit of pique, Laura omits a key ingredient from the recipe. It comes as no surprise that Millie's dip is not as good as Laura's dip.

Inadequate attention to the independent variable has serious repercussions for the quality of your research. First, without a clear, comprehensive description of the independent variable, others who read your work will not understand how you brought about changes in the dependent variable. Remember, the purpose of research is to contribute to the knowledge base in your field of study. This will not happen without devoting sufficient attention to the independent variable. Second, you must make sure that all aspects of the independent variable are in effect at predetermined levels. Like Millie's version of Laura's recipe, the omission of a key step, whether deliberately or by accident, means that the independent variable you delivered is not the one you had planned.

It is not sufficient to simply report that you exposed your subjects to the independent variable. You have to plan for (and provide documentation of) its delivery, similar to the manner in which you plan to demonstrate reliable changes in the dependent variable.

In this chapter, we will present a definition for the independent variable and discuss different types. We will also discuss the importance of describing the independent variable in clear, concise terms. Finally, we make recommendations for measuring the consistency and accuracy of its delivery.

TYPES OF INDEPENDENT VARIABLES

An independent variable refers to the conditions that you will vary or manipulate to produce a change in the dependent variable. Kazdin (1997) described three types of independent variables. The first type is an environmental or situational variable which involves doing something to, with, or by the subject. For instance, you can assign a treatment or task to some subjects but not to others. One group may receive a new medication or participate in an exercise program while others do not. You may also decide to give different amounts of the task or condition to the subjects. For example, you could vary dosage levels or the number of minutes spent in daily walks.

Finally, you could provide two distinct tasks or treatments to different groups of subjects. For example, some subjects would receive Drug A; others would receive Drug B.

The second type of independent variable is an instructional variable. Don't be misled by the name; it does not refer to an intervention or training program. It means that subjects are given an instruction or a piece of information designed to change their perceptions. Kazdin (1997) posed the following question to illustrate this variable: Do therapists who were told a projective test was completed by an individual with a personality disorder evaluate it any differently than therapists who were told it was completed by a person functioning within normal limits?

The third type of independent variable is a subject or individual difference variable, which refers to an attribute or characteristic of a person. Examples include intelligence, gender, socioeconomic status, or aptitude. Obviously, you cannot directly control these variables, but you can choose subjects according to how they vary across these dimensions. For example, you can study whether men and women perform differently on the same task, or whether people in white collar occupations experience higher levels of stress than blue collar workers.

Describing Your Independent Variable

Having selected the independent variable you will manipulate, you now need to define it clearly so that an outside observer can determine its effectiveness. Independent variables that involve subject or individual differences are defined rather easily. Gender is usually obvious. You can use standardized instruments such as intelligence tests to measure other subject variables. Similarly, it is easy to define an instructional variable instruction designed to alter perception by writing out the exact statement you intend to use. More challenging, however, is the description of an environmental or situational variable. Here you need to develop a concise, comprehensive description of every aspect of your intervention or treatment program. This means that you describe your independent variable in sufficient detail to allow a reader interested in replication to implement precisely the same strategy and produce the same result. You cannot tell others that your independent variable will be a job-training program for parolees, an exercise program for overweight people, or occupational therapy for persons with cerebral palsy. Different counselors, personal fitness trainers, and occupational therapists will have their own interpretation of such casual descriptions. Only by clearly operationalizing all features of the independent variable can you be sure others will understand exactly how you intend to produce changes in the dependent variable.

Your literature review should have addressed not only the dependent variable you are focusing on in your study, but it should have included other independent variables used previously to change it. Thus, you should already have a fairly good idea of what your intervention or treatment will include. For example, you may be interested in testing the impact of a social skills training program on the ability of children born addicted to crack cocaine to accept and respond to criticism. However, as we suggested earlier, this description is too vague. To develop it, we suggest you refer back to your literature review which may have highlighted other procedures that have been successful or unsuccessful in developing this skill in other populations. However, since these children have only recently entered the public school system, little empirical work is available to shed light on their unique needs. Therefore, your program will be a combination and modification of techniques you think will benefit them. Your program may include an explanation of the importance of the skill, a demonstration, a task analysis, role play, social reinforcement, corrective feedback, and homework. You have already improved your description enormously, but it still requires further clarification. Table 10.1 lists some questions that you can use to develop a clear and complete description. We used them in our own work involving the development of figurative language skills in students with hearing impairments. The independent variable we used in one of our studies is presented in Table 10.2

Table 10.1 Developing a Clear and Complete Description

Responses to the following questions can help you develop a concise, comprehensive, clear, and complete description.

1. What are the components of your intervention?
2. What is the sequence in which these components will be used?
3. Can a component be broken down into smaller steps?
4. What will you do or say when the subject performs appropriately?
5. How will you correct a mistake?
6. How long will a treatment session last?
7. What will the treatment setting look like?
8. Will training be conducted individually or in groups?
9. What materials will subjects have available to them?
10. Who will provide the independent variable?

Table 10.2 An Example of a Clear and Complete Description

A group of four students received 30 minutes of instruction per day, four days per week, in a therapy room at a speech and hearing clinic. The experimenter was a master level teacher with a degree in Deaf Education. All sessions were conducted using sign language. Students were at a table and played Monopoly following all the standard directions with one exception. Before a student could move the number of spaces indicated on the dice, he or she responded to a card containing an example of a metaphor. For example, the card presented the following vignette:

"She dyed her hair before she read the directions on the box. Now her hair is green." The student was instructed to identify and explain the metaphor illustrated. A correct response elicited the following:

Teacher: Good. You said, "Fools rush in where wise men fear to tread."

Teacher or student: The metaphor means that a foolish person does things quickly and often makes mistakes. It is the correct metaphor because she foolishly did not read the directions.

Teacher: You may move your game piece all the way.

An incorrect response triggered the following correction procedure.

Teacher: No, the correct metaphor is "Fools rush in where wise men fear to tread." The metaphor means that a foolish person does things quickly and often makes mistakes. It is the correct metaphor because she foolishly did not read the directions. What is the correct metaphor?

Student: (States the metaphor.)

Teacher: What is the rule?

Student: (States the rule.)

Teacher: How does the metaphor compare to the story?

Student: (States the comparison.)

Teacher: Good. You may move your game piece the number of spaces on the lower die.

Developing a Clear and Complete Description

A major benefit of a clear and complete description of the independent variable is that it allows you to minimize therapist drift. Chances are that you or some other person acting as your assistant will be responsible for exposing your subjects to the intervention or treatment. Because we are human, we are prone to making the occasional mistake. You or your assistant may "drift away" from the original procedures you had planned to use. For example, your assistant could forget a step in the program, or reverse the order of two steps in a sequence. Subjects in that group would not be experiencing the independent variable you had designed. If you and your assistant take turns implementing the independent variable to the same group, then subjects in that experimental condition could actually be experiencing two versions of the treatment.

Therapist drift also has major implications for conclusions you will draw at the end of your study. In one scenario, the independent variable you claim changed behavior may, in fact, bear little resemblance to the independent variable you originally planned to use. A treatment could be judged as effective when, in fact, it is not. You may be successful in publishing your work; however, your conclusions may be flawed, and your contribution questionable. It may take some time for subsequent manuscripts describing a failure to replicate to appear in the literature. In another scenario, it is possible that drifting away from your procedure as originally described means that you implemented a treatment less effective than you had anticipated. At the end of your study, you may report lack of significance and abandon what may have been a promising line of inquiry (Peterson, Homer, & Wonderlich, 1982).

Measuring the Reliability of the Independent Variable

In Chapter 9 we defined several ways to ensure the reliability of an instrument used to measure the dependent variables. Options included test-retest reliability, alternate forms, and split half procedures. There are also ways you can ensure the reliability of the independent variables.

For some studies it may be useful to have an outside observer verify that you, in fact, provided instruction or treatment as prescribed in the research report. In the most simple form, you can ask a research assistant to periodically observe the treatment and record specific steps or procedures that conform to the protocol as well as steps or procedures that violate the protocol.

Billingsley and Munson (1980) and Peterson, Homer, and Wonderlich (1982), have described a more precise method for measuring the reliability of the environmental or situational variables. Their procedures are as follows:

1. Develop a clear and complete description of the treatment or intervention.
2. Develop a data sheet that outlines key elements in the independent variable.
3. Have an observer watch the experimenter as the independent variable is delivered. Write a "+" or a "−" to indicate whether a procedure is used correctly and in the proper order.
4. Calculate procedural reliability. The following formula was proposed by Billingsley, White, and Munson (1980).

$$\text{Procedural Reliability} = (TA \times 100)/TT$$

where TA = the number of teacher behaviors emitted in correspondence with the plan, as judged by the independent observer;

TT = the total number of behaviors which could have been emitted in accord with the plan.

Skill	Trial Number									
	1	2	3	4	5	6	7	8	9	10
Card Presented	—	—	—	—	—	—	—	—	—	—
Student Responds	—	—	—	—	—	—	—	—	—	—
(For a Correct Response)										
Social Reinforcement	—	—	—	—	—	—	—	—	—	—
Metaphor Identified	—	—	—	—	—	—	—	—	—	—
Rule Explained	—	—	—	—	—	—	—	—	—	—
Consequence	—	—	—	—	—	—	—	—	—	—
(For an Incorrect Response)										
Corrective Feedback	—	—	—	—	—	—	—	—	—	—
Metaphor Identified	—	—	—	—	—	—	—	—	—	—
Student Response	—	—	—	—	—	—	—	—	—	—
Rule Explained	—	—	—	—	—	—	—	—	—	—
Consequence	—	—	—	—	—	—	—	—	—	—

Figure 10.1 Sample Calculations of Procedural Reliability

Figure 10.1 presents an example of procedural reliability. As a rule of thumb, 90 percent or higher is acceptable. Lower percentages indicate there is a problem. We will suggest ways to address problems in the next section.

Training the Treatment Agents

Obviously, the results of your procedural reliability will be greatly affected by the skills of the person delivering the independent variable. In most cases, we assume that person is you. It is your study, and you are responsible for all aspects of developing and carrying it out. However, depending on your resources, timelines, and the number of groups, you may decide to ask or hire another person to assist with some aspects of your study. Turning all or part of the delivery of the independent variable over to someone else is certainly an option. Before doing so, think this decision through very carefully. Although you will not leave an assistant to his or her own devices, you are placing a very important part of your study in someone else's hands. You should consider their qualifications and pay close attention to their training.

The person you select to assist in the delivery of the independent variable does not need to be seeking the same degree. For example, just because you are completing a Ph.D. in school psychology does not mean your assistant must also be a Ph.D. candidate in the same program. However, if your intervention involves counseling, you will need someone who is skilled in this area. Before hiring an assistant, make sure he or she has those skills. You will also want to ensure he or she will be available when needed for the duration of the study.

Once your assistant has been selected, you need to train him or her in the delivery of the independent variable. We recommend you adhere to the following guidelines.

1. Develop a training protocol. It should contain a complete description of the independent variable. For example, you may script a typical intervention session that your assistant can review.

2. Demonstrate what you expect the assistant to do. A verbal description may not convey all the subtleties of your intervention. A demonstration allows your assistant to see the independent variable in action.

3. Encourage the assistant to ask questions and clarify any misunderstandings.

4. Have the assistant role play implementation of the independent variable. Observe and provide feedback. It is very helpful to videotape performance and review it together.

5. During your study, conduct periodic checks of procedural reliability. You may want to have two observers, one who checks the reliability of the dependent variable and another who checks for procedural reliability. Do not let the assistant know which observer is collecting which piece of data. Awareness of being observed may change the assistant's behavior. It is ideal to conduct your study in a setting that has a one-way mirror, but this option is not always practical or possible. You may want to consider videotaping all sessions but not let the assistant know when a tape will be reviewed. He or she is more likely to deliver the independent variable accurately and consistently.

6. Use the results of procedural reliability checks to determine whether additional training is needed.

7. Familiarize your assistant with guidelines governing ethical behavior. He or she should also be made aware of confidentiality issues.

8. Document every step in the sequence and include it in your final report.

Training Data Collectors

You may have someone assisting you in the delivery of your independent variables. You are even more likely to have one or more people assisting with data collection. Even if you intend to collect your own data, an observer is still needed to collect reliability information on the dependent variable. As was true for the independent variable, the observers need not come from the degree program in which you are enrolled. Most people can serve as an observer. You will need to train them to increase the accuracy of the data and your ability to document the effects of the independent variable. We recommend the following guidelines.

1. Develop a manual that includes definitions of your dependent variables and forms to be used for data collection.

2. As much as possible, keep observers naive to the purposes of the study. Knowing what you are anticipating may change the way they record data, albeit unconsciously.

3. Familiarize them with ethical and confidentiality issues.

4. Discuss proper observer etiquette. For example, observers should not call undue attention to themselves as they enter and exit an observation site. You should also discuss manner of dress, hairstyle, and jewelry.

5. Observers should be given sufficient time to memorize definitions and familiarize themselves with observational procedures and data collection forms.

6. Test them on their knowledge of the contents of the manual. You can use oral drills, paper and pencil tests, and scoring vignettes.

7. Demonstrate how to collect data. Respond to any questions they may have.

8. Observers should practice collecting data using videotapes or role-playing.

9. Provide feedback regarding performance, and discuss procedural problems and confusion.

10. Continue practicing until observers are 100 percent reliable.

11. Practice in the setting in which data will be collected.

12. During actual data collection sessions, observers should use pens rather than pencils so that it is difficult to change a data sheet. This could happen if there are two observers collecting data simultaneously and one feels less confident about his or her skills. Two observers should not sit near each other, nor should they calculate their own reliability.

13. During the study, review observer performance and retrain as needs dictate.

14. Document every step in the sequence and include it in your final report.

SUMMARY

This chapter focused on describing the independent variable. There are three types of independent variables, including environmental or situational variables that call for an intervention to be implemented, instructional variables that change subjects' perceptions, and subject or individual difference variables that describe an attribute or a characteristic. The independent variable you choose to study needs to be clearly defined, regardless of its exact nature. Readers of your work must have a complete understanding of the event that produced a change in the dependent variable. Of the three types, environmental or situational independent variables are the most difficult to define. In response, we recommended clear and complete descriptions that minimize therapist drift and the possibility that you will unknowingly over or underestimate the effect of your independent variable. We presented guidelines for writing clear and complete descriptions and illustrated them with an example from our own research.

We also discussed the importance of measuring the reliability of the delivery of the independent variable. Again, environmental or situational independent variables presented the greatest challenge. We recommended using procedural reliability and offered guidelines for its use.

Finally, we discussed the importance of adequately training other treatment agents and data collectors. These individuals can substantially decrease your workload but only if they are properly trained.

REFERENCES

Billingsley, F., White, O. R., & Munson, R. (1980). Procedural reliability: A rationale and an example. *Behavioral Assessment, 2,* 229–241.

Kazdin, A. E. (1997). *Research design in clinical psychology* (2nd ed.). Needham Heights, MA: Allyn & Bacon.

Peterson, L., Homer, A. L., & Wonderlich, S. A. (1982). The integrity of independent variables in behavior analysis. *Journal of Applied Behavior Analysis, 15,* 477–492.

FURTHER READINGS

Examples of Studies Containing Clear and Complete Descriptions and Procedural Reliability

Israelite, N., Schloss, P., & Smith, M. A. (1986). Teaching proverb use through a modified table game. *Volta Review, 88,* 195–207.

Lockhart, J., & Law, M. (1994). The effectiveness of multisensory writing programme for improving cursive writing ability in children with sensori-motor difficulties. *Canadian Journal of Occupational Therapy, 61,* 206–214.

11

Organizing and Describing Data

INTRODUCTION

How valuable would the United States Census Data be if it were only tabled in the order in which it was collected? Questions as simple as, How many Americans represent minority groups? What is the average family income? and Where are the population centers of the country? could not begin to be answered. Answering these questions from raw data presented in random form would be analogous to locating an 8mm screw in a pile of scrap metal. The item or answer is contained in the pile of raw data, but neither is accessible through a cursory review.

A team of workers may organize the scrap metal by type and function. An inventory system may be used to map the location of items. The 8mm screw, or any other part included in the inventory, could then be easily located. Similarly, raw data from the census could be organized by

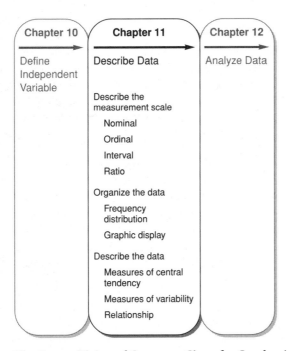

The Scope, Plan, and Sequence Chart for Conducting Research: The Eighth Step in the Research Process

geographical region, race, income status, and so on. Answers to social and political questions could subsequently be obtained through a brief data scan.

To carry our analogy a step further, what if a visitor to our hypothetical scrap yard picked up a handful of screws and noted that one was cross-threaded? Would it be proper for the visitor to conclude that parts obtained from our scrap pile were typically defective?

A mathematician may establish an objective rule for determining the pervasiveness of defects. He or she may determine the probability that a number of defects in a small sample would suggest that a proportional number of defects existed in the population of all parts. Having done this, you may conclude that the single defect was predictive or not predictive of what would be found in the inventory of scrap parts.

In Chapter 5 we described research designs to use when working with large numbers of subjects. This chapter describes methods for organizing raw data obtained during studies using these designs. We will review scales of measurement and their implications for the selection of data management procedures. We will also describe the use of graphic displays and descriptive statistics.

SCALES OF MEASUREMENT

We have suggested a wide range of methods for translating observations into numeric descriptions. Criterion referenced tests yield numbers that indicate the extent to which performance objectives were attained by subjects. Standardized tests yield numbers that indicate the relative performance of a subject against a normative sample. Observational procedures indicate the frequency or duration of responses. Scales reveal the strength of attitudes or opinions.

The method by which data are obtained has major implications for the way that data can be summarized and interpreted. Therefore, we will describe the levels of measurement common to the social and behavioral sciences. The taxonomy we will use was originally proposed by Stevens (1946, 1951) and is the most frequently cited scheme for classifying measurement.

Nominal scale

The nominal scale is the most basic and least informative level of measurement. Nominal measurement simply "names" categories of events, items, or individuals. Reliability of measurement is judged solely by the accuracy with which categorization occurs. A reliable nominal scaling of "gender" accurately distinguishes between men and women. A reliable nominal scaling of hair color reliably categorizes individuals as being brunettes, blondes, and redheads. Finally, the reliable nominal scaling of language utterance may include the categories declarative and interrogatory.

To be reliable, nominal scales must include two or more mutually exclusive categories. These categories must be based on objective standards. Finally, they cannot be numerically related in any manner other than being different. Values such as greater than/less than, older/younger, and bigger/smaller should not be relevant to the categories.

While numbers are often used in nominal measurement, the actual numeric value offers no meaning. To be a true nominal scale, numbers are used only to indicate the name of the category. Type 1 and type 2 personality, for example, indicates nominal scaling since the numbers 1 and 2 simply name the category. Room numbers or street addresses similarly indicate nominal scaling. Finally, a researcher may use numbers to designate categories of individuals for computer management of data. The label 1 may be used to identify all individuals living on the East Coast, 2 may correspond with the Midwest, 3 may correspond with the West Coast, and so on.

Note that the numbers in the preceding example imply no relative value. The only relationship between type 1 and type 2 personality is that they represent exclusive sets of characteristics. The number 1 does not imply that the personality type comes first, is smaller, or is less significant.

Manipulation of numbers from nominal scaling is limited to the simple reporting of frequencies within the category. It is inappropriate to use arithmetic manipulations including addition, subtraction, multiplication, or division on nominal data. Imagine the misinterpretation that would result from subtracting baseball players' uniform numbers to produce conclusions about team status. Uniform numbers simply "name" players. They suggest no quantitative or value difference.

Ordinal Scale

The ordinal scale provides the next higher level of information. Beyond identifying objects, events, or individuals, the ordinal scale identifies relative position. Reliability of measurement is judged by the accuracy with which relative positions are established. A reliable ordinal scaling of "beauty" accurately orders objects or individuals from unattractive to attractive. A reliable ordinal scaling of "team performance" accurately orders teams from worst to best. Finally, a reliable ordinal scaling of "wealth" accurately orders individuals from poor to wealthy.

To be reliable, ordinal scales must include an objective criterion for ordering objects, events, or individuals. This criterion must conform with the transitivity postulate. This postulate is illustrated by the expression: If *a* is greater than *b,* and *b* is greater than *c,* then *a* is greater than *c.* Depending on the objective standard, the transitivity postulate may include the value statements: "less than," "more recent than," "bigger than," or "older than."

As in nominal scales, ordinal scales commonly use numeric designations. Again, however, the manner in which numbers are manipulated is limited by the level of measurement. The numbers 1 and 2 are differentiated only in that 1 precedes 2 or possesses less of some characteristic. The number 1 does not imply that the item, event, or person has half the characteristic possessed by the item, event, or person with the designation 2. It is improper to say that the difference between the number 1 rated coffee pot and the number 2 rated coffee pot is the same as the difference between the numbers 9 and 10 coffee pots. One can only say that the rank order difference between the two pairs is the same. The rank order difference between 1 and 2, and 9 and 10, is one position. The relative arithmetic difference can range from being less than, equal to, or greater than each other.

To emphasize, the only consideration in an ordinal scale is relative position. It is misleading to compute or report differences between numbers or the ratio of numbers. Consequently, statistical methods for summarizing ordinal data are limited to those not assuming equal interval measurement between scale positions such as median (middle score in a set of scores) and rank correlation (relative position of scores in associated data sets). As we noted earlier, arithmetic manipulations are not used with nominal data. Therefore, methods appropriate for nominal data are also appropriate for ordinal data.

Interval Scale

This level of measurement provides information not available in ordinal and nominal scales. Interval measurement, as is implied by the name, provides uniform differences between scale units. The 0 value on the scale is established through convention.

The Fahrenheit scale exemplifies interval measurement. The difference between 30 and 40 degrees is 10 Fahrenheit. The difference between 15 and 20 degrees Fahrenheit is 5 degrees. The temperature associated with 0 Fahrenheit is arbitrary and is a uniformly agreed upon standard that has no objective basis. It does not imply an absence of temperature as 0 centimeters implies an absence of length or 0 grams implies an absence of weight.

Using another example, a player's golf handicap of 10 is seven greater than that of a player with a handicap of three. It is 10 greater than a "scratch" player. As in Fahrenheit measurement, the 0 value is not based on an objective standard; it is determined by convention. The United

States Golf Association can easily change the standard (possibly to account for better equipment or courses) so that the current 0 handicap becomes a handicap of one or two. This will not alter the accuracy of numeric differences between handicaps, only the convention for establishing the zero point on the scale.

Because the zero point is arbitrary, it is misleading to form comparisons based on ratios. We can say that the difference between an IQ of 60 and 120 is 60 IQ points. Since the IQ value of 0 is arbitrary (e.g., there is no objective standard for an absence of intelligence), we cannot say that the person with an IQ of 120 is twice as smart as the person with an IQ of 60.

We will use a brief example to illustrate this limitation of interval scaling. Let's assume that we construct a criterion referenced measure of mathematics. The instrument includes 10 items. One child obtains a score of 5 and another obtains a score of 10. We would be tempted to say that the first student was half as proficient as the second. However, because we arbitrarily determine the 0 point by the nature of items included in the exam, this statement would be incorrect. To demonstrate this, we could add 5 very easy items to the exam. This would change the first youth's score to 10 and the second's score to 15. Using the same erroneous logic, we would say that the first youth was a third as proficient as the second. This change in judgment resulted solely from moving the arbitrary zero point. No actual change in performance occurred.

We must emphasize that interval scaling not only results from equal numeric differences in the measuring instrument, but also from equal differences in the characteristic being assessed. For example, we could develop the following attitude scale item:

How often do you think children should say silent prayers?

(1)	(2)	(3)	(4)
Hourly	Daily	Weekly	Never

Although numeric values with equal interval spacing are used, it is clear that equal spacing does not exist for the attitude being measured. Most people would agree that the difference between believing in hourly prayer and daily prayer is substantially closer than the difference between weekly prayer and no prayer. In this case, the scale is actually ordinal since the numbers do not indicate true equal interval differences.

The most common statistical methods are appropriately used with interval scaling. Computing mean, variance, standard deviation, and conducting t tests, analysis of variance, and regression require equal interval assumptions but do not require the assumption of a fixed zero point.

Ratio Scale

This is the highest and most complete form of measurement. Not only are equal intervals provided, but there is also a true zero point as an anchor to the scale. Ratio scaling is not common in social and behavioral sciences. Those that do exist generally involve the measurement of physical properties such as length, weight, volume, speed, and force. In each example, there is an objective zero point corresponding with the absence of the property. Since this objective zero point exists, one can confidently claim that a child is twice as tall, twice as heavy, twice as fast, twice as strong, and so on, as another child.

Because of the completeness of information in a ratio scale, all statistical procedures can be used effectively. As with interval scaling, these include procedures that involve the use of addition and subtraction. Unlike interval scaling, procedures may also include the use of multiplication and division.

ORGANIZING RAW DATA

The raw data you collected during your research project must be organized prior to analysis and interpretation. Frequency distributions and graphic displays are most commonly used to organize data. We will discuss these procedures separately.

Frequency Distributions

An *array,* the most basic frequency distribution, is appropriate for very small data sets. It includes a single column listing the scores of all subjects in an ascending or descending order. Figure 11.1 illustrates the use of an array for the efficiency ratings of 10 businesses. Note that the range is from 100 to 87 and the median or middle rating is 93. Note also that several stores had the same rating of 93. As will be discussed later, this is described as the modal rating.

Rank Order Distribution

The rank order distribution, also for limited data sets, is slightly more complex but easier to interpret. Figure 11.2 is a rank order distribution that includes a table of quiz grades for 11 students. The rank order distribution includes three columns. The first column identifies all possible test scores ordered from the lowest to the highest. The second column includes one tally for each subject obtaining the associated score. The third column includes the number of tallies for the score. Note that the tallies offer a crude graphic representation of the frequency distribution. One can easily see that the median, or middle score, and the modal, or most common score, was 7.

Grouped Frequency Distribution

The grouped frequency distribution is the final and most complex method of constructing a frequency distribution. It is appropriate for larger data sets (e.g., 20 subjects or more). The first column includes a series of carefully constructed class intervals. The second column includes tallies

Store Efficiency Ratings	
Location	Rating
Gettysburg	100
State College	98
Chambersburg	96
Harrisburg	93
York	93
Lancaster	93
Reading	91
Intercourse	89
Bloomsburg	88
Snow Shoe	87

Figure 11.1 **Array of Efficiency Ratings**

for each class interval. The third column includes a frequency for each interval. Figure 11.3 illustrates the use of a grouped frequency distribution for summarizing weight loss data for clients of a nutrition center.

To establish class intervals, determine the optimum number of intervals. Generally, between 10 and 20 are appropriate. An excessive number of intervals will "flatten" the distribution,

Score	Tally	Frequency
10	/	1
9	//	2
8	//	2
7	////	4
6	//	2
5	/	1
4	/	1
3		0
2		0
1		0

Figure 11.2 Rank Order Distribution Quiz Grades

Weight loss	Tally	Frequency
91–100 lbs.	//	2
81–90	///	3
71–80	/////	5
61–70	//////	6
51–60	////////	8
41–50	/////////	9
31–40	//////////	10
21–30	//////	6
11–20	//	2
1–10	/	1

Figure 11.3 Grouped Frequency Distribution
for Weight Loss Data

making it difficult to interpret. Having too few will obscure meaningful differences. Next, determine the width of the interval. Subtract the lowest score from the highest score to obtain the range in raw scores. Divide this value by the number of intervals and round to the nearest whole number. Odd interval widths are preferred because they produce a whole number for the midpoint of the interval. When interval widths are 10 or more, multiples of five are recommended.

Additional columns may be added to a frequency distribution for clarity of data summary or to support specific conclusions. For example, Figure 11.4 includes a column reporting cumulative frequencies. Figure 11.5 reports the percentage of subjects within each interval. Also, classes can be formed using descriptions of demographic features as opposed to numeric values as is illustrated in Figure 11.6.

GRAPHIC DISPLAY

You can communicate pages of textual information through a single graphic display. Such displays facilitate the development of effective result and discussion sections for research reports.

Histograms

Histograms are the most commonly used method for graphically representing data. A histogram is a two dimensional representation of the frequency of occurrence for each score. The vertical axis

Test Score	Frequency per Interval	Cumulative Frequency
13–15	7	40
10–12	10	33
7–9	13	23
4–6	6	10
0–3	4	4

Figure 11.4 **Frequency Distribution Reporting Cumulative Frequencies**

Consumer Satisfaction Ratings	Frequency	Percentage
41–50	15	10%
31–40	33	22
21–30	42	28
11–20	36	24
0–10	24	16

Figure 11.5 **Frequency Distribution Including Percentage of Subjects Within Each Interval**

Demographic Features	Frequency	Percentage
Sex		
Male	121	30%
Female	279	70
Age		
5–9	113	28
10–14	147	37
15–19	140	35
IQ Level		
81–90	33	8
91–100	47	12
101–110	131	33
111–120	102	26
121–130	87	22
Grade Average		
0–.9	11	3
1–1.9	36	9
2–2.9	76	19
3–3.9	145	36
4–5	132	33

Figure 11.6 Frequency Distribution Using Descriptions of Demographic Features

depicts frequencies, while the horizontal axis depicts lowest to highest rank ordered scores. Figure 11.7 illustrates a basic histogram. Figure 11.8 demonstrates the use of a histogram to compare scores. Notice that frequencies for each score interval are indicated for two conditions, urban and rural.

Frequency Polygons

Frequency polygons are also commonly used to display data. Frequency polygons are similar to histograms except that single points are used instead of bars. These points may be connected by

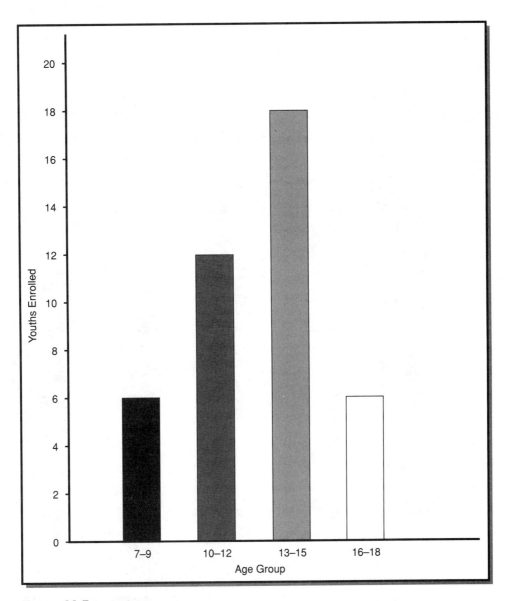

Figure 11.7 A Basic Histogram

straight lines to illustrated trends in the data. Figure 11.9 is a frequency polygon using the same data used in the histogram depicted in Figure 11.7.

Be aware that the vertical scale may distort or misrepresent frequency data. Note that while Figures 11.7 and 11.9 report the same data, we have used different vertical scales. The scale in Figure 11.7 magnifies differences between scores, while the scale in Figure 11.9 minimizes differences. The critical reader must judge the appropriateness of the frequency scale before making judgments from the pictorial representation.

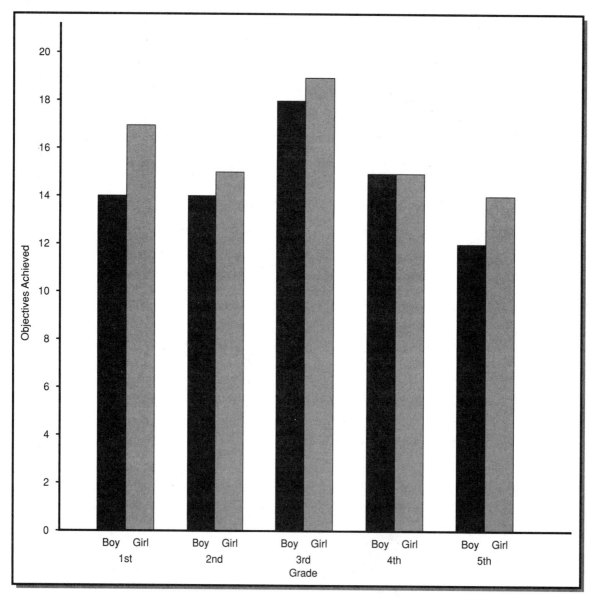

Figure 11.8 A Histogram Used to Compare Groups

Cumulative Frequency Curves

Cumulative frequency curves are similar to frequency polygons except that the cumulative number of subjects within each score range is reported from the lowest to the highest class interval. Cumulative frequency curves are useful for indicating the overall position of a subject in a group as opposed to the shape of the distribution. Figure 11.10 illustrates the use of a cumulative frequency curve.

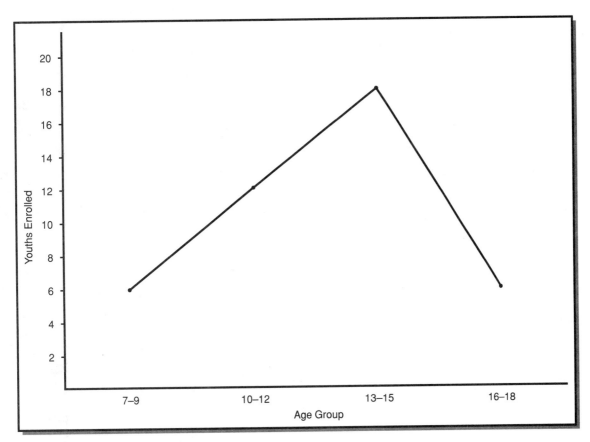

Figure 11.9 A Frequency Polygon

Scatterplot Diagrams

Scatterplot diagrams graphically represent the relationship between two variables. The vertical, or *y*, axis indicates performance on one variable. The horizontal, or *x*, axis indicates performance on another variable. Each point is the intersection of the two scores for an individual subject. The scatterplot diagram A in Figure 11.11 illustrates a strong positive relationship. Subjects with low performance on the *x* variable have low performance on the *y* variable. Subjects with high performance on the *x* variable have high performance on the *y* variable. Scatterplot diagram B illustrates no relationship between the *x* and *y* variables. Low performance on the *x* variable is equally likely to correspond with high, medium, or low performance on the *y* variable. Scatterplot diagram C illustrates a strong negative relationship. Subjects with low performance on the *x* variable have high performance on the *y* variable. Subjects with high performance on the *x* variable have low performance on the *y* variable. Finally, scatterplot diagram D illustrates a curvilinear relationship in which *y* is high only when *x* is low or high.

Note that the closer the points are to the trend line, the stronger the relationship. Diagram A in Figure 11.12 illustrates a strong positive relationship when contrasted with the modest positive relationship depicted in diagram B.

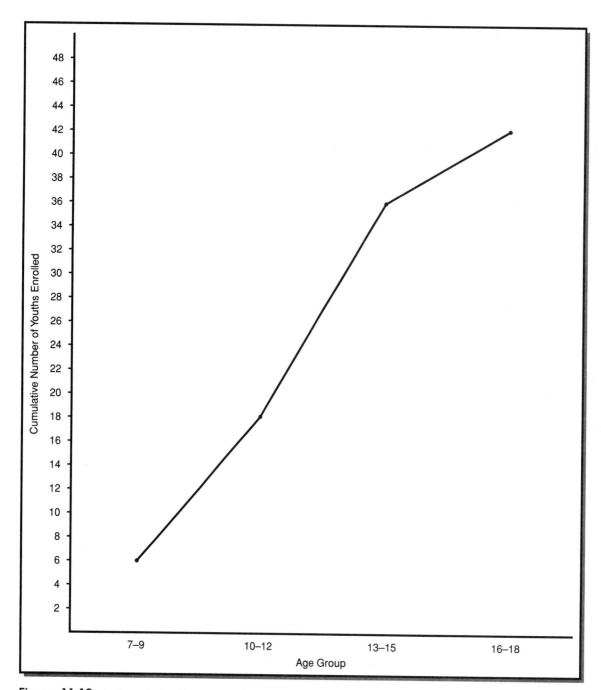

Figure 11.10 A Cumulative Frequency Curve

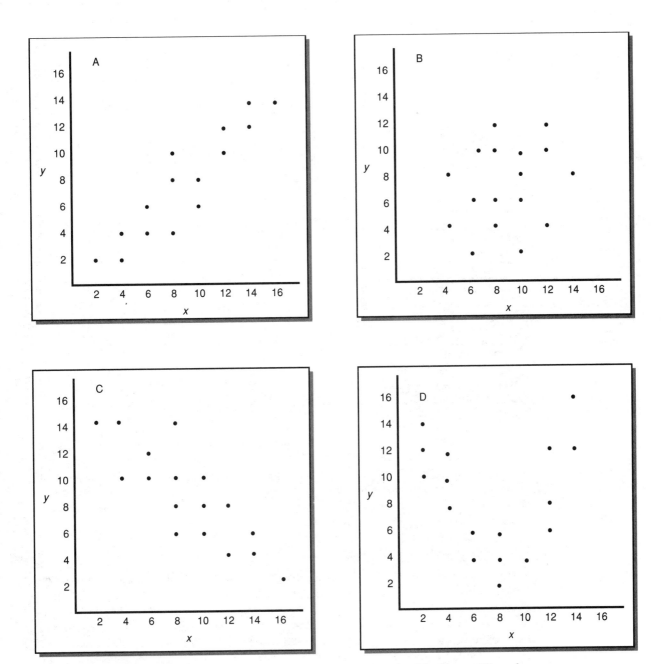

Figure 11.11 Scatter Plot Diagrams Depicting Positive (A), Negative (C), Absent (B), and Curvilinear (D) Relationships

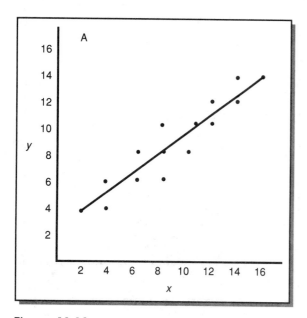 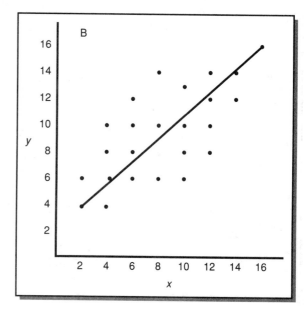

Figure 11.12 Scatter Plot Diagrams Depicting Strong (A) and Weak (B) Positive Relationships

DESCRIPTIVE STATISTICS

Single numbers or indexes can also be used to summarize data. Baseball aficionados quickly recognize the qualities of a hitter with a .300 batting average. The batter makes a base hit 30 times in 100 attempts. We will review the most commonly used descriptive statistics. They include measures of central tendency (specifically, the mean, median, and mode) and measures of variability (specifically, range, quartile deviation, variance, and standard deviation). Finally, they also include correlation as a measure of relationship.

Measures of Central Tendency

The measure of central tendency is a score that represents the typical, or most probable, score from a sample. The *mean* is the most frequently used measure of central tendency. It is also referred to as the *arithmetic average.* It is computed by summing all scores and dividing by the number of scores. Since the computation of mean involves addition of individual scores, it requires interval or ratio data and is not appropriately used with nominal or ordinal data. The *median* is the midpoint in distribution. Fifty percent of the cases lie above the median, and 50 percent lie below the median. Since the size of individual scores is not considered in computing the median, it is appropriate for use with ordinal data. The *mode* is the most frequently occurring score in a distribution. In some cases, a distribution may have two or more high frequency occurrences. This distribution is referred to as a bimodal, or multimodal, distribution. Though seldom used in educational research, mode can be applied to nominal scales. Figure 11.13 illustrates the computation of mean, median, and mode for a small data set.

Measures of Variability

Besides knowing the typical score from a sample, you may also find it useful to summarize the level of variability in scores. A grade point average of 3.0 may mean that the student "always"

```
Raw Data:   2, 4, 4, 6, 6, 6, 8, 8, 9

Mean:       2 + 4 + 4 + 6 + 6 + 6 + 8 + 8 + 9 = 5.9
            ─────────────────────────────────
                          9

Median:   2   4   4   6   6̲   6   8   8   9 = 6

Mode:     2   4   4   6̲   6̲   6̲   8   8   9 = 6
```

Figure 11.13 Computation of Mean, Median, and Mode for a Sample Data Set

earns B's. Alternately, it may mean that he earns a substantial number of A's with a few D's and C's.

Imagine contracting with a steelworks firm to build a nuclear reactor containment building. Would you be content to know that a company's average quality rating was "superior" without also knowing the range of performance? You would hope that there was minimal variability in ratings (e.g., ratings were uniformly superior) as opposed to being dispersed (e.g., substandard ratings being offset by higher ratings).

The most basic and easily understood measure of variability is *range*. Range is the difference between the lowest score and the highest score. For example, the range in geographical size of the 50 states is 560,899 square miles, from 1,054 square miles for Rhode Island to 570,833 for Alaska. The range in population is 26,568,000 people, from 512,000 for Wyoming to 27,080,000 for California.

As you can see from the preceding example, range is very easy to compute. Only the lowest and highest scores for the sample are required. Mathematical calculations are limited to subtraction. Unfortunately, the range may not be an adequate measure of variability for many data sets. The range only accounts for the most extreme scores; it does not account for scores closer to the mean. An atypically high or low score can leave the appearance of a highly variable data set when the data are actually very similar. For example, indicating a mean of 11 and range of 10 suggests wide variability in data. In fact, if a single extreme score is excluded, the numbers may be very homogeneous (e.g., 4, 4, 4, 5, 5, 5, 5, 6, 6, 16).

Quartile Deviation

Quartile deviation overcomes this limitation of range by using additional data in the computation of variability. Quartile deviation is one half of the difference between the higher and lower quartiles in the data set. Assuming a higher quartile of 12 and a lower quartile of 4, the quartile deviation is 4. The higher quartile is the point above which 25 percent of the cases lie (i.e., the 75th percentile). The middle quartile, corresponding to the median, is the point at which an equal number of cases is higher and lower. The lower quartile is the point below which 25 percent of the cases lie (i.e., the 25th percentile).

Variance and Standard Deviation

Variance and standard deviation are the most complete measure of variability. They require interval data as both the location and magnitude of each score is included in the computation.

Variance is the mean of squared deviation scores. A deviation score is the difference between a single score in the data set and the mean for the data set. Deviation scores are squared because, by definition, the sum of deviations from the mean is always 0. For example, the mean for the data set 2, 4, 4, 6, 8, 9, and 9 is 6. The deviations from 6 are $+4, +2, +2, 0, -2, -3,$ and -3 respectively. The sum of these deviations is 0. Squares of both positive and negative numbers are positive so that the sum of squared deviations will retain the relative magnitude of differences from the mean as well as a positive sign. The squared deviations from the preceding example are 16, 4, 4, 0, 4, 9, and 9. The sum of the squared deviations is 46. Finally, the mean of the sum of squared deviations, or variance, is 6.6.

The formula for these computations is as follows:

$$S^2 = \frac{\Sigma x^2}{N - 1}$$

S^2 = variance
Σ = sum
x = deviation score
N = number of scores in the data set

As noted earlier, variance is the sum of the squared deviation scores. Since deviation scores are squared, the resulting value is not in the same measurement scale that comprised the original data set. This makes the variance of a data set difficult to interpret.

Standard deviation is the square root of the variance score. It is an alternative that includes all of the favorable aspects of variance while retaining the original measurement scale. Because of these attributes, it is the most commonly used measure of variability.

Consider the data set 2, 4, 8, 8, 16, 16, 16, 19, 19, and 22. The mean is 13 and the respective deviation scores are 11, 9, 5, 5, $-3, -3, -3, -6, -6,$ and -9. The squares of the deviation scores are 121, 81, 25, 25, 9, 9, 9, 36, 36, and 81. The mean of the squared deviation scores, or variance, is 43.2. The square root of the variance, or standard deviation, is 6.6. Given the common measurement scale, one can say that the average score is 6.6 units from the mean of the data set. The formula for the preceding computations is as follows:

$$S = \sqrt{\frac{\Sigma x^2}{N - 1}}$$

S = standard deviation
Σ = sum
x = deviation score
N = number of scores in the data set

Statisticians have developed an alternative formula that is more easily used when the mean of the data set is not a round number. This formula is as follows:

$$S = \sqrt{\frac{\Sigma x^2 - \frac{(\Sigma x)^2}{N}}{N - 1}}$$

S = standard deviation
Σx^2 = sum of the squares of each score (i.e., square all scores and add)
$(\Sigma x)^2$ = sum of scores squared (i.e., add all scores and then square)
N = number of scores in the data set

It is important to note that both standard deviation and variance are based not only on the relative position but also on measurement differences between points. Therefore, they can be used only with interval or ratio data. When ordinal data are used, only range and quartile deviation can be used.

STANDARD SCORES

Researchers and practitioners often wish to judge the relative performance of individuals on difference measures. This is difficult if means and standard deviations for the measures are different. Consider the admissions judgments of colleges and universities that accept both the American College Test and the Scholastic Aptitude Test. If the ACT cutoff score is 18, what should the SAT cutoff score be? Is a student with an SAT score of 580 a better admissions risk than a student with an ACT score of 24?

To answer these questions, test scores can be translated through use of a standard metric, *z score*. A z-score is defined as the distance in standard deviation units of an individual score. A score that is one standard deviation above the mean is a z score of $+1$. A score two standard deviations above the mean is a z score of $+2$. A score one standard deviation below the mean is a z score of -1. A score two standard deviations below the mean is a z score of -2. Finally, a score that coincides with the mean produces a z score of 0.

The following formula is used to compute z scores:

$$z = \frac{X - \overline{X}}{S} = \frac{x}{S}$$

X = individual score
$\overline{X}$ = mean of all scores
S = standard deviation of all scores
x = distance of the individual score from the mean $(X - \overline{X})$

As you have seen, z scores below the mean are reported as negative numbers. A similar descriptive statistic, the *t* score, was developed to overcome this limitation. While z scores have a mean of 0 and a standard deviation of 1 *t* (allowing for a score 1 standard deviation below the mean to be a z score of -1), *t* scores have a mean of 50 and a standard deviation of 10. A z score of -1 corresponds with a *t* score of 40 and a standard deviation of -1. A z score of 3 corresponds with a *t* score of 80 and a standard deviation of 3. The discussion of the normal curve and Figure 11.14 provides additional information on the relationship between these scores.

The scatterplots described earlier in this chapter are pictorial representations of the relationship between data sets. Statistics that indicate a relationship are referred to as *correlation coefficients*. A correlation coefficient summarizes these data into a single number.

As illustrated in Table 11.1, there are a number of types of correlation coefficients. Each serves a specific function based on the nature of data being correlated. Regardless of the type, all correlation coefficients are interpreted in the same manner. They can range from 0 (denoting no relationship between data sets) to $+1$ (indicating an exact positive relationship) to -1 (indicating an exact negative relationship).

For most research purposes, a correlation coefficient of 0 to 0.40 demonstrates too low of a relationship to be of practical importance. Correlations in the 0.30 to 0.40 range may, however, have theoretical implications. Correlations over 0.41 are generally judged to be sufficiently strong to have practical or theoretical value. It should be noted that while correlations in the 0.80 to 1.0 range identify a very strong relationship, they are seldom obtained in research on human performance.

Table 11.1 Characteristics and Uses of Common Correlational Methods

Product-moment correlation (r)

Used to produce stable estimates of relationship when both variables are continuous.

Rank-difference correlation or Rho (ρ)

Used to estimate relationship in larger sets of numbers (e.g., 10 to 30) when both variables are ordinal.

Kendall's Tau (τ)

Used to estimate a relationship in smaller number sets (e.g., fewer than ten) when both variables are ordinal.

Biserial correlation (r_{bis})

Used to estimate a relationship when one variable is artificially dichotomous and the other is continuous. Biserial correlation is often used to analyze items in test construction. Correlation coefficients may exceed 1.

Point-biserial correlation (r_{pbis})

Used to estimate a relationship when one variable is truly dichotomous and the other is continuous. Point-biserial correlation is also used to analyze items in test construction. Correlation coefficients are smaller than those found in biserial correlation.

Tetrachoric correlation (r_t)

Used to estimate a relationship when both variables are artificially dichotomous.

Phi coefficient (ϕ)

Used to estimate a relationship when both variables are truly dichotomous. Often used to calculate inter-item correlations on multiple choice test items.

Correlations are used to make predictions from one set of data to another. For example, a strong positive relationship exists between salary and investment spending. The higher a person's earnings, the larger his or her investment portfolio. The stronger the correlation, the more confident you may be in the prediction or estimation. If a perfect relationship (or correlation of +1) exists, you can predict the precise size of the portfolio based on the individual's salary. If no relationship (or a correlation of 0) exists, investment spending is completely random as related to earning, and one set of data cannot be predicted from the other.

Strong negative correlations are just as effective in making predictions as strong positive correlations. The only difference between the two is in the direction of prediction. In a strong negative correlation, a high value for one variable predicts a low value for the other variable. This may be exemplified by the correlation between body weight and foot speed. The larger the body weight, the slower the foot speed.

Care should be taken in selecting an appropriate correlational statistic. *The Pearson product moment correlation* is the most commonly used measure of relationship. As noted in Table 11.1, however, it requires interval or ratio measurement and is not appropriately used with ordinal data. *Spearman rho correlation coefficient* is used for ordinal data. To assess the relationship between a continuous interval or ratio variable and an artificial dichotomous nominal variable, *biserial correlations* are used. Relationships between two artificial dichotomous nominal variables requires

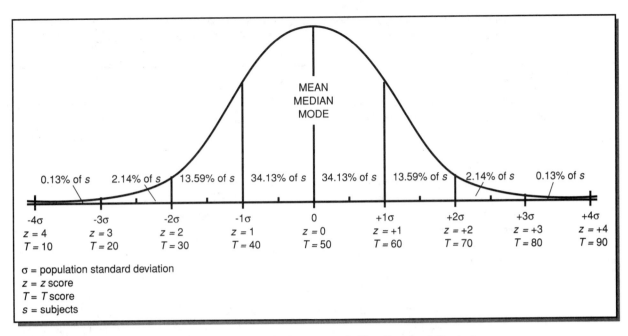

Figure 11.14 Characteristics of the Normal Distribution Including Standard Deviations, *z* Scores and *T* Scores

the use of *Tetrachoric correlation.* Relationships between two artificial dichotomous nominal variables requires the use of *Phi coefficient.* A true dichotomous variable represents a factual distinction without imposition of an arbitrary rule. For example, male/female, correct/incorrect, won/loss, rejected/retained, and so on are true dichotomous variables. Artificial dichotomous variables are derived by establishing a demarcation point on a continuous scale. Examples include high achieving/low achieving, tall/short, heavy/light, active/passive.

A high correlation between two variables does not indicate that one variable caused the other. Rather, it simply means that the two variables are associated. This association can be caused by any number of third variables. For example, birth weight and intelligence may correlate positively. The heavier an infant at birth, the more likely he or she will produce a high intelligence score. One cannot say that birth weight causes intelligence. As an alternative explanation, high birth weight and intelligence can both be the product of the third variable, prenatal care.

The size of a correlation coefficient must be judged with reference to the variability of scores being correlated. All things being equal, the more diverse the distribution of scores being correlated, the larger the correlation coefficient. The less diverse, the smaller the correlation. One would expect weak correlations between scores on parallel criterion referenced tests that are administered following instruction. This results from the restriction of the distributions at the upper range. A larger correlation may be obtained prior to instruction, since a wide range in scores is included in the samples.

Similarly, the size of the correlation must be judged against the purpose for which the data are being used. Higher correlation coefficients should be expected of instruments used to restrict personal liberty (e.g., admission to college, hospitalization, or professional licensing). Instruments used to provide guidance may not be held to the same standard for predictive ability.

A correlation coefficient cannot be interpreted to indicate the percentage of correspondence between variables. For example, a Pearson of 0.50 does not mean that the prediction is half that found in a Pearson of 1.0 or twice as strong as a Pearson of 0.25. Similarly, a Spearman rho correlation of 0.75 does not indicate accurate predictions three-fourths of the time.

THE NORMAL CURVE

The vast majority of human characteristics (e.g., height, weight, intelligence, academic achievement, etc.) distribute on a normal curve. The normal curve is a frequency polygon in which the curve's height at a point representing a given score shows the number of cases obtaining that score.

As shown in Figure 11.14, knowing that scores distribute normally helps interpret descriptive statistics and standard scores. For scores that distribute within a normal curve, the largest number of cases occur in the middle of the distribution. The further one goes in either direction (representing progressively larger and smaller scores), the fewer the cases obtaining the score. Specific characteristics of the normal curve are that the mean, or average score, is also the mode, or most frequently obtained score, and the median, or middle score. Further, the normal curve is symmetrical. That is, the probability of obtaining a score a given number of units above the mean is equal to the probability of obtaining a score the same number of units below the mean.

Scores under the normal curve can be divided into equal units, each a standard deviation in length, to assist in summarizing and interpreting data. Each standard deviation includes a constant number of scores. As illustrated in Figure 11.14, a score that is one standard deviation above the mean includes 84.13 percent of all cases. A score that is three standard deviations above the mean includes 99.87 percent of all cases. Of all cases, 68.26 percent are within a standard deviation of the mean, while 95.44 percent of all cases are within two standard deviations of the mean.

As discussed earlier, standard scores are derived from standard deviation units. You will note in Figure 11.15 that a z score of 1 and a T score of 60 correspond with one standard deviation above the mean. A z score of 0 and T score of 50 represent the mean. Finally, a z score of 3 and a T score of 80 correspond with a location 3 standard deviations above the mean.

As emphasized earlier, methods reviewed in this section are used to describe and depict raw data. Methods for drawing objective conclusions from the raw data are discussed in the following chapter.

SUMMARY

Descriptive statistics and graphic displays are used to organize, summarize, and interpret raw data. The selection of specific methods for organizing and describing data depend in part on the level of measurement employed in data collection. We described four major levels of measurement. Nominal scaling is the most basic and least informative. It simply involves identifying items, individuals, or events by name. Use of arithmetic manipulations entries within a category is not appropriate. Ordinal scaling is the next higher level of measurement. Entries on an ordinal scale are distinguished by their relative positions. As with nominal scaling, it is inappropriate to compute relative differences between items within an ordinal scale. We are limited to indicating procedures that simply rank order observations (i.e., indicate the number of observations above a given rank, or indicate changes in rank order). Interval scaling, unlike nominal and ordinal scaling, includes information on relative differences between entries in a data set. We can indicate the precise difference in scale units between observations. Consequently, arithmetic manipulations that underlie the vast majority of parametric tests can be used with interval data. Interval measurement is limited, however, in that the 0 point on the scale is established through convention. Ratio scaling is the most complete form of measurement. It possesses all of the properties of interval measurement. In addition, ratio scaling includes an objective "0" point. All statistical procedures used in interval measurement can be used in ratio measurement. Procedures involving the use of multiplication and division in forming ratios are also appropriate.

Frequency distributions and graphic displays are commonly used to organize and present data. Arrays are the most commonly used method for constructing a frequency distribution in small data sets. Rank order distributions are commonly used for larger data sets. Grouped frequency distributions are similar to rank order distributions except that they include a range of scores as opposed to discrete scores. Graphic displays are used to pictorially represent data trends. Options include histograms, frequency polygons, cumulative frequency curves, and scatterplot diagrams.

Data are also summarized using descriptive statistics. There are two major sets of descriptive statistics. The first, measures of central tendency, represents the most probable score from a data set. These measures include the mean, or the arithmetic average, the median, or the midpoint of all scores, and the mode, or the most frequently occurring score in the distribution. The second class of descriptive statistics, which includes measures of variability such as range and quartile deviation, overcomes this limitation by reporting one half of the difference between the higher and lower quartiles in the data.

Variance and standard deviation are the most complete measure of variability. Variance is the mean of squared deviation scores for the data set. Deviation scores are computed by determining the difference between all scores and the average score for the data set. Standard deviation is the square root of the deviation score. It is preferred in many cases to variance since it retains the original measurement scale. Computation of variance and standard deviation require interval and ratio data.

Standard scores are used to judge the relative performance of individuals on different measures. To meet this objective, scores that may be reported using different scales must be reported within a common scale. The z score is the most commonly used standard score. A z score is the distance between scores in standard deviation units.

Measures of relationship, or correlation coefficients, are used to indicate the extent to which two sets of scores are related. Correlations may range from $+1$, indicating a highly positive relationship, to -1, indicating a highly negative relationship. A correlation of 0 indicates the absence of a relationship between the data sets.

REFERENCES

Stevens, S. S. (1946). On the theory of scales of measurement. *Science, 103,* 677–680.

Stevens, S. S. (1951). *Mathematics, measurement, and psychophysics.* In S. S. Stevens (Ed.). *Handbook of experimental psychology.* New York: John Wiley & Sons, Inc.

FURTHER READINGS

Ghauri, P. N., Gronhaug, K., & Kristianslund, I. (1995). *Research methods in business studies: A practical guide.* Upper Saddle River, NJ: Merrill/Prentice Hall.

Graziano, A. M., & Raulin, M. L. (1996). *Research methods: A process of inquiry.* (3rd ed.) New York: Harper and Row.

Johnson, J. B., & Joslyn, R. A. (1994). *Political science research methods* (3rd ed.). Washington, DC: CQ Press.

Johnson, E. S. (1981). *Research methods in criminology and criminal justice.* Upper Saddle River, NJ: Merrill/Prentice Hall.

Manheim, J. B., & Rich, R. C. (1994). *Empirical political analysis: Research methods in political science.* (4th ed.) New York: Longman.

Webb, J. R. (1992). *Understanding and designing marketing research.* San Diego: Academic Press.

Zikmund, W. G. (1996). *Business research methods* (5th ed.). Chicago: Dryden Press.

12

Analyzing Data from Large Group Quantitative Research

INTRODUCTION

Information from the Chapter 11 is useful in summarizing large amounts of data. Frequency distributions, graphic displays, measures of variability, central tendency, use of standard scores, and measures of relationship assist the researcher and research consumers in describing complex research outcomes. We use these methods to indicate patterns of responding and the strength of responses within and between groups. Common examples of their use are seen in sports statistics. A baseball player is described as hitting 49 home runs and having a batting average of .289 (almost 3 hits every 10 times at bat). A football team averages 14 points a game while holding other teams to 7 points a game. The field goal rate for a basketball team is 48 percent or 48 shots made for every 100 shots attempted.

Descriptive statistics used alone do not allow us to evaluate hypotheses; they only describe outcomes. While humans will never be omniscient or infallible, we often possess sufficient

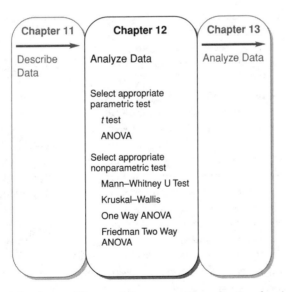

The Scope, Plan, and Sequence Chart for Conducting
Research: The Ninth Step of the Research Process

information to produce reasonable decisions. For example, school district administrators may know the precise number and length of bus runs that will occur in a school year. Estimation based on a limited sample of data is not required as school personnel possess all the data needed to make transportation funding decisions. Similarly, a dietitian may know the precise number of meals required in a nursing home during a calendar year. Confident budget and purchasing decisions can be made directly from these data. In each case, descriptive statistics including frequency, mean, and variance may be sufficient to make decisions.

In many areas, however, all the data from which to make reasonable decisions are not available. It is not likely that we will ever know the consumer preferences of all Americans. We will never know the factors that produce criminal conduct in adolescents. We will not be able to identify the specific methods that enhance reading achievement for all elementary school students.

We often study a sample of individuals when it is not possible to obtain information from all individuals in the population. We then generalize knowledge gained from the limited sample to the broader population. The principal tools used in making these generalizations are referred to as inferential statistics.

This chapter describes strategies used in making inferences from a sample to a population. Special attention is given to the nature and effect of sampling error, the role of the null hypothesis, probability error in testing the null hypothesis, the level of significance, and specific statistical tests.

THE SAMPLING DISTRIBUTION AND SAMPLING ERROR

Any time we make inferences based on a limited number of observations, we introduce the possibility of sampling error. This error is the difference between information obtained from the limited number of observations and the true number that may be obtained if observations were made with all possible cases. For example, it is not possible to know the exact amount of unreported earnings for all hospitality workers in the United States. In the absence of all inclusive data, we are limited to surveying a small number of randomly selected hospitality workers. Those surveyed are described as the *random sample*. The total group of all hospitality workers are described as the *target population*.

Assuming that we obtained an accurate measure of unreported income for each member of the sample, we may conclude that the mean value for the sample is similar to the mean value for the population. Any difference between the mean level of unreported income indicated by our sample and the actual level of unreported income for the population of all hospitality workers would be *sampling error*.

We cannot simply assume that a sample mean represents the population mean. Imagine deciding that all teenagers should have mandatory curfews based on the mean delinquency rate reported for a sample of 12 individuals. How confident would you be in quality ratings of automobiles if the rate of sample defects expected in all cars were based on the study of only a few vehicles?

Statisticians have studied the relationship between sample means and population means. Based on their work, we are able to estimate the degree of sampling error that one may expect based on the size of the sample and the population. The principle that underlies this estimate is referred to as the *central limit theorem*.

The central limit theorem has several major implications for the estimation of sampling error. First, *sample size and sampling error are negatively correlated.* As sample size increases, sampling error decreases. Second, regardless of whether or not the target population is normally distributed, *means of equal-sized samples will distribute normally.* Third, *the mean of all equal-sized sample means is the same as the mean of the target population.* Finally, *the standard deviation of equal-sized sample means describes the standard error of the mean.*

The actual mean of the target population may not be known to the researcher. However, computation of the standard error of the mean provides a reasonable estimate of the probability that a given sample mean emulates the mean for the target population.

Probability Testing

One major function of inferential statistics is to determine if a sample mean accurately reflects a given population mean. We can hypothesize that a pair of dice is "loaded," i.e., doesn't roll fairly. To illustrate this example, we agree that a pair of dice is loaded if 7 turns up in 5 of 10 trials. Therefore, the hypothesized population mean of 5 indicates the average number of times 7 turns up in an infinite number of sets of 10 rolls. Since it is not possible (or necessary) to roll the dice an infinite number of times, we agree to a sample of 30 sets of 10 rolls. If our hypothesis is correct, the average for the 30 sets of 10 rolls should be approximately 5. This would indicate that the sample mean was the same as the hypothesized population mean.

We record that the actual average for the 30 sets of 10 rolls is 1. Do we now conclude that the sample mean of 1 reflects the hypothesized population mean of 5? Probably not.

The word "probably" was carefully selected. You will recall that the central limit theorem indicates that sample data will distribute normally around the population mean. By chance alone, some of the samples will yield an average of 1 even when the population mean is 5.

Inferential Statistics

Inferential statistics indicate how likely it is for a sample to yield an average rate of one 7 in 10 trials. In this case, it would be very unlikely for a sample mean of 1 to be drawn from a population with a mean of 5. Based on the central limit theorem, the largest number of samples would have a mean of 5, and the more disparate the sample mean is from 5, the less common. In fact, since the standard error of the mean for dice rolling is relatively small, a sample mean of 1 would appear in fewer than one percent of all cases.

Returning to our original question, would we conclude that the sample we obtained was drawn from the hypothesized population? In other words, did the performance of the dice indicate that they were from a population of "loaded dice" or "fair dice"?

To answer this question objectively, we need a decision rule indicating the level of probability at which we will no longer accept that a sample represents the hypothesized population. To avoid bias and enhance objectivity, this rule is established in advance of collecting data. As will be discussed later, most researchers accept 0.05 as the level of probability beyond which a sample is concluded as being drawn from a population other than the hypothesized population. In our case, the sample mean of 1 would be expected in fewer than 5 in 100 samples given a population mean of 5. Therefore, we reject the hypothesis indicating that the dice were loaded and conclude that they are fair.

THE NULL HYPOTHESIS

We emphasized in the preceding example that differences between the sample and hypothesized population could be explained by two phenomena. First, differences could be due to chance alone. This was also referred to as sampling error. Second, differences could be due to the sample not actually representing the hypothesized population. In other words, the sample is drawn from a population of fair dice as opposed to loaded dice.

Since it is not possible to know the actual mean for all samples using fair and loaded dice, we can never be 100 percent certain which population the dice represent. As we noted, we do not indicate our conclusion with absolute certainty. Rather, we indicate that it is sufficiently unlikely that sampling error alone produced the differences in the sample and population means; therefore, the most probable explanation is that they represent different populations.

The explanation based on chance differences between the sample and population means is referred to as the null hypothesis. If differences between the means are easily explained by chance variation in samples (i.e., sampling error), we can say that there is no difference between the sample and the population.

The preceding test of fair or loaded dice was conducted to reject the null hypothesis (i.e., to indicate a small probability that differences are due to sampling error). Stated as an alternate hypothesis, the test was conducted to support the alternative hypothesis. The alternative hypothesis indicates the population that the sample represents if it is not likely that the sample represents the population indicated by the null hypothesis. The outcome of the test of dice was the rejection of the null hypothesis (differences were not attributable to chance alone) and the acceptance of the alternative hypothesis (differences were attributable to the dice not being loaded).

It is important to emphasize that inferential statistics are used in the preceding example as an objective method for rejecting or failing to reject the null hypothesis. They do not lead to the acceptance of a null hypothesis. The test of the null hypothesis determines the probability that the sample mean is different from the population mean. The statistical test does not identify the probability that they are the same.

As noted previously, the failure to detect differences can be attributed to a wide range of other factors (e.g., sample size, precision of measurement, effect size, and homogeneity of the sample). These factors establish statistical power or the probability that an experiment will detect differences that actually exist. The failure to reject the null hypothesis can therefore be explained through limitations of statistical power as opposed to chance differences or the actual absence of differences in sample and population means.

ERRORS IN TESTS OF SIGNIFICANCE

We have emphasized that decision making using inferential statistics is based on limited information. Consequently, resulting decisions are subject to error. Two major errors may occur in inferential tests. They are illustrated in Figure 12.1.

Type I Error

As mentioned in Chapter 1, this error is defined as rejecting a null hypothesis that is actually true. You predict no differences between groups but detect differences that exist through sampling error alone. To emphasize, there are actually no differences attributable to the phenomena under study. Differences are attributed to the chance selection of subjects with disparate scores.

The probability of a Type I is established prior to data collection by determining the level of significance at which the hypothesis will be tested. The level of significance is referred to as *alpha*. Alpha is commonly set at 0.05 through convention. A 0.05 level of confidence indicates that a Type I error will occur in 5 out of 100 samples.

You may use any other alpha level that is consistent with the risks of rejecting a null hypothesis that is actually true. If the consequence of a Type I error is highly damaging, you may establish the alpha level substantially lower than 0.05. For example, setting alpha at 0.001 would result in rejecting a null hypothesis that is actually true only one in 1,000 times. If the consequence of a Type I error is fairly benign, alpha may be set at a level higher than 0.05. For example, setting alpha at 0.10 would result in rejecting a null hypothesis that is actually true 1 in 10 times.

Actual Conclusion Based
on All Possible Samples
from the Population

	Null hypothesis is true	Null hypothesis is false
Rejects Null	Type I Error	No Error
Fails to Reject Null	No Error	Type II Error

Conclusion Based on Given Sample and the Statistical Analysis

Figure 12.1 Type I and Type II Errors

Note that as the alpha level becomes more conservative, the ability to detect actual differences decreases. You must strike a balance between selecting an alpha level that is consistent with the risks of committing a Type I error and still having sufficient statistical power to detect differences when they actually occur.

To illustrate this balance, a study is designed to determine if sprinters eating a protein rich diet are faster than those on a carbohydrate rich diet. Speeds of runners in the two groups are contrasted using a *t* test. Based on the outcome, we may conclude that it is likely or unlikely that the two groups represent distinct populations as defined by the two diets.

Stated in the null form, the researcher predicts no differences between performance in the 100 meter dash for the two groups. The alpha level, or the probability of a Type I error, is set at the .05 level of confidence. This indicates a 5 in 100 chance of rejecting a null hypothesis that is actually true.

Results of the *t* test indicate that (given no actual differences in the two diets), group times are sufficiently different to occur in 5 or fewer of 100 samples. The researcher concludes that since the chance of two groups from the same population producing these times is so low, the groups must represent different populations. That is, sprinters on a protein rich diet and those on a carbohydrate rich diet represent separate populations when judged by their time in the 100 meter dash.

Let's say a number of researchers attempt to replicate this finding using the same methodology and differing only in the specific subjects selected. Each subsequent study results in a failure to reject the null hypothesis (e.g., concluding that there are no differences between groups). In viewing all of the studies, one is left to conclude that the rejection of the null hypothesis in the initial analysis was the result of a Type I error. The null hypothesis was rejected due to sampling error and not because actual differences occurred as a function of diet.

Type II Error

A Type II error occurs when a false null hypothesis is accepted. While two groups do actually represent distinct populations, the researcher fails to detect differences that are sufficiently large and improbable to support this conclusion. Failure to detect differences is a function of the research design and statistical power. Statistical power, as discussed in Chapter 8, is the probability of making a Type II error. It is the actual ability of a study to detect actual differences. Major factors that contribute to power and influence the likelihood of a Type II error are sample size, homogeneity of the sample, measurement precision, alpha level, power efficiency of the statistical procedure, and effect size.

A study is designed to determine if special class placement is superior to placement in mainstream classes. Twenty-four high school students with retardation are studied. Twelve are placed in special classes and 12 are educated in regular classes. Following six weeks of instruction, students are asked to take a standardized achievement test. Differences between groups are analyzed using a t test. This analysis is conducted to determine the likelihood that the mainstream and special class groups represent the population of students with mental retardation in general, or if they represent distinct populations as defined by the two instructional arrangements.

Stated in the null form, the researcher predicts no differences between performance on the achievement test for the two groups. The alpha level, or the probability of a Type I error, is set at .05 by convention. The probability of a Type II error is a function of numerous aspects of the research design and requires knowledge of the anticipated effect size, variance in the dependent measure, and sample size.

Results of the t test indicate that group achievement test scores are not sufficiently different to only occur in 5 or fewer of 100 samples given no actual differences in the two instructional arrangements. The researcher concludes that since the scores of the two groups are easily explained by chance variation in sampling, the groups must represent the same population. Students served in regular and special classes represent the population of students in general, and no differences exist in the two subgroups.

Following this initial study, a number of researchers attempt to replicate the findings. They change the methodology to increase statistical power (i.e., reduce the likelihood of a Type II error). The researchers increase the sample size to 60 in a group. They use curriculum-based measures that are more sensitive to learning. Finally, they extend the length of the educational program to nine months, allowing time for an increased effect size. The subsequent studies result in differences that are expected in fewer than 5 in 100 samples. This leads to the rejection of the null hypothesis (e.g., concluding that differences do exist).

In viewing all of the studies, one is left to conclude that failure to reject the null hypothesis in the initial analysis was the result of a Type II error. The null hypothesis was not rejected due to limited statistical power and not because of the absence of actual differences.

It should be apparent from the preceding discussion that Type I errors lead to the acceptance of ideas or methods that are inaccurate or ineffective. Type II errors lead to the rejection of ideas or methods that are accurate or effective. Type I errors are typically recognized by the failure to support findings of an initial study in subsequent investigations. Type II errors may also be recognized by the failure to replicate findings.

Even prior to replication, a simple analysis of the research methodology may indicate a high probability of a Type II error in studies that fail to detect differences. Knowing that a study has only a 20 percent chance of detecting differences that actually exist at a given effect size may lead you to conclude that the failure to detect differences was due to the design of the study and not the lack of the phenomena's validity.

DIRECTION OF THE STATISTICAL TEST

The region of rejection, or area in which the null is rejected, can be established entirely at one end of the sampling distribution or at both ends of the distribution. An alternative hypothesis may stipulate that men who are dieting will be more aggressive than those who are not dieting. This hypothesis suggests that the null hypothesis will be rejected only if scores on an aggressiveness scale fall at the top 0.05 level of the distribution (assuming that the test is conducted with an alpha of 0.05). Conversely, the hypothesis may indicate simply that there will be differences in aggressiveness between men who are dieting. In this case, alpha of 0.05 is divided into a 0.025 region of rejection at the top of the distribution and 0.025 at the bottom of the region of rejection.

Figure 12.2 illustrates the region of rejection for a one-tailed test. The first sampling distribution is consistent with an alternative hypothesis in which the sample data are expected to be higher than expected in the population. The second sampling distribution is consistent with an alternative hypothesis indicating simply that there will be differences, but the direction of the differences cannot be specified.

A nondirectional statistical test has less power, that is, greater probability of a Type II error when considering only the upper or lower rejection region. Therefore, it is important to specify the direction of the test when research literature or past experiences permit a confident prediction.

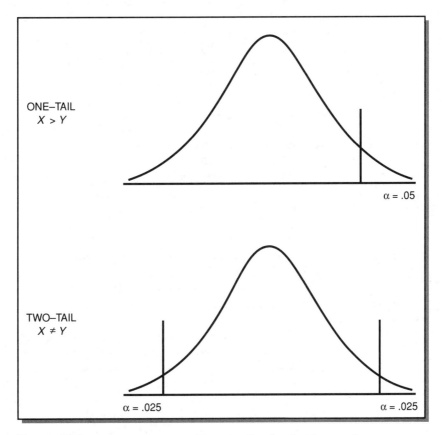

Figure 12.2 Hypothetical Sampling Distribution for One- and Two-Tailed Statistical Tests

PARAMETRIC AND NONPARAMETRIC STATISTICAL TESTS

Statisticians over the past few decades have developed a number of methods for comparing and contrasting data sets. The common goal of each procedure is to determine the probability that the data sets are derived from the same or different populations. A comprehensive analysis of these procedures is beyond the scope of this text. However, we will review the three most commonly used statistical tests. They include the *t* test, one-way analysis of variance, and factorial analysis of variance.

Commonly used statistical tests can be described as being *parametric* or *nonparametric*. Parametric tests rely on the hypothetical sampling distribution discussed previously to make probability judgments. Nonparametric tests make probability judgments without hypothetical distributions. We will describe tests under each category.

Parametric Tests

These tests are the most frequently used research statistics. They are applicable when a set of parametric assumptions are met. First, data being analyzed must at least be on an interval scale. Second, data from each subject must be independent, that is, one person's data must not be affected by another person's data. Third, scores must be normally distributed if a small sample size (e.g., less than 30) is used. Finally, when more than one population is being compared, the populations must have homogeneous distributions.

The *t test* is the most frequently used parametric statistic for comparing two groups. Sample means and standard deviations are used in an equation that yields a *t* value. The *t* value is entered in a table indicating the probability that the two samples are drawn from the same population. Use of the table requires that the researcher stipulate whether a one- or two-tailed test is being conducted. The alpha level and the degrees of freedom (number of scores or observations in the sample that are free to vary) are also required.

Variations of the formula are used depending on whether independent means or dependent means are being contrasted. The *t test for independent means* is used when all subjects in one group are unrelated to those in the second group. This usually results from subjects being drawn at random from a population and being randomly assigned to one of two groups. Independence may also result from subjects being selected at random from distinct populations.

The *t test for dependent means* is used when subjects in the two groups are related. The relationship may result from pre and posttest data for the same subjects. The relationship may also result from matching subjects in the two groups.

While group comparisons comprise the major use of the *t* test, it may serve several other functions. A sample mean can be compared to a single number. For example, the mean weight of members of a junior football league may be compared to an accepted standard for safe participation of 100 pounds. Scores in collegiate golf matches may be compared to par for the courses on which the courses were played.

The *t* test may also establish that a correlation coefficient is substantially different from 0. A correlation coefficient of 0.40, for example, indicates some level of relationship. Viewed in isolation, one cannot judge whether the relationship is explained by chance or is a real function of the relationship between the two scores. The *t* test indicates the probability of the relationship existing by chance.

Finally, *t* tests can be used to determine if two groups differ in dispersion or variability. For example, an anthropologist may be interested in knowing if the height of members of two different cultures was more or less variable. Upon computing a *t* test for variance, he or she may report that members of one culture fall within a narrower range of height than members of the other culture. In other words, greater extremes in height are found in one culture when compared to the other.

One Way Analysis of Variance

One Way Analysis of Variance (ANOVA) is used when two or more means are to be compared under a single independent variable. ANOVA is a preferred alternative to conducting multiple t tests since the alpha level can be set at a specific level for the aggregate of all contrasts. For example, one may wish to compare the tensile strength of three different samples of wire (S1, S2, and S3). Three separate t tests could contrast S1 with S2, S2 with S3, and S1 with S3. Aside from the analysis being very cumbersome, the experiment-wide alpha level would not be controlled. A single one way analysis of variance would produce each contrast while controlling the experiment-wide error rate at a single alpha level.

An ANOVA involves the calculation of an F statistic as opposed to a t statistic. The F statistic is a ratio of variance in scores within groups and between groups, hence the title analysis of variance. A large F ratio for a contrast between two groups indicates that the variance for the contrasts is greater than would be expected based on the variance for subjects in all groups. A small F ratio indicates that the between group variance is similar to the within group variance.

Statistical significance of an F ratio is determined using the F table appended to most statistics books. The F table indicates the probability of obtaining a given value depending on the degrees of freedom in the numerator and denominator of the F ratio. The degrees of freedom for the numerator is one less than the number of samples being contrasted ($k - 1$ where k is the number of samples). The degrees of freedom for the denominator is the total number of subjects in all groups minus the number of samples being contrasted ($N - k$ where N is the total number of subjects and k is the number of samples). For example, if we conducted an analysis of variance for five groups ($k = 5$) with 20 subjects in each ($N = 100$), the numerator degrees of freedom would be 4 ($k - 1 = 4$), and the denominator degrees of freedom would be 95 ($N - k = 95$).

The first examples involved one independent variable, or factor, and three groups. The second involved one independent variable and five groups. The analyses are labeled 1 X 3 and 1 X 5 ANOVAs, indicating three or five groups under one independent variable.

Analysis of variance can also be conducted with more than one independent variable or factor. This is referred to as a factorial analysis of variance. For example, a 2 X 3 factorial analysis of variance involves three groups under two independent variables. This may be exemplified by the comparison of adolescents and adults (two independent variables) who are subjected in three different levels of television viewing (three groups).

Figure 12.3 illustrates a 1 X 3 and 2 X 3 analysis of variance. Note that the 1 X 3 design simply contrasts sales performance for agents described as rookies, mid-career, and veteran. The 2 X 3 extends this analysis by including an educational level factor (bachelor's degree and master's degree). The 1 X 3 allows three separate contrasts, rookie vs. mid-career, mid-career vs. veteran, and rookie vs. veteran.

The 2 X 3 ANOVA allows for each of these comparisons by averaging across educational level groups. It also allows for a comparison between educational levels by averaging across experience groups. Finally, the 2 X 3 ANOVA allows one to identify performance at any one education and experience level when contrasted with any other education and experience level. This is referred to as an interaction.

The overall F ratio in a one way or factorial analysis of variance simply determines the probability that all groups are not the same. Since more than one combination of groups is being evaluated, one cannot tell when one or more contrasts are significant. *Post hoc comparisons* or *multiple comparisons* are used to evaluate all possible sets of means. The most widely used multiple comparison tests are Duncan's new multiple range, Fisher's LSD, Newman-Keuls, Scheffe's, and

One-way (Three levels of experience)		Experience		
		Rookie	Mid-Career	Veteran
		_____	_____	_____

Two-way (Three levels of experience and two levels of education)		Experience		
		Rookie	Mid-Career	Veteran
Education	BS	_____	_____	_____
	MS	_____	_____	_____

Figure 12.3 Illustration of One-Way and Factorial (Two-Way) Analysis of Variance

Tukey's HSD. The most conservative (i.e., unlikely to produce a Type I error but likely to detect differences that actually exist) is Scheffe's test. The most liberal is Fisher's LSD.

Nonparametric Tests

Not all data sets meet the assumptions that underlie the use of parametric statistics. For example, many psychometric scales produce nominal or ordinal data, performance measures such as reaction time and foot speed are not normally distributed, and sample distributions of students with disabilities are not often homogeneous. While parametric tests may be robust against violations of these assumptions, discrepancies may be so severe that use of nonparametric statistics (that do not rely on these assumptions) is warranted.

A nonparametric test exists for every purpose served by a parametric test. The _median test_ and _Mann-Whitney U test_ are analogous to the independent samples _t_ test. The _sign test_ and the _Wilcoxon matched-pairs signed-ranks test_ are analogous to the dependent samples _t_ test. The _Kruskal-Wallis one way analysis of variance_ is analogous to the one way analysis of variance. Finally, the _Friedman two way analysis of variance_ is analogous to the two way analysis of variance.

Computational procedures and methods for determining probability levels differ for nonparametric tests and their parametric analogues. While parametric tests depend on a hypothetical sampling distribution, nonparametric procedures use the actual sample data to form a distribution. Use of actual sample data makes the analysis and interpretation substantially more intuitive and direct than the use of a hypothetical distribution.

Unfortunately, the utility and simplicity of nonparametric procedures also come at a cost. Nonparametric tests are generally less powerful than their parametric counterparts; therefore, they are less than likely to detect actual differences.

SUMMARY

Inferential statistics are used to make judgments about a population based on sample data. Samples drawn from a population will seldom mirror the population precisely. Any discrepancy between sample and population data is described as sampling error. The central limit theorem provides essential information about sample characteristics and the likelihood of sampling error.

Inferential statistics build upon the central limit theorem to determine if it is likely that a given sample is a member of the population or instead represents another population. This is done by determining the probability that the sample would be drawn from the population. The null hypothesis indicates that there is no difference between the sample and the population. Rejecting the null hypothesis indicates that it is sufficiently improbable for the sample to have come from the population and that the sample must have been drawn from an alternate population.

Since inferential statistics are based on probability and not fact, error can occur. The first error, or Type I error, occurs when the null hypothesis is falsely rejected. The second error, or Type II error, occurs when the null hypothesis is falsely accepted. There are two major classes of inferential statistics, parametric and nonparametric tests. Parametric tests establish the probability of an outcome by comparing sample data to a hypothetical sampling distribution. The most commonly used parametric statistics include the t test, one way analysis of variance, and factorial analysis of variance. Nonparametric statistics establish probabilities directly from the sample data. Commonly used procedures that are analogous to parametric tests include the median test, Mann-Whitney U test, sign test, Wilcoxon matched-pairs signed-ranks test, and Kruskal-Wallis one way ANOVA of ranks.

FURTHER READINGS

Churchill, G. A. (1991). *Basic marketing research* (2nd ed.). Fort Worth: Dryden Press-Harcourt Brace Jovanovich College Publisher.

Ghauri, P. N., Gronhaug, K., & Kristianslund, I. (1995). *Research methods in business studies: A practical guide.* Upper Saddle River, NJ: Merrill/Prentice Hall.

Graziano, A. M., & Raulin, M. L. (1996). *Research methods: A process of inquiry.* (3rd ed.) New York: Harper and Row.

Johnson, E. S. (1981). *Research methods in criminology and criminal justice.* Upper Saddle River, NJ: Merrill/Prentice Hall.

Kinnear, T. C., & Taylor, J. R. (1995). *Marketing research: An applied approach.* 5th ed. New York: McGraw-Hill, Inc.

Manheim, J. B., & Rich, R. C. (1994). *Empirical political analysis: Research methods in political science.* (4th ed.) New York: Longman.

Silverman, F. H. (1997). *Research design and evaluation in speech-language pathology and audiology* (4th ed.). Needham Heights, MA: Allyn & Bacon.

Tull, D. S., & Hawkins, D. I. (1988). *Marketing research: Measurement and methods* (4th ed.). New York: Macmillan.

Zikmund, W. G. (1996). *Business Research Methods* (5th ed.). Chicago: Dryden Press.

13

Analyzing Data from Single Subject Designs

INTRODUCTION

Just as there are methods for determining the importance (or significance) of data obtained through procedures involving group designs, so too are there methods for determining the importance of data gathered using single subject design methodology. Chapter 6 highlighted how the use of single subject design methodology could demonstrate a functional relationship between implementation of the independent variable and subsequent changes in the dependent variable. The question was, did performance change only when the independent variable was in effect? In most investigations involving single subject designs, you can answer this question through visual inspection of the data displayed on the graphs maintained throughout the study.

According to Neuman and McCormick (1995), we use visual inspection for several reasons. First, graphed data allow for an ongoing view of your participants' performance as your study

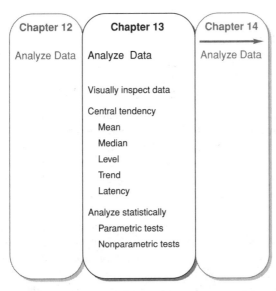

The Scope, Plan, and Sequence Chart for Conducting
Research: The Ninth Step in the Research Process

progresses. You can make data-based decisions throughout the study to make sure participants are benefiting from their involvement. Second, visual inspection does not require any expertise in statistics and yields quick conclusions and hypotheses. Third, visual inspection allows an individual to judge the social significance of a treatment effect. Unlike statistics, visual analysis does not specify preset levels of significance. We look at educational and social significance rather than at the statistical significance of the results. On a related note, visual analysis presents a conservative view of the data, because findings that could be, or are, statistically significant may not be interpreted as strong and stable. Finally, visual inspection may yield findings of interest not directly related to your original research question.

Despite these advantages, some authors (Gentile, Roden, & Klein, 1972; Shine & Bower, 1971) have argued that visual inspection is insufficient for determining the significance of results obtained using single subject designs. This methodology is well suited for use in applied settings; however; these settings make it difficult to control extraneous factors that can influence performance. As a result, there are disadvantages in using visual inspection (Kazdin, 1982). For example, the intervention has to have a clear effect on behavior or conclusions will be shaky. Thus, subtle differences are not received as positively, if they are perceived at all. Also, there is a possibility that you will discard a weak intervention on the basis of visual inspection rather than devote more time and effort to enhance it (DeProspero & Cohen, 1979). Bear in mind that advocates of visual inspection argue that statistical significance does not necessarily mean an effect is important in applied settings. In addition, they point to the lack or limited number of statistical techniques appropriate for use with data from single subject designs.

Baer (1977) argued that visual inspection and statistical procedures are not fundamentally different with respect to their underlying rationale. Both want to avoid Type I (i.e., rejecting the null hypothesis when it is true) and Type II (i.e., not rejecting the null hypothesis when it is false) errors. Therefore, rather than as an alternative, statistical procedures should be a supplement or a replacement for visual analysis to permit us to draw conclusions about the consistency of change. This chapter describes procedures for visual inspection and statistical analysis of data from single subject designs.

VISUAL INSPECTION

The heart of visual inspection is a comparison of either data points gathered during a baseline phase to those gathered during a treatment phase, or data points gathered during two interventions. It is important to know the trend your data show during baseline, and the trend you anticipate will be produced by the independent variable. It is also important to know any little idiosyncrasies associated with the independent variable. A perfect example is the use of planned ignoring, or extinction, by teachers. This technique is used to decrease nondangerous behaviors previously maintained by attention, usually from the teacher. The data collected by the teacher using extinction will indicate, to her dismay, that the behavior has increased. It does not mean that extinction is not working; in fact, it is working quite well as will be demonstrated by data collected in subsequent sessions. The teacher need only survive this extinction burst. This example highlights the importance of being thoroughly familiar with the features of your independent variable.

Generally, you can use two types of criteria to evaluate data: experimental and therapeutic (Barlow & Hersen, 1984). With the experimental criterion, you want to decide if a change has been demonstrated and if it can be attributed to the intervention. The experimental criterion includes four techniques: *measures of central tendency, level, trend,* and *latency.* With the therapeutic criterion, you are looking for clinical or applied significance, that is, that the results have made an important change in the participant's life. Social comparison is the technique used as the therapeutic criterion. We recommend examining your data using all five techniques and reporting all of them in your results section. Remember, however, that idiosyncratic features of your independent variable may make analyses by some of these techniques more relevant than others when determining the effectiveness of your independent variable.

We think it would be helpful to explain these techniques and then apply them to an example. Figure 13.1 presents a hypothetical analysis of an intervention program using an ABAB design. The independent variable is a technique called differential reinforcement of lower rates, a procedure that reduces a behavior to a more acceptable level. The dependent variable is the number of questions asked by a preschooler during a two and a half hour school day. Obviously,

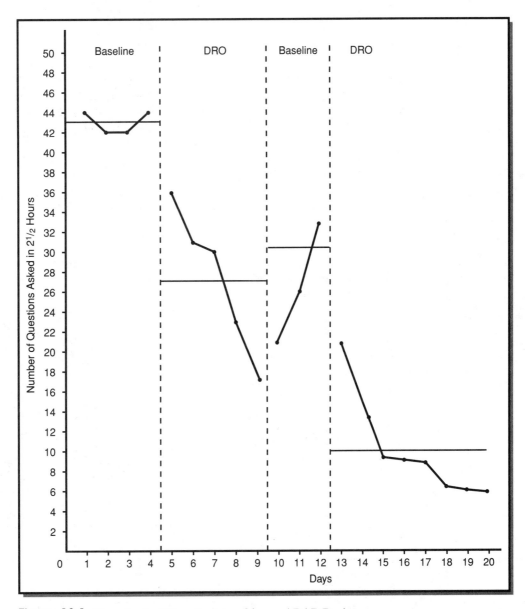

Figure 13.1 Hypothetical Data Evaluated by an ABAB Design

asking questions is not an unacceptable behavior, but asking too many of them in a short period of time can be a problem for the busy preschool teacher. The student's behavior should be reduced, not eliminated. We encourage you to refer to this figure frequently as you read through the next sections.

MEASURES OF CENTRAL TENDENCY

Measures of central tendency summarize performance on the dependent variable across each phase of the study. The two most commonly used measures are *mean* and *median.*

Mean

For each phase of your study, add the value of the data points and divide by the total number of data points to get the mean. Compare these numbers across phases. If you had anticipated that the independent variable would increase the dependent variable, then the means during treatment phases should be higher than the means during baseline phases. In the example in Figure 13.2, we anticipate that the independent variable would decrease the dependent variable. The mean for the first baseline is 43; for the first treatment phase the mean is 27. During the reversal phase, the mean increases to 30.6; it falls to 10.75 during the final treatment phase. This method of visual inspection highlights the functional relationship between the independent and dependent variables. Kazdin (1982) suggested the mean line for each phase be drawn. You can see our mean lines in Figure 13.2.

Median

This standard is used if the data are highly variable or unstable. Rank order the data within a phase and divide by two. The value for the observation occurring at that middle rank is the median. Compare medians across adjacent phases. If you had anticipated that the independent variable would increase the dependent variable, then the median during treatment phases should be higher than the median during baseline phases. Conversely, if the treatment was expected to decrease the dependent variable, then the median during treatment phases should be lower than the median during baseline phases. The medians for each phase in Figure 13.2 are 42, 30, 26, and 10. Each baseline median is higher than the median for the treatment phase that follows it, an outcome that supports a functional relationship.

Level

Measures of central tendency require several data points in each phase. Thus, some time may pass before you have solid indications that your independent variable is functioning as hypothesized. A more immediate technique for visual inspection is level. This technique requires a comparison of the last data point of one phase to the first data point of the next phase. The smaller value is subtracted from the larger number to determine if the change is in an improving or a decaying direction. A large, positive change is evidence of a powerful intervention.

In Figure 13.2, the last data point of baseline is 44, and the first data point of treatment is 36. Subtracting 36 from 44 leaves 8, indicating that the independent variable had a strong effect in the desired direction. The last data point of treatment is 18, and the first data point of the reversal phase is 20. Subtracting 18 from 20 leaves 2, indicating that removal of the independent variable had an effect in the undesired direction. Finally, the last data point of the second baseline is 34, and the first data point of final treatment phase is 20. Subtracting 20 from 34 leaves 14, indicating that reinstatement of the independent variable had a strong effect in the desired direction.

Two cautions should be noted when using level. First, reliance on a single data point from each phase can obscure variability. Second, data points from one phase can overlap with data points from another phase. The more the overlap, the less solid your conclusions about a functional relationship.

Trend

Trend refers to the direction of the data path. Generally, there are three types of trend lines. The first is an ascending trend, which indicates a dependent variable is increasing. The second is a descending trend, which indicates the dependent variable is decreasing. The third is actually no trend at all; the data are stable (i.e., zero celeration). We remind you of the importance of knowing whether the dependent variable is something that must be increased or decreased. A low and stable trend or a descending baseline trend for a dependent variable you want to increase is ideal. Hopefully, implementing the independent variable will produce data with an ascending trend. Conversely, a high and stable trend, or an ascending baseline trend for a dependent variable you want to decrease, is ideal. Your hope then is that implementing the independent variable will produce data with a descending trend.

Unlike the data in Figure 13.1, your data will probably have some variability. Rarely will your data produce a single line whose direction can be easily determined. In this case, we recommend you use the split middle technique to draw trend lines for each phase. Follow these steps.

1. Count the number of data points in your first baseline phase and divide in half. If you have an even number of data points, then you will have an even number of data points in both halves. If you have an odd number of data points, then there will be some overlap. For example, if there are five data points, you will use the first, second, and third data points in one half, and the third, fourth, and fifth data points in the other half. In Figure 13.1, you can see that we have four data points, an even number.

2. Average each half. In our example, 44 plus 42 divided by two is 43. For the remaining portion of baseline, 42 plus 44 divided by two is 43.

3. 43 and 43 are the first and last points of the new trend line for the baseline phase. Draw this line in your graph and label the trend. As we show in Figure 13.2, our data yielded a high and stable trend.

4. Repeat Steps 1–3 and draw a trend line for the first treatment phase. Our data yielded a decreasing trend, as you can see in Figure 13.2.

5. Determine the effectiveness of the independent variable by comparing trend lines across adjacent phases. In our example, the dependent variable was high and stable, a trend we hoped our independent variable would decrease. The descending trend line in the treatment phase of Figure 13.2 indicates we achieved our goal.

6. Repeat Steps 1–5 with remaining phases. As you can see in Figure 13.2, the trend line during the reversal phase ascends in the undesired direction, indicating the preschooler's behavior was getting worse. Reinstating the independent variable in the final treatment phase produced a descending trend in the desired direction.

Latency

This final criteria, latency, is the period between the onset of a phase and changes in the dependent variable. Confidence in the strength of your independent variable is increased if latency is short. Ideally, the independent variable should have an immediate effect upon the dependent variable. Inspection of the data in Figure 13.1 indicates that the preschooler's behavior began to change five days into the study, on the first day of the intervention. Her behavior regressed on

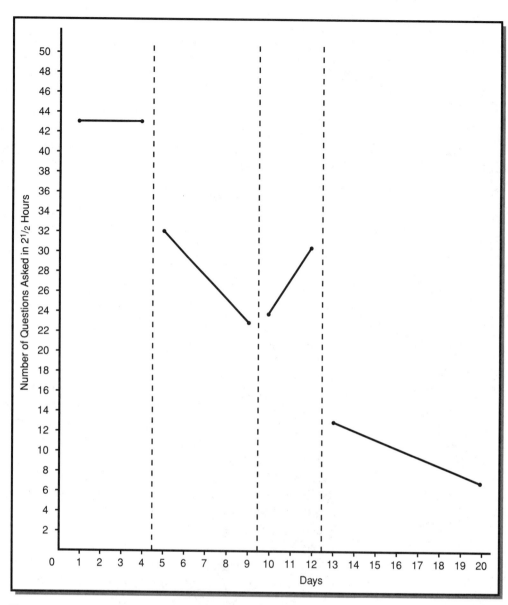

Figure 13.2 Trend Lines for the Data Presented in Figure 13.2

the tenth day of the study, on the first day of the reversal phase. Finally, behavior improved on the thirteenth day of the intervention, on the first day the independent variable was reinstated.

SOCIAL COMPARISON

While it is important to know that an independent variable produced desired changes in the dependent variable, you should also want to know how well a participant is performing in relation to others. Social comparison (Wolf, 1978) allows us to make this determination. Follow these steps to gather, graph, and use social comparison data:

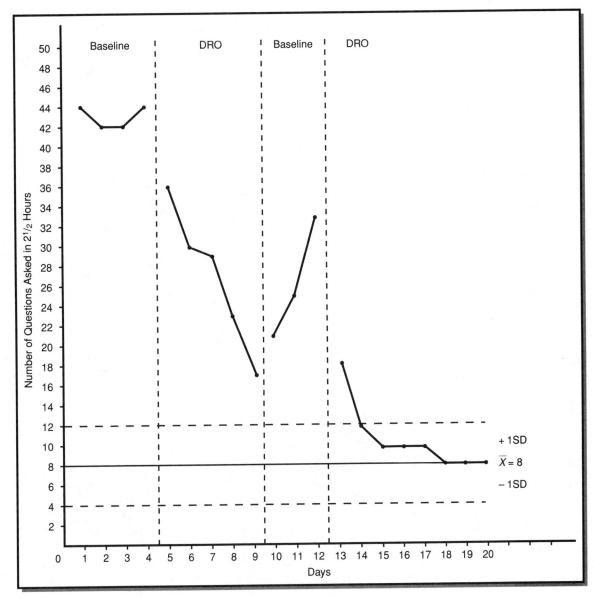

Figure 13.3 Social Comparison Data for the Data Presented in Figure 13.2

1. Graph the participant's data.
2. Identify a small sample of individuals who are not participating in your study but whose behavior appears typical.
3. Use the recording system you have already developed to collect data on the amount of the dependent variable demonstrated by these individuals.
4. Average these data and compute the standard deviation.
5. Use a solid horizontal line to draw a mean line on your graph. Use broken lines to indicate one standard deviation above and below the mean. Our mean and standard

deviations lines on Figure 13.3 indicate that other preschoolers were asking an average of eight questions, with a range of 4 to 12.

6. Examine your participant's performance to see if it is within the range of the social comparison data. As you can see in Figure 13.3, the independent variable brought the preschooler's behavior to within acceptable levels.

STATISTICAL ANALYSIS OF DATA FROM SINGLE SUBJECT DESIGNS

At the beginning of this chapter, we referred to a difference of opinion regarding the adequacy of visual inspection for analyzing data from single subject designs. Given the problems with visual inspection, some researchers (Gentile, Roden, & Klein, 1972) recommend data from single subject designs be analyzed by statistical methods.

The idea has not been embraced with enthusiasm. There are several arguments against use of statistics. First, such procedures would allow for the detection of significant differences that would have been disregarded by visual inspection; thus, visual inspection is the more stringent or conservative criterion against which change produced by an independent variable is judged. Second, a statistically significant result is not necessarily socially or educationally important. Third, the development of statistical procedures appropriate for use with data from single subject designs has lagged behind the development of procedures for group research.

Unfortunately, using statistics intended for group research can pose many problems. First, single subject design data are neither independent nor interval, two major assumptions on which traditional statistical tests are based. Second, some statistical procedures require special conditions that may limit their usefulness in investigations incorporating single subject designs. For example, some procedures require experimental conditions be assigned randomly, a requirement that can only be met by one single subject design, the alternating treatments design. Another procedure requires the independent variable be implemented randomly across subjects, settings, or behavior. We make this selection on the basis of which subject, behavior, or setting is most in need of the intervention. Third, single subject designs allow us flexibility in meeting participants' needs; yet use of some statistical tests require careful planning at the outset. We usually hope for substantial differences in across phases that can be identified by visual inspection. It's only when this doesn't happen that we may decide to use statistics. By then, it may be too late to meet the requirements or assumptions associated with them. Finally, Michael (1974a, 1974b) warns that if the significance test is valued above all other judgmental aids, investigators are likely to try and design their experiments so that a significance test can be computed, an obvious loss in experimenter flexibility.

If the results of visual inspection of data from single subject design are definitive, there is little need to employ statistical tests. However, if ideal patterns do not emerge, then statistical procedures may offer some advantages. Following are the conditions governing their use:

1. Visual inspection does not provide a convincing demonstration of the effects of the independent variable one way or the other.

2. You are interested in identifying any "elusive" effects that may be overlooked by visual inspection, particularly if your independent variable is the beginning of a new line of research, and you are unfamiliar with conditions that maximize its efficacy. Statistical procedures may identify variables that warrant further investigation.

3. You have been unable to get a stable baseline, and the design calls for one, or your data show considerable variability within and across phases.

4. You may have noticed moderate improvement in the dependent variable during baseline. Using statistics might reveal that continued improvement during treatment is educationally significant.

If employed, statistical procedures are usually used in combination with visual inspection to answer the research question. Their use is the exception rather than the rule in single subject design methodology. Kazdin (1982) and Neuman and McCormick (1995) summarized the statistical procedures most commonly used.

PARAMETRIC TESTS

Analysis of variance can be used to demonstrate statistical significance between the conditions of an ABAB or a multiple baseline design. A *t* test can be used if your research question is about differences between all baseline data and all treatment data. Analysis of variance answers questions about trends across all four conditions. Gentile et al. (1972) tried to make the case for using the one way analysis of variance with reversal design: Collapse the data from the four conditions of a typical reversal design into two treatment levels. Preferably, each condition contains an equal number of data points. They suggested the treatment effects be the between-subjects effects, and the observations be the within-subjects effects. The results can tell you whether the treatment effects were significant for a participant. Both a *t* test and an analysis of variance assume the data points within a phase are independent of each other. Therefore, you will need to calculate a procedure called an *autocorrelation* for each phase. Significant autocorrelations indicate the data are dependent. Different procedures such as randomization tests or nonparametrics must be used.

A times series analysis could also be used even when autocorrelations are significant. This procedure compares data over time for separate phases for a single individual or a group of individuals. It can be used to evaluate single subject design data when the purpose is to compare alternative phases such as baseline and intervention phases. The test examines whether there are statistically significant changes in level and trend from one phase to the next.

NONPARAMETRIC TESTS

Nonparametric tests do not require the data to be independent or that subjects be chosen randomly from a population. One nonparametric test that is appropriate for use with an alternating treatments design is a randomization test. As discussed in Chapter 6, an alternating treatments design requires you to schedule randomly the delivery of two or more independent variables. A *t* test or an *F* is calculated for the data and for repeated orderings of the data. The proportion of significant results is the test statistic used to determine how rarely a test statistic as extreme as the experimental value would result from random assignment alone, that is, if there were no treatment effects. The data are randomized and the statistic is run again until all possible combinations have been tested.

The Rn Test of Ranks is suitable for evaluating data obtained from multiple baseline designs, where data have been gathered across several different baselines. An assumption of this test is that the subject, behavior, or setting being exposed to the independent variable has been selected at random rather than on the basis of greatest need. Whether the intervention produces a statistically reliable effect is determined by evaluating the baseline performance of each subject, setting, or behavior at the point at which the independent variable is introduced. In a multiple baseline across individuals, you rank scores of each participant at the point when any one of the participants is exposed to the independent variable. When an intervention is first introduced, the performance of all participants is ranked, including those from whom treatment is withheld. The next time the intervention is introduced to a participant, that participant's performance, and the performance of others not yet receiving the intervention, is ranked. Rn is formed by summing the ranks at the point where treatment is introduced. If the independent variable produces no significant effects, then the combination of ranks will be randomly distributed.

SUMMARY

In this chapter, we presented procedures you can use to strengthen your conclusions about the functional relationship between independent and dependent variables established by single subject designs. These procedures fall into two categories: visual inspection and statistics. Visual inspection involves four experimental criteria, including measures of central tendency, level, trend, and latency. It also includes social comparison to address a therapeutic criterion. Visual inspection techniques are easy to use, and they allow you to react to your data (and your participants' needs). They are also a very conservative judgment aid. Only those interventions that produce strong changes are likely to be viewed as significant.

Although visual inspection is the more commonly used category, several investigators have called for the application of statistical procedures to analyze data from single subject designs. Not many researchers have responded favorably, possibly due to satisfaction with visual inspection techniques and the lack of statistical procedures designed especially for the unique characteristics of single subject designs. Nonetheless, statistical procedures may be useful when the results of visual inspection are not convincing.

REFERENCES

Baer, D. M. (1977). Perhaps it would be better not to know everything. *Journal of Applied Behavior Analysis, 10,* 167–172.

Barlow, D. H., & Hersen, M. (1984). *Single case experimental design: Strategies for studying behavior change* (2nd ed.). New York: Pergamon.

Deprospero, A., & Cohen, S. (1979). Inconsistent visual analysis of intrasubject data. *Journal of Applied Behavior Analysis, 12,* 573–579.

Gentile, J. R., Roden, A. H., & Klein, D. (1972). An analysis of variance model for the intrasubject replication design. *Journal of Applied Behavior Analysis, 5,* 193–198.

Kazdin, A. E. (1982). *Single-case research designs.* New York: Oxford University Press.

Michael, J. (1974a). Statistical inference for individual organism research: Some reactions to a suggestion by Gentile, Roden, and Klein. *Journal of Applied Behavior Analysis, 7,* 627–628.

Michael, J. (1974b). Statistical inference for individual organism research: Mixed blessing or curse? *Journal of Applied Behavior Analysis, 7,* 647–653.

Neuman, S. B., & McCormick, S. (1995). *Single subject experimental research: Applications for literacy.* Newark, DE: International Reading Association.

Shine, L. C., & Bower, S. M. (1971). A one-way analysis of variance for single subject designs. *Educational and Psychological Measurement, 31,* 105–113.

Wolf, M. M. (1978). Social validity: The case for subjective evaluation, or How applied behavior analysis is finding its heart. *Journal of Applied Behavior Analysis, 11,* 203–214.

FURTHER READINGS

Use of Visual Inspection

Killeen, P. R. (1978). Stability criteria. *Journal of the Experimental Analysis of Behavior, 29,* 17–25.

See articles listed in the *Further Readings* section of Chapter 6.

Use of Statistics with Single Subject Design Data

Gentile, J. R., Roden, A. H., & Klein, D. (1972). An analysis of variance model for the intrasubject replication design. *Journal of Applied Behavior Analysis, 5,* 193–198.

Hartmann, D. P. (1974). Forcing square pegs into round holes: Some comments on, "An analysis of variance model for the intrasubject replication design." *Journal of Applied Behavior Analysis, 7,* 635–638.

Kazdin, A. E. (1980). Obstacles in using randomization tests in single-case experimentation. *Journal of Education Statistics, 5,* 253–260.

Kesselman, H. J., & Leventhal, L. (1974). Concerning the statistical procedures enumerated by Gentile et al.: Another perspective. *Journal of Applied Behavior Analysis, 7,* 643–645.

Kratochwill, T. R., Alsen, K., Demuth, D., Dawson, D., Panicucci, D., Arnston, P., McMurray, N., Hempstead, J., & Levin, J. A. (1974). A further consideration of the application of the analysis of variance model for the intrasubject replication design. *Journal of Applied Behavior Analysis, 7,* 629–633.

Shine, L. C., & Bower, S. M. (1971). A one-way analysis of variance for single subject designs. *Educational and Psychological Measurement, 31,* 105–113.

Thoreson, C. E., & Elashoff, J. D. (1974). An analysis of variance model for intrasubject replication designs: Some additional comments. *Journal of Applied Behavior Analysis, 7,* 639–641.

14

Analyzing Data from Qualitative Research Approaches

INTRODUCTION

In Chapters 12 and 13, we discussed procedures for analyzing data from experimental, quasi-experimental, correlational, survey, and single subject research. These procedures involved statistical or visual inspection methods that enabled you to accept or reject a hypothesis about the relationship between dependent and independent variables. From this hypothesis you could then make generalizations to a population. However, you cannot use these techniques to analyze the results of a qualitative research study. Rather than numbers, results of qualitative research usually take the form of written accounts of your observations. Your goal is to describe as accurately as possible what your participants said and what you observed them do. The purpose of your analysis is to discover broad themes and patterns.

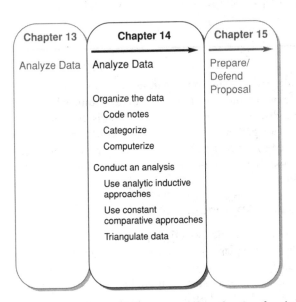

The Scope, Plan, and Sequence Chart for Conducting Research: The Ninth Step in the Research Process

This chapter highlights techniques you can use to analyze data from qualitative studies. We remind you of a unique feature of qualitative data; that is, you can collect and analyze them simultaneously. Data analysis should occur over time and be inductive and recursive in nature.

ORGANIZING THE DATA

Observations and field notes will produce a large amount of data, primarily composed of verbal descriptions. You need to analyze these items for themes and patterns which you describe and illustrate with examples that include quotes from individuals and excerpts from documents.

Coding Notes

Review transcripts and identify categories of content as they emerge. A coding system can be refined to facilitate sorting and reviewing new data.

Organizing by Categories

Categories may result from reading and re-reading field notes and noting regularities. They may reflect groupings of people, settings, activities, and administrative structures (Stainback & Stainback, 1988). Having selected categories, review the field notes, and sort the data into them. It may be necessary to revise categories as you collect and analyze more data.

Computerized Data Processing

The numeric quality of data from quantitative research makes using a computer invaluable for data analysis. Qualitative data, however, involve verbal descriptions. The development of computer programs suitable for use with this type of data is still in its infancy. There are a handful of programs available for coding, searching, and sorting qualitative data. One example is Ethnograph (Tesch, 1990). However, applications of computer technology can assist in other aspects of your study. Word processing programs can help you manage field notes. Spreadsheets can help keep track of participant and setting characteristics. Graphics packages can create charts, tables, and diagrams.

DATA ANALYSIS

Analysis of qualitative data involves organization, classification, categorization, a search for patterns, and synthesis. Through analysis you can determine whether data are missing and if additional work is needed. The analysis is recursive, that is, findings are generated and constructed as new pieces of data are gathered. There are no guidelines for determining how much data and data analysis are needed to support your conclusions. Typically, qualitative researchers do not claim their interpretations have been proven; rather, they demonstrate plausible support (Stainback & Stainback, 1988).

Analytic Inductive Approaches

Katz (1983) described analytic inductive approaches as a method for arriving at a reasonable fit between your data and explanations of a social phenomenon. Use this strategy if you have a specific problem, question, or issue in mind and want to develop a theory or hypothesis about it. Denzin (1989) identified seven steps that are included in an analytic inductive approach. These are presented in Table 14.1 and each is illustrated here.

The first step requires establishing a rough definition of the event being studied. For example, you may be interested in the factors that make inclusion in general education successful for some students with disabilities. Define inclusion as the placement of students with disabili-

Table 14.1 Steps for Using Analytic Induction

Denzin (1978) recommended following these steps to complete an analytic induction of qualitative data.

1. Define the event you are studying.
2. Develop a tentative hypothesis to explain the outcome.
3. Evaluate another case to see if it supports your hypothesis.
4. If needed, reconsider and restate.
5. Evaluate cases that may disprove your hypothesis.
6. Reformulate the hypothesis based on these observations.
7. Continue until the hypothesis is confirmed.

ties in the general education classroom. Conduct participant observations in an inclusive setting you consider successful for a particular student. Also, interview the classroom teacher.

Second, examine the data and note that the teacher spoke very highly of the amount of support that she and the student received. You hypothesize that successful inclusion results from providing necessary support services for students and their teachers.

Third, determine if there is a fit between your data and this tentative hypothesis. Networking can help select another inclusive site. For example, the first teacher you observed recommends visiting another colleague's classroom to observe and collect additional data. Upon visiting this site, conduct more participant observations; interview the staff, student, and parents; and examine school records such as the Individualized Education Plan (IEP).

Fourth, examine these data for information that can be used to refine the original hypothesis. For example, the data may reveal that the classroom is perceived as a successful placement for this student, and there are indeed a number of support services available.

Fifth, select a case that you suspect could disprove the hypothesis. For example, network to find a classroom in which inclusion is not as successful despite the availability of support services, and collect data in this setting. Data from this negative case should help refine the hypothesis. For example, the data may indicate that the student appears to function at a level comparable to that of other students you have observed, and that he receives similar support services. However, data from interviews indicate that the teacher feels isolated in her attempts to provide effective programming for the student. At this point, you may suspect that your concept of support needs to be extended to include not just the provision of services but emotional support and encouragement for staff and student.

Sixth, revise your hypothesis to emphasize the importance of staff receiving emotional support and encouragement from administrative personnel, colleagues, and students' parents.

Seventh, continue collecting data and adjusting your hypothesis until you can find no case to which it does not apply.

Constant Comparative Approaches

This approach also allows you to develop and refine a hypothesis; however, it differs in that you collect data from several cases before developing a hypothesis. Your hypothesis will develop upon examination of the data for categories, patterns, consistencies, and inconsistencies (Stainback & Stainback, 1988). Bogdan and Biklen (1982), Taylor and Bogdan (1998), and Stainback and Stainback (1988) outlined steps to follow in using a constant comparison strategy. We present these steps in Table 14.2 and illustrate them here.

Table 14.2 Steps for Using a Constant Comparative Strategy

Bogdan and Biklen (1997), Taylor and Bogdan (1998), and Stainback and Stainback (1988) recommended following these steps to use a constant comparative strategy in analyzing qualitative data.

1. Collect data from several cases.

2. Identify important issues and recurring events; use them to create categories.

3. Collect additional data to provide many examples for each category. Elaborate on the dimensions within any given category.

4. Write about the categories, and describe how they can account for all events you have documented. Reformulate some categories and delete others as the data dictate.

5. Identify patterns and relationships.

6. Develop a theory by continuing to collect and compare data and refining categories and relationships.

Let's use the qualitative study we described in the previous section. To use the constant comparison strategy, you first collect data in several general education classrooms in which students with disabilities are placed. You conduct participant observations. You interview teachers, support staff, students, family members, and administrative personnel. You examine IEPs, school records, and notes between the school and home.

Next, examine your data and place main issues or recurring events into categories. For example, you may note that some students vary in the nature and degree of their disability. This is one category. Some receive a substantial number of support services, while others do not. This is a second category. Teachers vary in the professional preparation programs they completed, a third category. Some teachers receive release time to plan effective programs and participate in multi-disciplinary and IEP team meetings, while others do not. This is a fourth category. Parents vary in their level of involvement, a sixth category. Continue until you have identified all the categories you think are relevant.

Continue to collect data so as to provide several instances or events for each category. You may also see what dimensions should be included within your categories. For example, the student disability category could have separate levels, each representing a handicapping condition. The second category could include the exact support services and the amount of time students receive each service. The teacher category could include highest degree earned, field of study, and number of years of professional experience.

Use the categories to describe and account for every event recorded in your data. You may need to reformulate a category. For example, the student disability category could be altered to address the severity of the handicapping condition.

Continue to collect and analyze your data, and assign them to categories. Over time, patterns and relationships will emerge. For example, you may see that some students whose inclusive placements are considered a success do receive a substantial number of support services. However, other students in placements considered equally as successful do not receive a comparable amount of support services. Still another group of students who do receive support services are not perceived as successful. At the same time, you notice that all students who are successful are placed with teachers who voluntarily agreed to work in an inclusive classroom and have parents who are actively involved in their education. Settings perceived as less successful are staffed by teachers who felt pressured into accepting students with disabilities.

Corroboration and Triangulation

Qualitative researchers corroborate their data to increase the likelihood that their findings will be perceived by others as credible. One method for doing this is triangulation. Triangulation may involve the convergence of multiple sources of data such as data collected from several subjects or in several settings. For example, if you were interested in studying perceptions about inter-racial adoptions, you may want to collect data from a variety of social workers employed at separate agencies.

Alternately, data collected from different procedures may be converged. To increase understanding of inter-racial adoption, you could examine data obtained from participant observations in social service agencies, interviews with social workers, and analyses of court documents and newspaper accounts.

SUMMARY

This chapter described how to analyze data collected during a qualitative study. There are two broad steps involved. First, you need to organize the data. This can be challenging because the amounts of data typically collected are massive and verbal in nature. We recommended coding your field notes and assigning them into categories. Second, you need to conduct your analysis.

We described three methods you can use to analyze your data. First, you can use the analytic induction method which requires you to generate a hypothesis then test it on a case by case basis. You start with positive examples that should support your hypothesis and move on to negative examples that refute it or suggest it needs modification. Your hypothesis testing is complete after each case available to you has been examined.

The second method is the constant comparative method. Unlike the preceding method, you do not generate a hypothesis early in the data collection process. Rather you use any combination of qualitative methods to collect data in several sites. These data are used to develop and refine categories and their dimensions. Additional data are gathered to support categories. Patterns, relationships, and theories emerge as categories are examined.

Third, you can triangulate the data. You can converge multiple sources of data such as data collected from several subjects or in several settings. Also, you can use methodological triangulation, in which data collected from different procedures are converged.

As a final note, we remind you of the recursive nature of qualitative data collection and analysis. Although we discussed them separately, data collection and analysis are not conducted separately in practice.

REFERENCES

Bogdan, R. C., & Biklin, S. K. (1997). *Qualitative research for education: An introduction to theory and methods.* (3rd ed.). Needham Heights, MA: Allyn & Bacon.

Denzin, N. (1989). *The research act: A theoretical introduction to sociological methods* (3rd ed.). New York: McGraw Hill.

Katz, J. (1983). *A theory of qualitative methodology: The social science system of analytic fieldwork.* In R. Emerson (Ed.). *Contemporary field research* (pp. 126–148). Boston: Little, Brown.

Marshall, C., & Rossman, G. B. (1994). *Designing qualitative research.* (2nd ed.). Newbury Park, CA: Sage Publications.

Stainback, S., & Stainback, W. (1988). *Understanding and conducting qualitative research.* Reston, VA: Council for Exceptional Children.

Taylor, S., & Bogdan, R. (1998). *Introduction to qualitative research methods: The search for meanings.* (3rd ed.). New York: John Wiley & Sons, Inc.

Tesch, R. (1990). *Qualitative research: Analysis types and software tools.* New York: The Falmer Press.

FURTHER READINGS

Denzin, N. K., & Lincoln, Y. S. (Eds.) (1994). *Handbook of qualitative research.* Thousand Oaks, CA: Sage Publications.

Ghauri, P. N., Gronhaug, K., & Kristianslund, I. (1995). *Research methods in business studies: A practical guide.* Upper Saddle River, NJ: Prentice Hall.

Glesne, C., & Peshkin, A. (1991). *Becoming qualitative researchers: An introduction.* NY: Longman.

Iwasiw, C. L., & Olsen, J. K. (1995). *Content analysis of nonprofessonal caregiver-patient interactions in long term care facilties.* Clinical Nursing Research, 4, 411–424.

Lincoln, Y. S., & Guba, E. G. (1985). *Naturalistic inquiry.* Newbury Park, CA: Sage Publications.

Liukkoner, A. (1995). Life in a nursing home for the frail elderly. *Clinical Nursing Research, 4,* 358–372.

Miles, M. B., & Huberman, A. M. (1997). *Qualitative data analysis* (2nd ed.). Thousand Oaks, CA: Sage Publications.

Rust, R. T., & Cooil, B. (1994). Reliability measures for qualitative data: Theory and implications. *Journal for Marketing Research, 31,* 1–14.

Sandelowski, M. (1995a). Qualitative analysis: What it is and how to begin. *Research in Nursing and Health, 18,* 569–574.

Sandelowski, M. (1995b). Triangle and crystals: On the geometry of qualitative research. *Research in Nursing and Health, 18,* 371–375.

Seymour, D. T. (1988). *Marketing research: Qualitative methods for the marketing professional.* Chicago: Probus.

Strauss, A., & Corbin, J. (1990). *Basics of qualitative research: Grounded theory procedures and techniques.* Newbury Park, CA: Sage Publications.

Valente, S. M. (1994). Messages of psychiatric patients who attempted or committed suicide. *Clinical Nursing Research, 3,* 316–333.

Walker, B. C. (1993). Computer analysis of qualitative data: A comparison of three packages. *Qualitative Health Research, 3,* 91–111.

15

Preparing and Defending a Research Proposal

INTRODUCTION

You now have the tools needed to study the topic that is of interest. You have refined one or more research questions, reviewed what other work has been conducted, and are reasonably confident that the work will contribute to the field. You have chosen a design to yield relevant data and selected a data analysis procedure that will summarize the findings. You have addressed methodological concerns by identifying a subject pool, selecting measurement techniques, and developing your intervention procedures. All you need now is permission to proceed with data collection. To do that, you must prepare a proposal and submit it to a committee of individuals who are in a position to approve the plan.

This chapter discusses how to prepare and defend a research proposal. In the first section, we identify a proposal's purpose and major characteristics, describe how the thesis or dissertation committee is chosen, suggest some writing ideas, and explain all the components needed in the

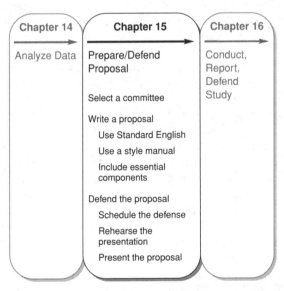

Chapter 14	Chapter 15	Chapter 16
Analyze Data	Prepare/Defend Proposal	Conduct, Report, Defend Study
	Select a committee	
	Write a proposal	
	Use Standard English	
	Use a style manual	
	Include essential components	
	Defend the proposal	
	Schedule the defense	
	Rehearse the presentation	
	Present the proposal	

The Scope, Plan, and Sequence Chart for Conducting Research: The Tenth Step in the Research Process

195

proposal. In the second section, we explain the importance of the proposal defense and suggest several ideas that may contribute to the success of the meeting.

PREPARING A PROPOSAL

Purpose of the Research Proposal

Research proposals communicate the purpose of the research. They not only describe in detail what is planned, but why it is planned. In addition to communication, the proposal demonstrates the researcher's credibility as a scholar. It shows that the researcher knows how to communicate in writing and that he or she has the potential for contributing to the professional literature, not just consuming it. It is also a reflection of competence and persistence, two essential characteristics for people who plan to engage in research. Finally, preparing a proposal enables a researcher to better anticipate decisions that must be made. Nothing is left to chance. There will be no waste of money, time, and energy on something that doesn't have a clear goal, a way to gather information, and an objective evaluation.

Leedy (1993) described three characteristics of an effective proposal. First, it should be a straightforward document that contains no extraneous material. Second, it is not a literary production. Its purpose is not to be artistic, but rather to communicate in clear, precise terms. Third, a proposal is clearly organized. We now turn our attention to activities that will enable you to write a proposal that meets Leedy's (1993) standards.

Enlisting Support for the Project

Although you are primarily responsible for developing and carrying out the project, you need not operate in a vacuum. There are resources available to help.

Your Committee. The study will be conducted under the supervision of a committee. Depending on university requirements, there will probably be three or four committee members. Rudestam and Newton (1992) presented an excellent discussion on selecting committee members. In the ideal universe, you would be able to choose people who can work together smoothly and lend support as you conduct the research. Unfortunately, even on the most cooperative committees, members will occasionally disagree with each other.

The most important decision is made first by choosing a major advisor. This is typically the person who has served as your academic advisor, but it doesn't have to be. Choose someone who has expertise in your area of interest, who has high standards, and who has a history of working effectively with students. Arrange an appointment during which you will share your idea and outline the tentative plans. Then ask the person to chair the committee. You may already know others that could serve on the committee. Before extending the invitation, check with your major advisor. You want people who will provide substantive feedback and occasional assistance as the research process unfolds. Your advisor should be able to help in choosing other committee members. He or she has worked with other faculty members and may have personal preferences. To be honest, you want to make sure your chairperson will be able to get along with other committee members.

Keep in touch with the committee members while developing the proposal and provide them with plenty of time to read and react to drafts. It is easier to ask when they will be able to provide feedback if you turn in sections of your proposal in a timely manner. Of course, never give anyone your only copy of anything.

Community/Administrative Support. Tentatively identify key people in the community who can assist with your project. Of specific interest are those who hold administrative positions at potential data collection sites. Make informal contact with them to introduce yourself, outline your tentative plan, provide a rationale, and discuss potential benefits to participants. Because you haven't received formal permission to proceed, they cannot consent to participate at this time. However, listen to their perceptions regarding your proposal. They may point out unique features of their setting that can have implications for your work. You can use this information to revise the plan if necessary. Such meetings can result in letters of support that contribute to the viability of the project.

Obtaining Permission. Secure the application forms required by your university's Human Subjects Review Board or Animal Use Committee. Formal action cannot be taken until the project is approved by the committee. Having all the paperwork done in advance will allow you to act quickly once permission has been granted.

Preparing for the Writing Task

The proposal writing task may initially appear very formidable. We agree that the preliminary procedure can appear quite daunting. Spooner and Heller (1993) developed a series of recommendations for researchers who are in the early stages of their careers. We think they make sense for students who are in the early stages of writing their proposal.

First, they recommend that you be at your physical best. This doesn't mean you should put off writing until you drop ten pounds or can run a five-minute mile. All it means is that you should get sufficient rest, eat right, and exercise regularly. Second, they recommend setting up a specific place to write and equip it with all the materials needed. Also, set aside a specific time each day for writing. Third, keep track of ideas that occur to you when not at your writing space. You never know when the perfect solution to that nagging writing problem will pop into your head. Fourth, let the ideas flow. Write phrases and incomplete sentences as they emerge. They can be fully developed later. Fifth, develop and use an outline. You don't have to adhere to it completely, but as long as there is a map, you won't be lost for long. Sixth, write the first draft. It doesn't have to be perfect; it's enough to get your ideas down on paper.

Format of the Proposal

Having selected a committee, established contacts in the community, and created a mind set, it is now time to get down to the nuts and bolts of your proposal.

Writing Style. You are not writing the next great American novel; you are writing as a scientist. Be direct and to the point, and use objective, unbiased language. Solid writing skills are very important. You need to be able to construct sentences, tie them together into a cohesive paragraph, organize paragraphs into a sequence, and make transitions from one paragraph to the next. There are a few tricks of the trade from which even experienced writers may benefit. Best (1997) and Borg, Gall, and Gall (1992) offer several style aides. We present them in Table 15.1.

Style Manual. There are many different style manuals for professional writing. One may have been adopted by your graduate school or department. Style manuals include very specific information regarding items such as abstracts, verb tense, person and voice, number use, and gender-free language. Although they all require documents be double spaced, these manuals can vary on other points such as paper size, width of margins, style and type of font, and references. We list some of these style manuals in Table 15.2. You should obtain a copy of the appropriate manual and follow its recommendations as the proposal is written.

Probably the most frequently used style manual is the Publication Manual of the American Psychological Association (4th ed.). Figure 15.1 is a short paper about this style, written according to APA guidelines.

Table 15.1   Style Aids

Best (1993) and Borg, Gall, and Gall (1993) offered several tips to enhance your writing style.

1. Use objective, unbiased language.
2. Use transition sentences to connect main ideas and topics.
3. Be very clear when you are expressing someone else's research findings (e.g., "Bodkin (1989) indicated that . . .").
4. Do not use a repetitive writing style (e.g., starting every sentence with the name of an author).
5. Avoid repeating the same word. Use synonyms interchangeably such as "subject," "participant," or "respondent."
6. Short simple sentences are better than long complex sentences that confuse the reader.
7. Avoid jargon.
8. Avoid slang.
9. In the interest of objectivity, do not use personal pronouns. Use "The data were analyzed . . ." rather than "I analyzed the data."
10. Use direct quotations sparingly.

Table 15.2   Style Manuals

Many style manuals are available to guide you in writing your proposal. The following is a list of the major style manuals used in the social sciences.

The ACS Style Guide: A Manual for Authors and Editors
American Chemical Society
1155 16th Street, NW
Washington, DC 20036
Publication Date: 1997

CBE Style Manual (5th ed.)
Council of Biology Editors, Inc.
Bethesda, MD 20814
Publication Date: 1994

The Chicago Manual of Style (14th ed.)
The University of Chicago Press
Chicago, IL 60637
Publication Date: 1993

A Manual for Writers of Term Papers, Theses, and Dissertations (5th ed.)
The University of Chicago Press,
Chicago, IL 60637
Publication Date: 1987

MLA Handbook for Writers of Research Papers (4th ed.)
Modern Language Association of America
10 Astor Place
New York, NY 10003
Publication Date: 1995

Publication Manual of the American Psychological Association (4th ed.)
American Psychological Association
750 First Avenue, NE
Washington, DC 20002
Publication Date: 1994

Running head: SAMPLE APA STYLE PAPER

The Title of Your Paper Goes Here

Your Name

Your Affiliation

Figure 15.1 A Paper Reflecting APA Style

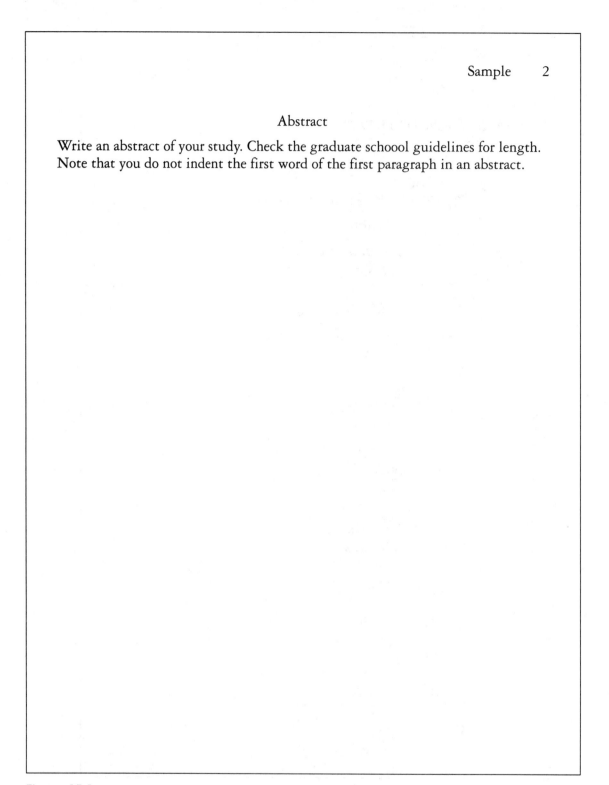

Abstract

Write an abstract of your study. Check the graduate schoool guidelines for length. Note that you do not indent the first word of the first paragraph in an abstract.

Figure 15.1 Continued

The Title of Your Paper Goes Here

You should begin writing with some general comments that introduce your paper and establish your purpose. Note that everything is double spaced. Note that margins are 1 inch all around. Don't justify both margins, only the left one. It may help to divide your paper into sections that are preceded by headings. For a thesis or dissertation, you may be required to use chapter names and numbers. Again, check graduate school requirements. There are several levels of headings in APA; you need to look at the manual for more information. In our own writing, we figure out headings last, after the paper is written.

You need to be very careful about references. The references listed in this text are in APA 4th ed. format. You also need to be very careful about citing references within the text of your paper. The next sentence is one example of how to paraphrase someone else's words and cite them at the same time. According to Smith and Jones (1988), the definition for exclusionary time out is the loss of the opportunity for reinforcement due to the removal of a child from the immediate environment to another separate setting. Please note that this is not a direct quote; I have paraphrased. This is neither my thought nor information that is already known to me or widely known by others. Therefore, I must include a citation. The next sentence is another way of paraphrasing and citing. The definition for exclusionary time out is the loss of the opportunity for reinforcement due to the removal of a child from the immediate environment to another separate setting (Smith & Jones, 1988). Note circumstances under which the "&" and the word "and" are used.

You need to be very careful about quoting. Don't include too many quotes because the paper is supposed to reflect your ability to integrate and synthesize the work of several authors. The next sentence is one way to quote. According to Smith and Jones (1988), the definition for exclusionary time out is "loss of the opportunity for reinforcement due to the removal of a child from the immediate environment to another separate setting" (p. 115). The next sentence is another way to quote. Exclusionary time out is "loss of the opportunity for reinforcement due to the removal of a child from the immediate environment to another separate setting" (Smith & Jones, 1988, p. 115). Pay close attention to quotation marks, location of authors' names, page number, and punctuation.

Figure 15.1 Continued

To quote over 40 words, use a freestanding block and omit the quotation marks. An example follows.

> For example, APA (1994,) suggests the following guidelines
>
> Start such a block quotation on a new line, and indent it five spaces from the left margin (in the same position as a new paragraph). Type subsequent lines flush with the indent.
>
> > If there are additional paragraphs within the quotation, indent the first line of each five spaces from the margin of the quotation. Type the entire quotation doublespaced. (p. 95)
>
> One thing you have to watch out for is a cite within a cite. Generally, don't do it. For example, if you are reading Smith and Jones (1988) and they mention Brown and Duke (1985), you cannot do any variation of the following sentence. According to Brown and Duke (1985) (cited in Smith & Jones, 1988), there are many disadvantages associated with the use of time out. Don't rely on what Smith and Jones have to say about Brown and Duke. Look at Smith and Jones reference list; find the Brown and Duke cite; go to the library; get Brown and Duke's publication; read it, and paraphrase or quote them, using them as your only source for that thought. The exception is when the original source is completely unavailable to you (it's printed in another language; it's an unpublished manuscript or unpublished data; it's a paper presented at a professional conference). Again, if it's in a journal or a book, use the resources at the library to get it.
>
> There must be a perfect match between the citations in your text and the references you list at the end of your paper. If you do not cite the author in the text, do not include the publication on the reference list.
>
> Paragraphs consist of more than one sentence, no matter how long that sentence is. If you have a one sentence paragraph, re-work it. Add another sentence that enhances the thought, or combine it with the previous or next paragraph.
>
> Despite the informal tone of this figure, personal referents (such as "I," "We," and "You" and contractions are not appropriate in an APA paper. Use something like, "In this writer's opinion . . ." or "It has been the experience of this writer . . .".

Figure 15.1 Continued

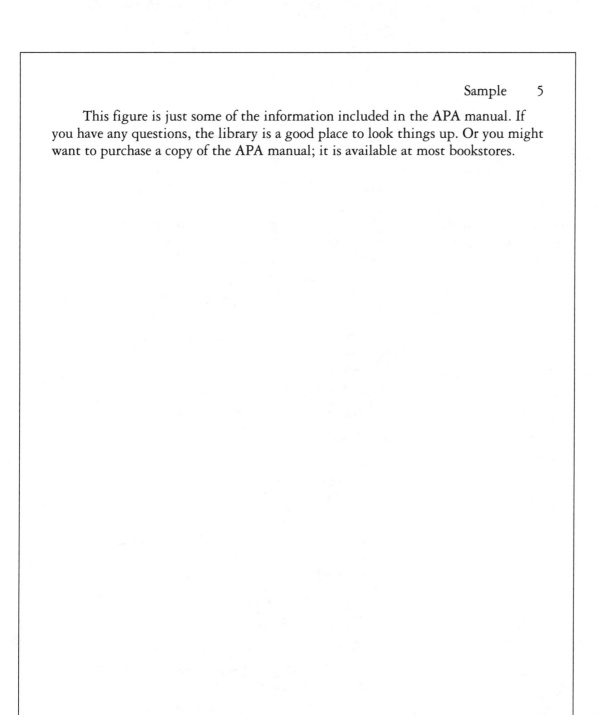

This figure is just some of the information included in the APA manual. If you have any questions, the library is a good place to look things up. Or you might want to purchase a copy of the APA manual; it is available at most bookstores.

Figure 15.1 Continued

References

(List your references here. Remember, there must be a perfect match between citations in the text and references on this page. List them alphabetically by the last name of the first author of the publication. If you have several publications by the same author or series of authors, list them chronologically. Be careful with punctuation, underlining, indenting, and capitalizing. You only need volume numbers for journals with continuous pages. For example, the first issue of the year ends on page 50; the second issue of the year starts on page 51. You need volume and issue numbers for journals with discontinuous pages; that is, each issue starts with page 1. Below are sample references for journals, books, edited books, print media, and electronic media. These are included on pp. 194-222 of the APA manual.)

Ansbacher, H. L. (1988). What is positive mental health? In D. G. Smith, Jr. & C. C. Jones (Eds.), *Prevention of psychopathology: Volume 2. Environmental influences* (pp. 3-6). Hanover, NH: Press of New England.

Barlow, D. H. (Ed.). (1991). Diagnosis, dimensions, and DSM-IV: The science of classification [Special issue]. *Journal of Abnormal Psychology, 100*(3).

Bekerian, D. A. (1993). In search of the typical eyewitness. *American Psychologist, 48,* 574-576.

Birney, A. J., & Hall, M. M. (1991). *Early identification of children with written language disabilities* (Report No. 81-1505). Washington, DC: National Education Association.

Central Vein Occlusion Study Group. (1993, October 2). Central vein occlusion study of photocoagulation: Manual of operations [675 paragraphs]. *On-line Journal of Current Clinical Trials* [On-line serial] Available: Doc. No. 92.

College bound seniors. (1989). Princeton, NJ: College Board Publications.

Compas, B. E., Wagner, B. M., Slavin, L. A., & Vannatta, K. (in press). A prospective study of life events. *American Journal of Psychology.*

Crystal, L. (Executive Producer). (1993, October 11). *The McNeil/Lehrer news hour.* New York and Washington, DC.: Public Broadcasting Service.

Dawson, B., De Armas, A., McGrath, M., & Kelly, J. A. (1995). *Cognitive problem-solving training to improve child-care.* Unpublished manuscript. University of Mississippi Medical Center.

Figure 15.1 Continued

Funder, D. C. (1994, March). Judgmental process and content: Commentary on base-rate [9 paragraphs]. *Psycoloquy* [On-line serial], 5(17). Available E-mail: psyc@puc Message: Get psyc 94-99

Gottfredson, L. S. (1990). How valid are occupational reinforcer pattern scores? (Report No. CSOS-R-292). Baltimore, MD: Johns Hopkins University, Center for Social Organization of Schools. (ERIC Document Reproductive Service No. ED 182 465).

Harrison, J. (Producer), & Scmiechen, R. (Director). (1992). The story of Evelyn Hooker [Film]. (Available from Changing Our Minds, Inc., 170 West Avenue, Suite 2, New York, NY 10023).

Lumsden, C. J., & Wilson, E. O. (1991). *Genes, mind, and culture: The coevolutionary process.* Cambridge, MA: Harvard University Press.

Meyer, A. S. (1992). The tip-of-the-tongue phenomenon: Blocking or partial activation? [On-line]. *Memory & Cognition, 20,* 715-726. Abstract from: DIALOG File: PsycINFO Item: 80-16351.

Meyer, A. S., & Bock, K. (1994). The tip-of-the-tongue phenomenon: A meta-analysis of the literature. {CD-ROM}. *Memory & Cognition, 30,* 255-299. Abstract from Silver Platter File: PsycINFO Item: 90-23485.

Miller, R. (Producer). (1991). *The mind.* New York: WNET.

National Health Interview Survey—Current health topics: 1991-Longitudinal study of aging (Version 4) {Electronic data tape}. (1992). Hyattsville, MD: National Center for Health Statistics [Producer and Distributor].

Posner, M. I. (1993, October 29). Seeing the mind. *Science, 262,* 673-674.

Ruby, J., & Fulton, C. (1993, June). *Beyond redlining: Editing software that works.* Poster session presented at the annual meeting of the Society for Scholarly Publishing, Washington, DC.

Sigel, I. E. (Ed.). (1995). *Parental belief systems: The psychological consequences for children.* San Francisco: Lawrence Erlbaum.

Slaughter, D. T. (1993). Early intervention and its effects on maternal and child development. *Monographs for the Society for Research in Child Development, 48* (4, Serial No. 202).

Spetch, M. L., & Wilkie, D. M. (1993). Subjective shortening: A model of pigeons' memory. *Journal of Experimental Psychology: Animal Behavior Processes, 9*(1), 14-30.

Figure 15.1 Continued

Graduate School Guidelines. You are encouraged to obtain a copy of the thesis or dissertation standards approved by the graduate school at your university. While the proposal components we will discuss next are fairly standard, you should make sure our components reflect your program's specific guidelines.

Components of the Proposal

Table 15.3 presents the components of a written proposal. They are very similar to those included in a thesis or dissertation report. In fact, they are very similar to the major sections of a published report. Fuchs and Fuchs (1993) noted that this format is deeply rooted in the scientific method. Although the format may appear inflexible and arbitrary to the novice, it ultimately enhances the dissemination of research. In your role as a research consumer, this format allows you to access information more quickly. In your role as a research contributor, this format makes writing easier, thereby increasing your communication effectiveness and efficiency.

Introduction or Identification of the Research Problem. The first chapter in your proposal is just a few pages in length. Start the introduction by describing the problem area. Shift to a brief overview of the literature that leads to a concise and straightforward statement of the problem. Indicate why the problem is worth exploring, that is, make it clear that it will contribute to theory or practice. You want the problem to stand out so it is clearly recognizable to your readers (Wiersma, 1995). At the end of the introduction, include definitions of terms used in subsequent sections of the proposal. Include all the variables in the question or hypothesis, characteristics of your sample, and theories or models.

Literature Review. The main purpose of your literature review is to put your hypothesis or research questions into a proper context. Obviously, readers of your proposal will have very sophisticated levels of knowledge and will probably be familiar with the topic and the literature to be reviewed. Length will vary, although many times the literature review is the longest section in a proposal. Wiersma (1995) suggested you remember the following points when constructing the literature review.

1. *Be selective.* Though an enormous amount of material has been digested, include only those studies that directly relate to the research question. Consult all the index cards and analysis forms you maintain, as recommended in Chapter 4.

2. *Highlight the relationship between your study and previous work.* This is not done by stringing together a series of paragraphs that describe previous studies. Instead, tie them together in a critique that emphasizes findings, and make their relevance clear.

3. *Point out gaps in the literature.* Make the case that the knowledge base is incomplete without the answer to the research question being posed.

4. *Organize your literature review.* Again, the index cards you used during the literature search can come in handy. Organize them by main points and themes. Decide how you will arrange the points, and use heading and subheadings to help the reader follow the flow of the discussion.

5. *Summarize the most salient points at the end of your review.*

Your literature review should lead to the statement of the hypothesis or research question. A quantitative study uses a null hypothesis that indicates there will be no significant difference between performance on measures of the dependent variables. Also useful may be a directional hypothesis in which the anticipated direction of results is identified. A question format is appropriate for survey research. For a qualitative research proposal, you can present foreshadowed

Table 15.3   A Checklist of Components That Should Be Included in a Research Proposal

When preparing your research proposal, make sure you can answer "yes" to each of these items.

Introduction

Did I start by identifying the problem?

Is my overview of the literature brief?

Have I described how this work will contribute?

Did I define all of the terms I am using?

Literature Review

Have I included all of the most important studies related to my topic?

Does my review highlight gaps in knowledge?

Does my review progress from one major theme to the next?

Methods

Sample

Did I describe a sampling procedure?

Did I identify how many subjects I will need?

Dependent Variables

Did I describe the dependent variable?

Did I describe how I will measure the dependent variable?

Did I include samples of measures I created?

Did I describe procedures for ensuring reliability?

Independent Variable

Did I define the independent variable?

Did I include a technological description?

Did I describe how I will train other therapist agents?

Did I describe procedures for ensuring procedural reliability?

Design

Did I identify an appropriate design?

Data Analysis

Did I identify how my data will be analyzed?

References

Is there an exact match between citations in my text and on the reference page?

Did I adhere to suggestions in the style manual?

---

problems, that is, broad, anticipated research questions that will be reformulated through data collection.

Methods. The methods section of your proposal is the section likely to receive the most scrutiny from committee members. It is your plan of action, and you need to specify exactly what will be accomplished. A common mistake we see is that a proposal lacks detail. It is important to spell out every aspect of acquiring, arranging, processing, and interpreting the data. Try to anticipate the questions of those reading the proposal and answer them in advance. Also, if you know of a weakness or anticipate problems, describe the method used to compensate. There are several components to a methods section. They vary slightly depending on whether you are conducting a quantitative study or a qualitative study.

In a quantitative study, a complete description of the population of interest is presented. At this point, the specific subjects may not be identified, but you should know how many will be needed. A power analysis may even be conducted. Also included may be a demographic data sheet in which basic information about the subject is recorded. Describe clearly how you will locate a pool of subjects and how participants will be selected from that pool. Chapter 8 addressed sampling designs. It may help to go back and review the procedures we described.

The next part of the methods section in quantitative study addresses your instrumentation. Describe the data collection procedures you will use to measure the dependent variable. Identify any standardized tests you will be using and discuss why they are an appropriate choice. Include reliability and validity information. Describe other measures such as surveys, questionnaires, and systematic observation, and how they will be conducted and scored. Attach copies of them in the appendix. You may find it helpful to review Chapter 9.

Next, you need to describe your independent variable or variables. If it is a subject or individual difference independent variable (such as intelligence), identify the standardized assessment procedure to be used for measurement. If it is an instructional independent variable that is intended to change perceptions, include the specific instruction to be given. If it is an environmental or situational independent variable, provide a clear and complete description. If someone else will be serving as a treatment agent, describe what their qualifications will be and how they will be trained. Review Chapter 10 for more information on defining the independent variables for a quantitative study.

When proposing a qualitative study, address specific methodological features. You should identify your proposed site, your research role, the settings, and the purposeful sampling strategy you will use. Identify when the study will be conducted and for how long. Describe how you plan to enter the field and record data.

Design. Identify the design you intend to use. The choice should be rational, ethical, defensible, and capable of yielding answers to the stated problem. For a quantitative research proposal, you can specify a design by name. For a qualitative study, identify the nature of the data to be gathered (e.g., participant observation field notes, interviews, content analysis of documents).

Data Analysis. For a large group quantitative study, identify and provide a rationale for the data analysis techniques to be used to test each hypothesis or answer each question. You may need to identify forms of data presentation, that is, the tables, figures, and charts to be used to organize and summarize the data. This section could be the most intimidating part of a proposal. However, it is easier to think about it now and have it worked out before data are collected. If assistance is needed, consult with your advisor.

For a qualitative study, emphasize that data collection and data analysis are simultaneous rather than sequential. Also, discuss whether to use an analytic inductive approach or a constant comparative approach.

Regardless of the nature of the study, indicate where the data will be stored. This may be a condition for obtaining permission to conduct the study from the university's human subject committee.

References. All the precautions taken to maintain high quality notes during the literature review will pay off here. The citations you used should be at the tips of your fingers. It is simply a matter of placing them in alphabetical order. Make sure you adhere to the guidelines stated in the style manual.

Appendixes. This section of your proposal can include devices created to measure the dependent variable, instructions you plan to give to your subjects, pilot studies, and a proposed timeline for completing the study.

Miscellaneous. Check the requirements of the graduate school to prepare items such as a cover page and an abstract.

Obtaining Feedback While Preparing the Proposal

Once you have completed each section of your proposal, you may want to set it aside for a day or two and then reread it. Leedy (1993) suggested that you review it critically and objectively, looking for coherence and comprehensiveness. Don't wait too long before distributing it to committee members. Yours is not the only committee in which they are involved, and the clock is ticking.

When a committee member has read a section or the entire proposal, make an appointment with him or her to discuss reactions, questions, concerns, and recommendations for change. All the reading you did for the literature review can really help now. You should be able to respond intelligently to concerns about any aspect of your proposal. Negotiate changes that should be made. On a related note, it is possible that two committee members will make conflicting recommendations for changes. Listen to their rationale and enlist the support of your committee chairperson.

DEFENDING YOUR PROPOSAL

The Relative Importance of a Proposal Defense

In the previous section, we discussed how to develop a proposal suitable for preliminary submission to the thesis or dissertation committee. We advised you to select your committee members with care and keep them apprised of your progress. We encouraged you to submit various sections of the proposal to committee members in a timely manner. This provides committee members with plenty of time to examine your work carefully and offer comments and suggestions. You, in turn, have time to consider their suggestions, review your work (especially the literature review), then make and resubmit revisions. We review this information for a purpose. At this point, be ready to schedule an oral proposal defense, and we do not advise "walking into it cold." Long before the day of your proposal defense, every effort should have been made to complete drafts in a timely manner and get crucial feedback. You should be reasonably confident that your meeting will go well. Unfortunately, things can still go wrong.

It is not surprising when, at several points during their academic careers in higher education, students express concern over a dissertation defense that is still semesters away. This focus on the dissertation could be due to the fact that it is the last milestone you must pass to earn your degree. In fact, of the two meetings, the proposal defense is more important. This is the meeting during which you explain and defend your ideas. Many of the skills you have been developing and fine tuning over the last several semesters are being tested. It is the last chance your committee members have to suggest, even require, changes before deciding whether they will grant you permission to move forward. While we have rarely heard of a student's dissertation being rejected after a defense, we have witnessed several occasions where a proposal was rejected as a result of events at the meeting. In this section, we discuss how to prepare for, and behave during, your proposal defense. We have to be honest up front and tell you that we cannot offer anything but advice. We have no references to the professional literature; we only have our experiences to share.

Providing Adequate Notice Prior to the Formal Meeting

Having addressed all the concerns and questions raised by your committee, you and your advisor should select a date to defend. Actually, you should pick several, then meet with committee members to compare schedules. Select a date and time that are mutually convenient and confirm both with committee members. In addition, you should see the department secretary to schedule a room, post an announcement, and obtain any necessary forms. Be aware that, depending on university policy, part or all of your defense is open to the public. A bulletin board is usually reserved for such announcements. Don't be surprised at the number of people who check the board regularly.

The department or the graduate school will need at least one form completed, signed, and dated by committee members to document the outcome of the meeting. You or your advisor should complete appropriate sections and hold onto the form until the meeting. You should also discuss the format of the meeting with your advisor. Find out how much time is typically allotted to you for your presentation and to committee members and the audience for questions. Ask if part of your meeting will be closed to the public and if you are expected to leave at the end of the question and answer period so that the committee can debate your fate.

Preparing for the Proposal Defense

Hopefully, you have attended other students' defenses and have made several formal presentations on your own. These experiences will be helpful as you plan to defend your proposal. Start early. Review your literature periodically to increase the fluency with which you make your presentation and the clarity and accuracy of your responses to questions. Review your proposal in order to be well versed in all of its aspects. We know that you wrote it and realize that you probably feel confident about its contents, but don't underestimate the power of last minute butterflies. It is a good idea to overlearn. Prepare an outline of the main points you intend to cover.

You should also prepare materials to help your audience understand what you are trying to do. Committee members should already have a copy of your proposal, but you may want to develop a handout listing major points for other audience members. You should also decide what your technological needs are. Will you be using an overhead? Are you skilled at using Microsoft PowerPoint? Make whatever materials you will need.

A Week Before the Meeting

If you have completed your proposal in a timely manner, then you will have the luxury of devoting more time to the preparation of your defense. Check out the room where your defense will be held. Find out what audio-visual equipment is typically available and make sure it, and all the outlets, are working. Report any problems to the department secretary. Also, you should determine if you have any particular equipment needs. For example, you may have decided to make a PowerPoint presentation. Ask the secretary where you can locate the proper equipment. One week should be plenty of notice for the instructional resources department. Oddly enough, you should also determine if the room has a working clock that is visible from where you will be presenting. If necessary, bring a travel alarm and place where it can be seen. It is much less distracting to glance at the clock than it is to continually check your wristwatch.

We also encourage you to start practicing your presentation, preferably in front of an audience. Ask family members, friends, colleagues, and other students to be your audience members. You can be sure that the Olympic-caliber gymnast frequently has an audience so that she becomes accustomed to performing in public. You, too, should prepare for your moment in the spotlight (or on the hot seat).

We also suggest that you find out if fellow students will be attending. They can assist during your defense, as we will discuss shortly. Finally, although stress is inevitable, we encourage rest, a good diet, and exercise.

Just Before the Proposal Meeting

The evening before your defense, we recommend reviewing your presentation to ensure that your graphics, whether high- or low-tech, are ready. This is a good time to decide what to wear. Remember, you want to portray yourself as a credible, competent researcher, so dress for the part. Appear professional but comfortable. Others attending the meeting, even your committee members, will probably be more casually dressed. That is their perogative, as they have nothing to lose and no one to impress.

Early on the day of your meeting, check the room to ensure that the necessary equipment is available and in good working order. Check with your chairperson for any final instructions or words of wisdom. Be certain that the necessary paperwork is available at the meeting. Go to the room a bit early so you are there before committee members or other observers arrive. Introduce yourself to unfamiliar people and make handouts available. Some students we know have brought light refreshments to their proposal meetings. Actually, fellow students could assist you by distributing handouts and passing out refreshments.

Your Responsibilities During the Proposal Meeting

The committee chair will get everyone's attention to start the meeting. He or she will probably make any necessary introductions, formally introduce you to the group, set a time limit for the presentation, then turn the meeting over to you. The time will pass very quickly. Here are the points to cover.

Establish the background for the study. Spend a moment describing how you became interested in the topic, but move quickly into the major outcomes of the literature review. Again, establish credibility. Don't review the results of every study. Rather, show how findings of important previous work merged into patterns and led to your hypothesis or question.

State the Objectives for the Research. Clearly identify and display the hypothesis being tested or question being posed. Emphasize how results can potentially contribute to theory, or practice, or both.

Identify the Methods. Explain who your subjects will be and how they will be selected for the study. Precisely explain what your dependent and independent variables are and how they will be measured. Identify the steps in applying the independent variable in their chronological order. Describe your design and data analysis procedures, and provide a rationale for selecting them.

Suggest Potential Outcomes. Speculate as to what you think the outcomes will be, based on information gleaned through the literature.

Solicit and be Responsive to Feedback. Before you know it, the allotted time will be up, and the committee chair will call for questions. Generally, he or she will ask other committee members to go first. One committee member may ask all of his or her questions before another speaks, or they may alternate. The committee chair may ask additional questions then call for questions or comments from other audience members.

Answer all Questions Clearly, Precisely, and Without Any Elaboration. Anyone who wants you to elaborate will ask. If you don't understand a question, ask for clarification. If you're still not sure, you can say, "As I understand the question, you are asking me. . . ." If you understand the question perfectly and still don't know the answer, say so. As long as the rest of your meeting went as planned, you will not undermine your credibility by admitting you occasionally don't have an answer. It is also possible that audience members will be asked to leave, and your committee members will continue to ask questions.

Taking Notes During the Meeting. A question you can't answer should signal you to take notes. Based on the questions and comments, your committee may have some specific recommendations for changing your proposal. You should document these as well. If you think it would be too difficult to hold a substantive discussion and take notes at the same time, then ask a fellow student to take notes for you. These notes are very important. You may need them to review the literature or revise your proposal.

The Decision

You should know in advance if you will be asked to leave while the committee makes its decision. Wait outside until your advisor asks you to rejoin the group and informs you of the decision. Hopefully, it will be good news. Make careful notes of any changes they are requesting. This amended proposal now constitutes an agreement between you and your committee regarding the exact nature of your project. This is why the proposal meeting is so important. You now need to do only those items you have agreed to do, nothing more, nothing less. Obtain any necessary signatures and go celebrate!

SUMMARY

Having completed all the tasks outlined in previous chapters, you are now ready to write and present a proposal. This proposal will enable you to communicate, not only what you intend to do, but why. It is an important step in establishing your credibility as an independent researcher.

This chapter had two major sections. First, we discussed procedures necessary to ensure that the proposal you develop meets the expectations of your committee members and the graduate school at your university. We suggested techniques to prepare you for the challenge of writing. We also advised you to adhere to a style manual and graduate school requirements as you write. We identified and described components of the proposal and provided a checklist to ensure they are included. Finally, we suggested how to obtain and respond to constructive criticism.

The second major section in this chapter described the importance of the proposal defense meeting. Frequently, students do not realize that the proposal defense is more important than the dissertation. It is the meeting at which you and your committee come to a formal agreement regarding the scope of your research project. We described several ideas you can implement to increase the likelihood of a positive outcome to your meeting.

REFERENCES

Best, J. W. (1997). *Research in education* (8th ed.). Upper Saddle River, NJ: Merrill/Prentice-Hall.

Borg, W. R., Gall, J. P., & Gall, M. D. (1992). *Applying educational research: A practical guide* (3rd. ed.). New York: Longman.

Fuchs, L. S., & Fuchs. D. (1993). Writing research reports for publication: Recommendations for new authors. *Remedial and Special Education, 14*(3), 39–46.

Leedy, P. D. (1996). *Practical research: Planning and design* (6th ed.). New York: Macmillan.

Rudestam, K. E., & Newton, R. R. (1992). *Surviving your dissertation: A comprehensive* guide to content and process (3rd ed.). Newbury Park, CA: Sage.

Spooner, F., & Heller, H. W. (1993). Writing for publication in journals for prac-titioners: Suggestions for teachers and early career researchers. *Remedial and Special Education, 14*(3), 47–52.

Wiersma, W. (1995). *Research methods in education: An introduction* (6th ed.). Needham Heights, MA: Allyn & Bacon.

FURTHER READINGS

Borg, W. R., & Gall, M. D. (1989). *Educational research: A guide for preparing a thesis or dissertation proposal in education.* New York: Longman.

Madsen, D. (1991). *Successful dissertations and theses: A guide to graduate student research from proposal to completion* (2nd ed.). San Francsco, CA: Jossey-Bass, Inc.

Manheim, J. B., & Rich, R. C. (1994). *Empirical political analysis: Research methods in political science* (4th ed.). New York: Longman.

McMillan, J. H., & Schumcher, S. (1996). *Research in education: A conceptual introduction* (4th ed.). New York: HarperCollins Publishers.

Mitchell, M., & Jolley, J. (1992). *Research design explained* (2nd ed.). Fort Worth, TX: Harcourt Brace Jovanovich College.

Pyrczak, F., & Bruce, R. R. (1992). *Writing empirical research reports: A basic guide for students of the social and behavioral sciences.* Los Angeles, CA: Pyrczak Publishing.

Silverman, F. H. (1997). *Research design and evaluation in speech-language pathology and audiology* (4th ed.). Needham Heights, MA: Allyn & Bacon.

Zikmund, W. G. (1996). *Business research methods* (5th ed.). Chicago: Research Press.

16

Conducting and Reporting Your Research Project

INTRODUCTION

We assume by now that you have recovered sufficiently from celebratory activities surrounding the successful defense of your thesis or dissertation proposal. Having completed some well deserved R & R, you need to get down to business. With your committee's blessing, you are about to conduct the study to which much time and energy has been devoted. It is no longer a matter of saying

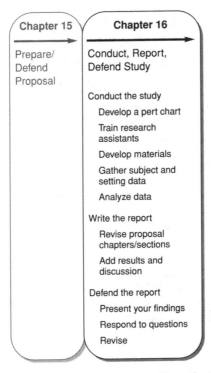

Chapter 15	Chapter 16
Prepare/ Defend Proposal	Conduct, Report, Defend Study

Conduct the study
  Develop a pert chart
  Train research assistants
  Develop materials
  Gather subject and setting data
  Analyze data

Write the report
  Revise proposal chapters/sections
  Add results and discussion

Defend the report
  Present your findings
  Respond to questions
  Revise

Scope, Plan, and Sequence Chart for Conducting Research: The Eleventh Step in the Research Process

what will be done; it's a matter of doing it. Hopefully, the discipline you have demonstrated over the last few months of proposal development will continue in the next phase of the research process.

This chapter is divided into three sections. First, we discuss how you should actually conduct your project. Next we discuss writing your thesis or dissertation. With modification, the three chapters in your proposal will serve as the first three chapters of the thesis or dissertation. We will discuss how to modify them, then direct our attention to the development of the results and discussion sections. We devote the third section to the dissertation defense.

CONDUCT YOUR STUDY

The activities that were described in the proposal and approved by your committee should fully guide your actions. As was the case during the proposal stage of your research, work closely with members of the committee, and keep members informed of your efforts. The fewer the surprises, the easier it should be to prepare and defend the dissertation. It is important to notify the committee of any problems or hindrance encountered as the study progresses, particularly those that may make it difficult to stay within the parameters specified in the proposal. While the intent is for you to conduct a study as an independent researcher, members of the committee are there to provide guidance if needed. Take advantage of their expertise; it's the reason they were invited to be on the committee in the first place.

Again, we highlight the possibility that members of the committee may disagree over how to handle changes. If conflict cannot be resolved between committee members, Rudestam and Newton (1992) suggest asking the chairperson to intervene on your behalf. They very wisely advise never to play one committee member against the other. You are the only one who will lose.

Before moving on, be sure to check the graduate school requirements to determine whether the composition of the committee changes as you move from the proposal stage to the implementation phase. For example, we know of one university where each dissertation proposal committee consists of two faculty members from the student's department (one acting as chairperson) and one faculty member from outside the department. For the thesis or dissertation, the student is required to add an outside reader, that is, someone else from another university who will read the dissertation and write a letter to attest to its quality. Students who have no such letter on record are not approved for graduation. Familiarize yourself with graduate school policies to avoid such unpleasant surprises at the last minute. If your committee changes, make sure you bring new members up to speed.

Develop a Pert Chart

The first activity of business after your proposal is accepted should be to develop a pert chart similar to the one presented in Figure 16.1. A pert chart is a visual representation of the timelines within which you expect to initiate and conduct activities related to your project. The left-hand column lists each component of your project. Columns on the right include spaces for noting when you anticipate starting work on that component and how long you expect work to continue. Think of a pert chart as your thesis or dissertation schedule at a glance. Keep it posted in a highly visible place to keep you going, particularly on those days when you feel as though you are just spinning your wheels. Update it as various tasks are completed. You may want to share it with your committee members to document your progress.

Obtain Permission

Now that your committee has approved your project, obtain permission from your university to conduct a study involving human subjects. We discussed this in detail in Chapter 2. Each university has its own application for approval. Obtain a copy, complete it, attach any materials

Objective	Month					
	2	4	6	8	10	12
Area of study		X				
Develop knowledge	X	X				
Research question			X			
Research hypothesis		X				
Experimental procedure			X			
Criteria for accepting hypothesis		X				
Key terms, assumptions, delimitations, limitations			X			
Present research plan			X			
Protect human subjects				X		
Carry out experiment			X	X	X	
Produce research report				X	X	
Defend research report						X

Figure 16.1 A Pert Chart

requested (e.g., sample letters to potential participants, a sample consent form, and copies or descriptions of instruments to measure the dependent variable), have your chairperson sign it, and put it in the mail. Upon approval of the university, you can re-initiate contact with administrative personnel at sites where you hope to collect data. You cannot start collecting data yet. The site has its own Human Subjects Committee to answer to, and they must give their stamp of approval. After securing permission, implement the sampling strategy described in the method section of your proposal, and distribute consent forms to those individuals who have been selected. Be prepared to wait while forms slowly return. A second batch of consent forms may need to be sent out.

Manage Personnel and Resources

While waiting for consent forms to trickle in, turn your attention to other aspects of the study. Depending on resources and topic, assistants may be needed. At the very least, you will need someone to conduct reliability checks on the dependent and independent variables. Someone else may help with data entry. Finally, another treatment agent may be needed, that is, another person who will deliver the independent variable. All of these individuals will require training. We refer you to the training procedures described in Chapter 10. Develop the training manual your observers will use. During training, make sure to note the exact sequence of events to be followed so you can include this information in your final report.

While a little time is still available, begin to assemble materials and equipment you will need for assessment and training activities. Materials can include a sufficient number of copies of standardized tests, systematic recording procedures, and worksheets.

Gather Subject and Setting Information. Start conducting the study as soon as you receive signed permission slips from all of your participants. Make sure you have subject's important demographic information such as age, gender, and ethnic background. Obtain this information; it may be difficult to locate subjects and retrieve it after the study is complete. You also need to describe the exact setting in which your study was conducted.

Pretest. If required, conduct pretest activities to measure each subject's current status on the dependent variable.

Assign Students to Groups. If you are using a group design, assign subjects to groups. Use the group assignment procedure you described in your proposal.

Implement the Independent Variable and Posttest. Your subjects have been selected, pretested, and assigned to groups, and data collectors have been trained. Now the independent variable can be applied. Conduct periodic reliability checks of the dependent and independent variable. Conduct posttesting at the end of your study.

Protect Data

As a condition for giving consent, the Human Subjects Committee at your university probably required that you ensure your subjects' confidentiality. They may also have required that your data be kept in a safe place for a specific number of years. You probably agreed to similar conditions when you received permission to conduct your study at the data collection site. As your data start to come in, you need to make good on those promises. Before they start to pile up, develop a system for storing data in a safe place accessible only to you. For example, you can place it in a file cabinet and keep the only key. You can provide additional safeguards by removing any identifying information from items such as worksheets, test booklets, and systematic recording sheets. Replace personal information with a code known only to you and possibly your advisor. Keep the master list of codes in a safe place other than the locked cabinet so that no one can come across both sets of materials.

Data Entry

It will be easier to manage your data on a daily basis than to wait until they start to accumulate. In fact, qualitative and single subject designs require daily attention to data to make decisions about your next course of action. It would be easy to let data from a quantitative study stockpile, but resist the urge. Chances are you're using a statistical package available on software or though the mainframe. You can begin data entry immediately.

Data Analysis

To analyze your data, simply carry out the procedures approved in your proposal. Qualitative data are collected and analyzed in a recursive process. Most single subject design data are analyzed through visual inspection, although less definitive results can be examined through statistical analysis. You may not have anticipated this analysis, so check with your advisor.

Update Your Literature Review

Obviously, time will elapse between the acceptance of your proposal and the defense of the thesis or dissertation. It is possible that a paper will be published that is related to the topic you are studying. Remain current by periodically checking selected preliminary resources to identify and obtain relevant primary resources as they become available over the course of your investigation.

Now that the data are in and analyzed, describe the results in writing. Do not start all over again; rather, build upon the three chapters included in the proposal, then add two more. A checklist may be helpful. Table 16.1 is an expansion of Table 15.3 presented in Chapter 15. As a reminder, just as you ensured the timely delivery of proposal drafts, make sure each committee member has copies of revised and new chapters. The more lead time you can provide, the more likely you are to receive detailed feedback.

Introduction or Statement of the Problem

Review your introduction to make sure it contains the necessary information. It is highly unlikely that this section of your report will change that much.

Literature Review

We recommended earlier that you keep abreast of new research that is related to your topic. Revise this section of your manuscript by integrating findings from recent relevant works.

Method Section

The method section has the potential for substantial changes. Remember, it is important to describe clearly every detail of your study so another person could replicate your efforts. Also, providing such detail will demonstrate your mastery of methodology.

Quantitative Studies. Describe everything using the past tense rather than the future tense. Assure your readers that standard procedures were followed for obtaining consent from both the university and the setting in which subjects were located. Identify the results of the sampling procedure, and describe the number and characteristics of the subjects. A table of demographic information may be useful. If two or more groups are used, report how many subjects were in each and how they were assigned. Provide a clear description of all treatment and control conditions including access to material and equipment. Report reliability for the dependent and independent variables. Finally, identify how long the independent variable lasted.

Qualitative Studies. Change the verb tense and verify that you obtained permission to conduct the study for qualitative studies as well. Report how you entered the field, selected the participants, and collected and recorded data. Identify the number of sites, settings, and participants involved, and provide detailed descriptions. Identify when the study was conducted and its duration. Describe the nature of the data collected, including observations, interviews, and whether corroborative procedures were used. Include the theoretical framework guiding the study, and your thoughts and perceptions during initial stages of the study and how they changed over time. The role of the researcher and the participants' reactions should be described.

Results

For quantitative studies, include basic information such as means and standard deviations for each group of subjects, followed by any correlations and inferential statistics. Discuss results separately for each hypothesis or question. If results were not statistically significant, then report only the procedure you used. If they were significant, then state the computed value of each statistic, the degrees of freedom, the level of significance, and the name of the test you used.

For single subject designs, include graphs and the results of visual inspection. With the knowledge and approval of your committee, use statistical procedures to clarify less definitive

Table 16.1   A Checklist of Components That Should Be Included in the Final Thesis or Dissertation Report

When preparing your thesis or dissertation report, make sure you can answer yes to each of these items.

Introduction

Did I start by identifying the problem?

Is my overview of the literature brief?

Have I described how this work will contribute?

Did I define all of the terms I am using?

Literature Review

Have I included all of the most important studies related to my topic?

Does my review highlight gaps in knowledge?

Does my review progress from one major theme to the next?

Methods

Did I obtain informed consent?

Sample

    Did I follow my sampling procedure?

    Did I identify how many subjects were involved?

    Did I describe the characteristics of my subjects?

Dependent Variables

    Did I describe the dependent variable?

    Did I describe how I measured the dependent variable?

    Did I include samples of measures I created?

    Did I report reliability?

results. For qualitative studies, include descriptions, analyses, interpretations of data, and any unexpected findings (Stainback & Stainback, 1988).

It may be helpful to use tables and figures that are well organized and give a clear and accurate impression of the results. For more information on figures and tables, refer to the style manual recommended by your graduate school.

Discussion

Begin your discussion by briefly restating the research problem and the main points of how the study was conducted. Provide an overview of the major findings of the study that were confirmed and those that were rejected. Integrate these findings with previous literature. State your con-

Table 16.1   Continued

Independent Variable

    Did I define the independent variable?

    Did I include a technological description?

    Did I describe the setting?

    Did I describe how I trained other therapist agents?

    Did I report procedural reliability?

Design

    Did I identify the design I used?

    Did I describe how subjects were assigned to groups?

Data Analysis

    Did I identify how my data were analyzed?

Results

    Did I provide descriptive information?

    Did I report results for each hypothesis?

    Did I include tables?

Discussion

    Did I identify the major findings of my work?

    Did I compare and contrast my findings to other studies?

    Did I indicate how these findings add to the research?

    Did I identify limitations?

    Did I include recommendations for future research?

References

    Is there an exact match between citations in my text and those on the reference page?

    Did I adhere to suggestions in the style manual?

clusions and interpretations. Do not deride the results, but clearly state if there are any limitations that affect confidence in your conclusions. Finally, offer suggestions for future research.

References and Appendixes

Any new articles included in the literature review should be included in the reference list. Testing information and sample consent forms are placed in the appendixes.

Miscellaneous Items

You will need to include a title page, an abstract, a table of contents, a list of figures, and, if desired, an acknowledgment. Check the graduate school guidelines for exact specifications.

Defend the Research Results

In the last chapter, we expressed our opinion that the proposal defense was more serious than the thesis or dissertation defense. You may not feel that way as the appointed time draws near. Certainly, it can be an anxiety-producing experience. The nature of a dissertation defense can range from a very perfunctory meeting, where approval is nearly rubber-stamped, to something downright unpleasant. A colleague who defended his dissertation fairly recently reported that such meetings on his campus are "free-for-alls," with faculty showing up to "take their last shots at you before you get out." It is likely that your defense meeting will be something in between these extremes. In this section, we describe how to prepare for a dissertation defense.

Reconvene the Committee

Use the procedures described in Chapter 15 to select a date and time for your defense. Inspect the room where you will be making your presentation. Again, make sure to provide members with the most recent copy of your thesis or dissertation well in advance of the meeting. It may also be advisable to arrange individual meetings with committee members in the days before the defense to review and discuss any concerns they may have. Don't forget to send a copy of your report to your outside committee member.

Present Your Findings

Credibility is still important, so review your work to be thoroughly familiar with the topic. Again, this meeting is open to the public. You're on stage, so it is important that you rehearse your part. The presentation will probably be limited to between 45 minutes to one hour. Be prepared to use visual aids to highlight your results.

Review the background, and state the hypothesis. At the proposal meeting, you already established your fluency with the literature and your credibility as a potential researcher. The committee is more interested in hearing what transpired over the course of the study. They are also interested in hearing what you have made of the results. Unless a recent study has particular implications for your literature review, you should not spend time doing more than a cursory review of the background.

Review Methodology. Your committee will be very interested in this portion of your presentation. They will want to know how closely you were able to adhere to the specifications of the proposal, whether problems occurred, and how they were handled.

Describe Results. Present your results, one hypothesis at a time.

Discuss Results. Relate your results to previous findings in the literature. Offer your interpretations of what happened.

Discuss Implications. Identify the contribution your study has made to the professional literature. Provide recommendations for future research.

Field Questions. Be prepared to spend part of your defense answering questions. We have yet to attend a defense where there wasn't at least one question the candidate couldn't answer. Occasionally, someone asks a question that is outside the scope of your research. It is perfectly acceptable to point that out. At the end of the questions, you will be asked to leave so that your committee can meet in private and make their decision. This is usually just a formality. It is highly unlikely your chairperson would have allowed you to schedule a defense if you were not ready. Request that all committee members autograph your signature sheet, which officially records the successful defense of your thesis dissertation.

REVISE YOUR FINAL MANUSCRIPT

Committee members may request minor revisions such as fixing a table, or major revisions that suggest more serious flaws in your work. The latter can be prevented by providing committee members copies of the work well before the defense. That way there will be time before the defense to make changes. Attend to revisions as soon as possible. Have your final draft bound and placed in the library; give a bound copy to each member of your committee.

Finally, you may also wish to acknowledge each committee member's contribution to your professional development. Although it is not required, it is not unusual to present him or her with a small gift as a token of your appreciation.

SUMMARY

Completing a thesis or dissertation means you have mastered the information in this text. We know it has been a slow process, but we hope your first foray into conducting research is by no means your last. As with any skill, the more you practice, the easier it gets.

REFERENCES

Rudestam, K. E. & Newton, R. R. (1992). *Surviving your dissertation: A comprehensive guide to content and process* (3rd ed). Newbury Park, CA: Sage.

Stainback, S., & Stainback, W. (1988). *Understanding and conducting qualitative research.* Reston, VA: Council for Exceptional Children.

FURTHER READINGS

Ghauri, P. N., Gronhaug, K., & Kristianslund, I. (1995). *Research methods in business studies: A practical guide.* Upper Saddle River, NJ: Prentice Hall.

Madsen, D. (1991). *Successful dissertations and theses: A guide to graduate student research from proposal to completion.* San Francisco: Josey-Bass, Inc.

Martin, R. (1980). *Writing and defending a thesis or dissertation in psychology and education.* Springfield, IL: Thomas.

Mitchell, M., & Jolley, J. (1992). *Research design explained* (2nd ed.). Fort Worth, TX: Harcourt Brace Jovanovich College.

Pyrczak, F., & Bruce, R. R. (1992). *Writing empirical research reports: A basic guide for students of the social and behavioral sciences.* Los Angeles, CA: Pyrczak Publishing.

Silverman, F. H. (1997). *Research design and evaluation in speech-language pathology and audiology* (4th ed.). Needham Heights, MA: Allyn & Bacon.

Webb, J. R. (1992). *Understanding and designing marketing research.* San Diego: Academic Press.

Wolcott, H. F. (1990). *Writing up qualitative research.* Newbury Park, CA: Sage.

Zikmund, W. G. (1996). *Business research methods* (5th ed.). Chicago: Dryden Press.

Glossary of Key Terms

As is true for any discipline, research has its own vocabulary. If you have taken or are taking research courses, then you may be familiar with some or all of these terms. Nonetheless, to make sure we are all playing in the same ballpark, we define and discuss some key terms used repeatedly throughout this text.

Applied research. Applied research shares many of the qualities of basic research. Both contribute to a knowledge base. Specific procedures are used to select subjects from the larger population. Statistical procedures can be used; however, its purpose is to directly improve a product or a process that enhances the participants' quality of life. The value of applied research is judged by the direct social importance of its consequences.

Basic research or pure research. Basic or pure research has as its goal the development of theories through the discovery of broad generalization or principles. Subjects included in basic research are selected using very careful sampling procedures so that the researcher can extend findings beyond the group or setting studied. Basic research is often conducted in highly controlled settings such as laboratories. While it advances theory, there is little direct utility to the field.

Dependent variable. A dependent variable is the variable you are interested in changing. For example, if you have a medical background, you may be interested in increasing the use of self-examination techniques for detecting cancer. If you are a social worker, you may want to increase your clients' employability or parenting skills. If you are a counselor, you may want to help someone kick a drug or alcohol problem. If you are a teacher, you may want to improve your students' reading performance.

Experimental control. A researcher has experimental control by demonstrating that the independent variable is the only event influencing the dependent variable. He or she selects participants at random, carefully defines and measures dependent variables of interest, and implements the independent variable. Data analysis indicates whether changes in the dependent variable can be attributed to chance alone or to the presence of the independent variable. Another term for experimental control is *functional relationship*.

Group design. A group design involves at least two groups of participants. Those in the experimental group are exposed to the independent variable so the researcher can measure if there is any effect on the dependent variable. Participants in the control group are not exposed to the independent variable. They are included so the effects on the dependent variables of factors other than the treatment or the intervention can be measured. For example, a psychologist randomly assigns patients with agoraphobia to either an experimental or a control group. She measures the self-reported levels of anxiety for both groups when they leave their homes (the dependent variable). Patients in Group A (the experimental group) participate in a new treatment program while patients in Group B do not. The data are evaluated to determine if there is a difference in anxiety scores reported by participants in each group.

Independent variable. An independent variable is the method you will use to effect or bring about changes in the dependent variable. You could be interested in simply seeing the effects of an independent variable already in place. For example, a coach or exercise physiologist may be interested in determining the effects of reaction time (independent variable) on batting average (dependent variable). You may also introduce one or more independent variables to all or some of your participants, then measure the effects on the dependent variable. In this situation, an independent variable is an intervention or a treatment program. For example, a medical researcher may give a new medication (the first independent variable) to half of the participants in his study and use a more traditional approach (the second independent variable) with the other half. He then measures their blood pressure (the dependent variable) to see if the new medication had a greater effect than the standard treatment. The independent variable could also be administered by degrees. Having established that the new medication is more effective than the traditionally prescribed medication, the researcher could experiment with dosage levels to determine the minimum amount necessary to reduce a patient's blood pressure.

Internal validity. Your study will have internal validity to the extent that you have controlled for variables, other than the independent variable, that could have contributed to changes in the dependent variable. Common threats to internal validity include history (an event occurring between pre and posttests, other than the independent variable), maturation (a change that occurs because a participant has grown older or gained more experience), and instrumentation (a change that occurs because the testing procedures are unreliable or have been altered unintentionally).

Null hypothesis. A null hypothesis is a restatement of the research hypothesis for statistical purposes. Statistical procedures allow you to determine whether any differences in your results occurred because of chance. Generally, you hope to be able to reject the null hypothesis and state that your results were due to the independent variable rather than chance. The examples used earlier can be restated as null hypotheses. There is no significant difference between the weight of obese people using Drug X and the weight of obese people not using it. There is no significant difference between the scores earned on district-wide science exams by students whose teachers use constructivist-based approaches and the scores earned by students whose teachers do not use it.

Population. The population is a group of people to whom you ultimately plan to apply your results. Examples include all students enrolled in a college or university, all students taking a particular course, all patients with skin cancer, all clients with panic disorders, or all employees of a particular hospital.

Qualitative research. An investigator uses qualitative research to study individuals and events in their natural state in great depth. It involves verbal descriptions and interpretations rather than statistical analysis of numerical data. Examples include historical studies and case studies.

Quantitative analysis. A quantitative analysis involves the use of statistical procedures to determine if changes in the dependent variable can be attributed to chance or to the presence or implementation of the independent variable. Data from both group designs and single case designs can be analyzed through the application of statistics.

Reliability, Reliability refers to the consistency of a measurement. Your test is considered reliable if your participants score similarly at another time or under different test conditions.

Research hypothesis. A research hypothesis is a formal statement you use to predict a single research outcome. Generally, it defines the relationship between dependent and independent variables. For example, obese persons using Drug X will lose more weight than obese people who do not use it. Students whose teachers use constructivist-based approaches will score better on district-wide science exams than students whose teachers do not use constructivist-based approaches.

Sample. Rarely is it feasible to recruit every member of a population to be in your study; therefore, you select a sample or a subgroup. For example, rather than survey all 7,000 students enrolled at a university, you randomly select and survey 200. You will make inferences about the larger population on the basis of your work with the sample.

Significance. You want to be sure that any difference you find in your results would be detected again if your study were repeated using other samples from the same population. Significance refers to the probability with which we are willing to risk rejecting a true null hypothesis (making a Type I error). It is a statement that a difference between group means resulting from chance when the population means are actually equal is less than or equal to a specified value. Most investigators choose either .05 or .01 as the point where they will reject the null hypothesis.

Single subject designs. Unlike group designs, single subject designs require that only one person, or a small number of persons, participate in the research project. Participants are not typically chosen at random; rather, they are selected on the basis of their need for an intervention. Several single subject designs are available, and they require the systematic application of the independent variable. Changes in the dependent variable that occur only after an independent variable is implemented indicate a relationship between both variables.

Type I error. You commit a Type I error by rejecting the null hypothesis when it is, in fact, true. You conclude there is a treatment effect when there is none.

Type II error. You commit a Type II error by not rejecting the null hypothesis when it is, in fact, false. You conclude there is no treatment effect when there was. A Type II error can occur when you have used an insufficient number of participants, and it may result in the abandonment of a potentially useful intervention.

Validity. Validity is the extent to which an instrument measures what it has been designed to measure. You want to be certain that the methods through which you measure the dependent variable do in fact assess the knowledge or skills in which you are interested. There are several ways to assess the validity of an instrument. Face validity is the degree to which a measure appears to assess what it claims to assess. Content validity is a comparison between your instrument and another organized body of knowledge such as a curriculum. Concurrent validity is the relationship between a given measure and another measure that purports to assess the same thing. Predictive validity is the extent to which the measure predicts a given outcome. Finally, construct validity is the extent to which an instrument measures a specific hypothetical construct such as intelligence or creativity.

Variable. A variable is anything in a research situation that varies. Variables can include characteristics of people such as intelligence scores; academic performance; physical prowess; height and weight; hair, eye, and skin color; gender, ethnic background, socioeconomic status, medical history, criminal record, anxiety level, and self-confidence. Variables can also include setting characteristics such as temperature, the amount of light, the size of the room, noise levels, the presence of others, and furniture. In addition, they can include access to instruction, medication, physical exercise, and counseling.

INDEX